Constitutionalism and Democracy

George Skouras

Constitutionalism and Democracy

The Supreme Court Power of Judicial Review v. We the People

Springer

George Skouras
Astoria, NY, USA

ISBN 978-3-031-66905-7 ISBN 978-3-031-66906-4 (eBook)
https://doi.org/10.1007/978-3-031-66906-4

This Springer imprint is published by the registered company Springer Nature Switzerland AG
The registered company address is: Gewerbestrasse 11, 6330 Cham, Switzerland

Contents

Chapter 1
Introduction: The Landscape and Implanting an Experimental Democracy in the New World

It should be made clear, straight away, that this work makes no novel claims, as to the determination of whether the Supreme Court acted properly or exceeded its authority by its application of judicial review power. I will not investigate each and every case that the Court ruled nor attempt to second guess the Court's opinions and behavior, under every single case, in the course of American history. Consequently, I will only be using a sample or a very small portion of Supreme Court history, as an example, which will hopefully illustrate the role the American Supreme Court plays as final arbiter and interpreter of the *Constitution*. The main point being that I am mostly interested in is whether there exists a legitimate reason that the Supreme Court should exercise such power and authority, in establishing a democratic state. The conclusion reached here is that it is illegitimate for the Court to have the power of judicial review.

It is of no concern to us whether the Supreme Court acted fairly, properly, or justly in its exercise of such authority. Whether it is a good steward of such power is beside the point. What I am essentially interested in is how such a power became lodged with this body of government, given the historical evidence that the British rejected such a power for their system. Was there anything special about the American system to suggest that such a power is good for America but not good for Britain?

Within the scope and focus on Supreme Court judicial review power, I will attempt to point out other instances that the separation of governmental power—divided branches of government—were susceptible to power grabs, with each division, from time to time in American history, attempting to poach power from the others. That is, the Montesquieu model of government failed to contain and properly demarcate the lines of division when the Founding Fathers incorporated it into the Constitution. So, poaching and power grabbing becomes a potential activity when a divided government comes to a standstill or is deadlocked. The Founders had a very good reason to divide government, the way they did, because history shows that investing all power in a King, Crown, or dictator can be very dangerous for *We the People*.

G. Skouras, *Constitutionalism and Democracy*,
https://doi.org/10.1007/978-3-031-66906-4_1

It is hoped within the context of the American governmental structure, we will discover how the Supreme Court usurped the power of judicial review and how the other branches—the Legislative and Executive—also tried to power grab, especially during emergency conditions. Hopefully, the lesson learned is that when there exists divided government—with checks and balances—regardless of how theoretically it is supposed to work—it can be detrimental to *We the People* in the opposite direction from monarchy, authoritarianism, or dictatorship, in that it can lead to chaos and anarchy. Whether it be from the Right or the Left of the political system, it is dangerous for *We the People.* The Founding Fathers were properly concerned about the concentration of power, but what they overlooked was the possible danger of having a divided government. With too many "checks and balances" and not enough headwind to drive the ship of state safely. What appears to be the case is that constitutionalism is being used to hide an aristocratic system by calling it "democracy." That is the creation of a "thick" constitutionalism as a cover for a "thin" democracy.

1.1 On the Status of Democracy and the American Class System

I hope to unbalance "experience" and "reason" in the telling of the implantation of an experimental system called "democracy" in the New World. Given the human animal is not primarily a bundle of logic but an amalgamation of senses and instinctual life. But, unlike purely empirical or conceptual attempts to place the human animal in the domain of historical space and time, I reserve a domain of mental space, namely the role of consciousness, in giving the human animal the wherewithal to not only be aware of the external world but its own internal state. The linear telling of the story will be interrupted by non-linear interventions. One might assume that the best way to get from point A to point B is to map out the most direct and efficient route. However, here, I will try to balance linearity with non-linear systems as we travel the domain of jurisprudence, philosophy, political science and much else. That is, I hope the reader stays with me as I try to read the signs and map out historical roads of how a legal system can dominate a people—*We the People.*[1] That is, I hope you stay with me as I attempt to build a case as to why the Supreme

[1]Who is "We the People"? I will roll out "We the People" concept over the course of this work. It should be no surprise that the use of this phrase/concept will appear over and over in the course of this work. Of course, this needs lots of unpacking and hopefully might be able to eventually convince the readers that although *We the People* has political power, its ultimate foundational status is metaphysical. Michelman says: "Among contemporary American constitutional theorists of populist inclination, Bruce Ackerman is one who has grappled most seriously with the question of what counts as an expression of the legislative will of the people. Ackerman quite convincingly maintains that, on any plausible conception of a people's constitutional will that is morally deserving of respect, that the will (or that "people") can never be corporately or instantaneously

Court of the United States of America should be stripped of the power of Judicial Review.

I will seek to carve out a historical space that allowed the foundational democratic systems to co-exist with non-democratic elements that have been incorporated into the American Constitution. The general conclusion reached is that the experimental system known as "democracy," in the Eighteenth century, was too speculative, untested, and unproven to be able to be established in the Constitution of the United States. That is to say, the civilizational conditions were not conducive to bring such a system to life in late Eighteenth century America.

How does the idea of "democracy" relate to the "power of judicial review"? What does the power of judicial review have to do with democracy?[2] This work will make the following claim: under the established political system, whether it be called 'Republicanism' at the framing of the American Constitution or 'Democracy' with increased political freedoms after the Civil War and the passage of the Civil War Amendments, the Supreme Court power of judicial review is the wrong toolset to give the Supreme Court because it gives the Justices rather than *We the People* the opportunity to direct American policy. In this work we will focus on one domain—property—in the period between the Gilded Age and the New Deal, but the use of this power is universal in the sense that the Court can use it to knock down any legislation it finds offensive to the Constitution. Of course, the exploration of the totality of this power, as used by the Court in many other domains, is beyond the scope of this work. However, if the conclusion is correct that the Supreme Court should never hold such power, then there is no need to go down each domain, exposing how the Court has become the ultimate guide of American politics. And, further, this power was appropriated by the Court under a theory that presupposed that a written Constitution needed a proper guardian and protector—the Supreme Court voted itself to be the proper entity to expound on the final meaning of the Constitution. That is, the power of judicial review was appropriated by the Court by fiat rather than found within the Constitution. The Supreme Court appropriated this power on its own terms, free of Congressional oversight or approval[3] nor with any

present but can only be represented by time-extended courses of political events." Michelman (1998), p. 76.

[2] Symposium (1981), p. 259; Kammen (1987), p. 31.

[3] Prakash and Yoo (2003), pp. 892, 893. It is clear that these authors (Prakash and Yoo) do believe that the Framers of the Constitution granted the power of judicial review to the Supreme Court. "[W]e believe that modern scholars who insist that the Founders never authorized judicial review of federal statutes are mistaken." (p. 892) Clearly, they point to many pieces of writing and actions of those in the Convention and especially outside of Convention that would have included such a provision in the Constitution. However, the fact remains even though some might have been strongly inclined to do so, they did not. So, the bottom line is the Founders were unclear as to whether they wanted to incorporate such a power in the Constitution. However, the two authors above beg to differ with me. According to them: "Our goal here is to show that the necessary predicate for these theories—the Constitution's authorization of judicial review—is on solid textual, structural, and historical grounds. In short, the original intent behind the Constitution (what the founders intended the Constitution to provide) and the Constitution's original public meaning (what

regard for the other elected bodies of government. Nevertheless, if it can be established that such a power does not belong to the Supreme Court, we will at least have won half the battle. The other half of the battle is to further plough the fields as to whether the domain of democracy is even feasible in our civilizational time. If democratic theory does not make any sense or it is simply a metaphysical product, then power grabs, like the one the Supreme Court conducted, is perfectly in line with many other non-democratic regimes throughout history. That is, authoritarian regimes, and other special interest actors, grabbing as much power as they can, and leaving *We the People* in the dustbins of history.

The power of judicial review cannot be brought under democratic control unless it is stripped from the Supreme Court and given to Congress. Here is how Dahl unpacks the power of judicial review as understood, debated, or intended for the operation of this power. Dahl makes clear that the Founders were unsure how this power of judicial review was to function within the new constitution. He says: "What the delegates intended in the way of judicial review will remain forever unclear; probably many delegates were unclear in their own minds, and to the extent that they discussed the question at all, they were not in full agreement. [N]evertheless, it is likely that a substantial majority intended that federal judges should not participate in making government laws and policies, a responsibility that clearly belonged not to the judiciary but to the legislative branch."[4] In short, Dahl goes on to say that the Virginia Plan, on giving the Executive and Judiciary veto power over the legislature failed.

Further, this work will maintain that: ideal "democracy" is utopianism.[5] The reason for attempts to set up a democracy is to try to give voice/vote to a wider range of the population. Be it a "thin" democracy or something more substantial has so far not proven fruitful anywhere in the world. Whether a "thin" democracy is possible we will further explore here. As to a "thick" democracy we will leave to the metaphysicians. One reason a "thick" democracy is not possible in our civilizational time is the dynamics between property and the democratic dynamic. The other more important reason we will leave to future analysts or the evolutionists, has to do with

---

the Constitution would have meant to a single, informed, objective reader in 1787-1788) show that the Constitution authorized judicial review."), p. 893.

[4]Dahl (2003), p. 18. Dahl goes on to say: "A judicial veto is one thing; judicial legislation is quite another. Whatever some delegates may have thought about the availability of justices sharing with the executive the authority to veto laws passed by Congress. I am fairly certain that none would have given the slightest support to a proposal that judges should themselves have the power to legislate, to make national policy. However, the upshot of their work was that in the guise of reviewing the constitutionality of state and congressional actions or inactions, the federal judiciary would later engage in what in some instances could only be called judicial policy-making—or, if you like, judicial legislation." (p. 19).

[5]In order to find out what "democracy" is, it will require pinning down a definition of it. This is tricky business but hopefully this work will make some attempt to pin it down and show why it is a metaphysical concept—but keep the hope open that some strip-down version is possible. Becker (1941), pp. 3–9; Dahl (2006), pp. 4–29, Chapter 2: "Is Political Equality a Reasonable Goal?" (Dahl links the idea of political equality to democracy.)

our evolutionary development and such a system not being able to be birthed in our civilizational time. We will explore a bit of the biologisms involved here but not with any depth. Democracy has eluded all that have tried to establish such a system so far. Of course, a skinny version of democracy or a more pragmatic form may be possible by overlooking the content and substance of a democratic state and settling for a "procedural" democracy. The question becomes whether some, perhaps pragmatic form of democracy,[6] can be salvaged from the threat of authoritarianism. Democracy, in its "ideal" form, has never existed and could never exist outside of utopia or metaphysical universe. So, the question arises as to whether some variation or stripped-down version of democracy is possible?[7] And if such a democracy can exist in some form or variation, whether it can be improved upon or doomed to failure under the pressures of authoritarian systems. That is, can a "practical" form of democracy emerge from the foundations of our civilization? Is it possible to have a stable variation of democracy or a "pragmatic democracy," and if so, can it be

---

[6]The tug of war between rationalism and empiricism as to which school has the upper hand in the representation of reality. Does 'democracy' fall within the domain of rationality and comport to the ideals of the mind or is 'democracy' an empirical institution capable to reductionism and fragmentation to be torn to pieces by such schools as sociology, political science, economics, etc.? Can the idea of 'democracy' stand up to empirical investigations? Can it survive 'rational' examination?

[7]Dahl (2003), p. 5. Dahl at the start of this book brings up an important point as to whether the Framers of the American Constitution created a "republic" or a "democracy"? (p. 5) Dahl relying on Madison in his work takes the view that the Framers created a "democracy" and not a "republic." I will not dwell on the point here and, hope eventually to point this work in the direction, that the Framers created a "Republic" and not a "Democracy." That is, I believe based on the *structure* of the Constitution that the Framers created a Republic. But this is not to say that America remained a Republic throughout its history. I will be arguing here for the thesis that although the Framers created a Republic, America took on many aspects of Democracy and moved towards democracy to a degree, but the American Constitution has a Republican infrastructure and plumbing system at its core. Further, I will attempt to segregate democracy as found in textbooks from real or actual democracy—theoretical democracy from practical democracy throughout this work. If theoretical/ideal democracy is not feasible and real/practical democracy is too messy, unworkable, or too fallen from the ideal, can there be a middle range democracy that can serve as some sort of serviceable entity or workable solution for the masses to be heard in the hallways of political power? The theme between democracy as an "ideal" and democracy in "reality/practice" will be a continues matter of revisitation throughout the book. But it is safe to say that "ideal" democracy is impossible or metaphysical because it suggests a group of people can assemble and direct themselves and select policies and set a course of direction by themselves or more plausibly by their representatives. I will have more to say on 'representative democracy' later in the book, but even representative democracy is incapable of meeting the above criteria of democracy free of assumptions as to what *We the People* want individually or as a collective. The basic problem is ascertaining the wants of the masses by way of filtration of their representatives. Representatives must make lots of assumptions as to what their constituents want. Therefore, there cannot be uniformity of policies over a divergence of independent moral agents with a plurality of wills and tastes. Of course, the use of the standard democratic technique of "majority" rule is the way of setting modern day policy. However, the concept of "majority" rule can be as difficult to grapple with as the concept of "democracy" itself. So, the conflation of the concept and the technique leads to additional misunderstanding of the modern 'experiment' in democracy. We will see how this intertwining plays out here.

salvaged and harvested for use by *We the People*? That is, under our civilizational time can an idea like "democracy" be birthed given the human animals' predispositions toward a rather ruthless existence? There does not appear to have been a time since the human animal came down from the trees, which is historical time within each passing civilizational time, including our own, that such an animal has not been knee deep in blood. Therefore, the social structure or ethics needed to build up democratic systems have been antithetical to such system within our civilizational time. Purcell does a great job expressing the status of ethics, political theory, and human behavior during the early part of the Twentieth century. That is, science or "naturalistic" science dashed the hopes of those hoping to establish ethical systems and political theory as to the foundations of democratic government. The methods of "induction" or "deduction" were sharply limited in their application to ethical and political theory. These behavioristic or scientific models deemed "higher law" legal doctrine simply a metaphysical enterprise parading as practical law.

> In the years after 1910 scientific naturalists strictly confined induction to observable, concrete phenomena and ruled it out as a method of proving the validity of any moral principles. At the same time, they sharply redefined the nature of deductive logic, always closely allied with rational ethical systems. By demonstrating its wholly abstract and formal nature, scientific naturalists denied it any authority in questions concerning the legitimacy of moral values. Rejecting the possibility of demonstrating the truth of ethical propositions by either induction or deduction, they left moral ideals without a rational, theoretical basis.[8]

The "naturalistic" scientific approach also questioned the possibility that citizens had sufficient "rationality" to participate in the democratic process. "[I]n empirically examining human behavior and the actual process of American politics, scientific naturalists came to question and often reject three cardinal principles of democratic government: the possibility of a government of laws rather than of men, the rationality of human behavior, and the practical possibility of popular government itself."[9] That is, human decision making was not simply a rational exercise but a muddle of various inputs that could not be justified scientifically. With the rise of psychology, during the early part of the Twentieth century, along with the other social sciences, it was revealed that the human animal is not a purely "rational" animal and that the instinctual and emotional domain could either take the lead or serve as decision-maker well before any rational analysis came to the fore.[10]

According to Becker, the assumption of the possibility for democracy is more than the procedural business of counting votes. There must also exist, along with procedure, the substance of democracy. Becker says these are the "necessary

---

[8]Purcell (1973), p. 11.

[9]Purcell (1973), p. 11.

[10]Purcell (1973), p. 11. "Psychologists found human behavior was largely irrational, especially in the complicated and emotional arena of politics. Most individuals, they maintained, were unable to fulfill the traditional democratic obligations of citizens. Students of politics learned that in practice small groups of insiders dominated the government and that popular control was an illusion. Democratic government did not work as its theory claimed it should. By the early thirties traditional democratic theory seemed largely untenable."

assumptions and the necessary preconditions" for democratic government. Becker list a series of requirements as preparatory ground to sound citizen voting.[11]

Can the assumptions mentioned by Becker be met? It seems that they are pretty-hefty assumptions. Let us list them:

1. Are citizens capable of managing their own affairs?
2. Can there be reconciliation of diverse opinions?
3. Is compromise possible in a world of diverse opinions?
4. Measures adopted for the common good. What is the common good?
5. Individual interests v. class interests?
6. The assumption of rationality and the rational citizen. Is the human animal a rational animal?
7. Citizens as sound judges of good policy. Is this possible?

The *principle* may be stated this way:

> Attempts to study human behavior can go so far and no further. Experimental scientists or behaviorists during the early part of the 20th century attempted to study human animal behavior using natural science methodology. It became clear in the later part of the 20th century that such a methodology is weak and incomplete in capturing the essence or true human behavior by mechanistically devised experiments and ignoring or leaving out the core of animal being—consciousness. These naturalistic efforts reduced the whole of ethics and political theory to the junk heap of history until they were resurrected in the later part of the 20th century.

Obviously, Becker has strong criteria for modern democracy. To what degree the above criteria can be met or possible, we will see. We will try to separate reality from myth to the extent it can be done. Or it might be argued that: if the substantive version of democracy is impossible, perhaps there is a "skinny" version that is doable? As mentioned earlier, some sort of "thin" democracy that preserves the right of the general public to cast a vote. Perhaps, a majoritarian democracy with procedures in place that allows each citizen to be heard and have their voice/vote accounted for in the polity. The idea of democracy has historically been kicked around but never taken seriously as a realistic goal by any previous society with a few exceptions. So, the revival of the idea of democracy in America was an 'experimental' effort to have a go of it.

What is clear is that the Framers of the American Constitution were not supporters of what generally goes under the label of 'democracy,' and did not highly appraise such a form of government. Although they embarked, for their times, on an 'experimental' journey going under the label 'democracy,' it could and should be more accurately labeled 'republicanism' or a 'republican' form of democracy. It was originally assumed that the Founders were liberal-individualist Lockeans until this view came under scrutiny. The challengers believed the Founders were also influenced by the republican communitarian tradition of Machiavelli. So, the assumption that Locke was the Founder's philosopher, that went unchallenged for

[11] Becker (1941), pp. 14–15.

a long time, came under challenge in the twentieth century. The liberal-Lockean individualism tradition facing off with a republican-communitarian tradition became contested ground in the twentieth century.[12] It seems that Machiavelli was just as important as Locke to the Founders.[13] We will not settle this debate here. We simply note the fact that the Founders, regardless of liberal or republican persuasion—simply could not have designed a democratic constitution.

We simply ask was the design and structure of the Constitution to facilitate democracy and democratic values or to facilitate aristocratic hierarchy and aristocratic values. What is clear is that for the Founders, the less democracy, the better, and they mostly held a highly negative view of democracy.[14] So, any form or semblance of democracy to emerge from the Constitutional Convention had to be a less than an ideal form that will be incorporated into the Constitution of the United States. And, further, democracy was boxed in by the need to protect property interests;[15] therefore, if any conflict arose between democracy and private property, democracy had to be curtailed to safeguard property.[16]

Since America was initially setup as a republic, the appropriation by the courts of the power of judicial review, was not very harmful to the interests of *We the People*, in any large scale at least.[17] However, over time with greater efforts made to democratize America, especially after the Civil War, and with the addition of the Civil War Amendments,[18] and, especially toward the final decades of the Nineteenth century, during the consolidation and monopolization stage of Industrial America[19] and early formation of monopoly enterprise,[20] it became clear and evident that the

[12]For a clash between liberalism and republicanism, see: Morone (1990), pp. 15–19.

[13]Morone (1990), p. 16. "To them, the spirit of Machiavelli runs as deep in Americans as that of John Locke."

[14]As to just how democratic America is, *see generally:* Rodgers (1987); Fishkin (1997); Morone (1990); Ackerman (1991, 1998, 2014); Levinson (2006).

[15]Siegan (2001); *see also*, Lockean philosophy on property rights protections.

[16]Charles Beard's work *An Economic Interpretation of the Constitution of the United States* (1913) has been controversial from its inception. It has generated counterarguments and counterclaims from the opposite side of the economic and political spectrum. This book has become something of a landmark for progressive groups and interests. So, it has been heavily attacked and scrutinized by more traditional and conservative interest groups throughout the twentieth century. Readers may want to examine and analyze his claims for themselves and see if they holdup or not. Some of my previous works cited here go into greater detail as to his claims and the counter-literature it generated; *see in particular*, Skouras (2011), pp. 37–58.

[17]The only exception to this was the pre-Civil War case of *Dread Scott v. Sanford* that eventually led to the killing of more than 600,000 Americans.

[18]13th, 14th, and 15th Amendments to the US Constitution, also known as the Civil War Amendments.

[19]For further views on Industrialism and capitalism during this period, see: Ginger (1975); Hobsbawn (1969); Diner (1998); Cochran and Miller (1942).

[20]Zunz (1990) for further analysis of this period—Industrialization & Monopolization of America, end of the nineteenth century: was there monopoly upsurge during this period? What was the nature of this business consolidation? Is this a contested truth given that America was undergoing

Supreme Court was using the power of judicial review as a check on any further push to democratize the economy by way of any reformist, regulatory, or legislative schemes that impinged on property values. That is, the basic fear of the Framers of the American Constitution was that of "democracy" interfering with property which was becoming a reality by the close of the Nineteenth century. But, instead of the Legislative branch stepping in to protect property interests, it was the Supreme Court. Now, who elected the Supreme Court to serve as the People's representative in these matters? What if *We the People* wanted change in the distribution of property? Is the Legislative branch or the Supreme Court the protector of property? Which branch of government has the final power as to how property is to function in any given age? Should property be a "fixed" concept and operate in the same manner under the Agricultural Age as in the Industrial Age?

The *principle* may be stated this way:

> Republicanism is not democracy. Republicanism is Aristocracy watered down. The Constitution being an Aristocratic Republican document only makes for provision of the protection of property, everything else is secondary or tertiary. Democracy is not the business of the American Constitution. That is, Montesquieu's model of democracy is a watered-down model of Aristocracy. Montesquieu was an Aristocrat; he understood matters via an aristocratic mind set. However, he made the effort to democratize aristocracy.

Nevertheless, the Supreme Court stepped into the breach to try to hold back *We the People* attempting to violate property rights via increased governmental regulations. The Court stepped in, using its self-appointed power of judicial review, to clean up any legislative efforts that rebalances property rights on the democratic side of the scale of justice. The threat to private property by the People, was deemed to be the

---

Industrialization, while shedding its agricultural workers; *See, United States v. Int. Harvester Co.*, 274 U.S. 693 (1927), *United States v. American Tobacco Co.*, 221 U.S. 106 (1911), oil industry (natural monopoly). John D. Rockefeller's *Standard Oil Company* cornered 90% of the market and was broken up in 1911; monopoly in the steel industry, Andrew Carnegie's company bought by J.P. Morgan and melded into *U.S. Steel* survived its monopoly battle under the *Sherman Act*; further instances of monopoly in 1) sugar, 2) tobacco, and 3) meat-packing; subsequently, the *Clayton Act* attempted to give further guidance and tighten up the Sherman Act by banning 1) interlocking directorates, 2) tie-in sales, and 3) certain mergers & acquisitions; *see further*, Areeda and Hovenkamp (2013) on antitrust; *see further*, Theodore Roosevelt and William Howard Taft and Progressive Era attempts to break up monopoly—*Northern Securities Co. v. United States*, 193 U.S. 197 (1904); *see further*, Sunstein (2004), p. 67. "For Berle, corporate power was a serious threat to both democracy and economic growth. He believed that corporations had increasingly obtained the status of monopolies and did violence to the old idea of free and open competition." *See also*, Cooper (1990), p. 11. Cooper says that between 1897–1903, over three hundred consolidations took place that totaled $7.5 billion in capitalization which involved 40% of the industrial output. "These consolidations became a vast horizontal integration that brought large segments of an industry, and sometimes the whole industry, under the control of a handful of firms. Railroads led the way, with 95 percent of all trackage controlled by six lines in 1899. Steel soon followed suit; the formation of the United States Steel Corporation in 1901 brought about 80 percent of production under one company. U.S. Steel, whose formation was announced on March 4, 1901, the same day as the inauguration of the president, was the first business in the world to be capitalized at $1 billion. Other fields, most notably aluminum, tobacco, and life insurance, soon underwent consolidations that left them comparably concentrated."

job of appointed justices to remedy rather than the representatives of the People. Probably the Framers, given the value they placed in private property protection, would not be opposed to the Supreme Court, using the power of judicial review, at least in cases involving property, to stopping the masses, especially during the Fuller Supreme Court, from interfering in the interests of private property. However, the power of judicial review is potentially universal in scope and would give the Court massive power to re-arrange American society, well beyond the economic and property interests. This might have been one reason as to why this power was not explicitly written into the Constitution. Even if some of the Founders were disposed to a judicial check or veto on Congress, but as Dahl pointed out, most of the Founders would have been shocked to learn that the Supreme Court was serving as the legislative and policy guide and regulator of Congress. The Founders might easily be concerned that the Court, with such a power, might refuse to yield to the Legislative and Executive branches, as co-equal branches, if such a power is explicitly stated in the Constitution. This would also make a mockery of Montesquieu's co-equal and balanced governance model,[21] since the Court was to be the final arbiter in the conduct of government.

Of course, Montesquieu was not the only aristocrat that also believed that the "better sort" of people ought to rule. It was the standard, not simply of the *Age of Enlightenment* of the Eighteenth century, but from time immemorial observation and experience dictated that the "better sort" of people, not only should rule but were obligated to rule, if a tribe, community, city, or state is to survive. One need not be a Darwinist to know that not "all" of the people are capable of leadership or rule of any given territory and society. Even at the start of Western Civilization the Greeks and Romans were of the opinion the "best," the "strongest," or the "wisest" were the most likely candidates for rulership. Of course, what "ideals" dictate and what "reality" necessitates are not one and the same thing. Each passing Civilization develops standards for its day or horizon. It should be no surprise that each passing Civilization will deploy those traits and values it adjudges suitable for those living in that time horizon. This means that no human being can escape his or her time horizon. Each human animal is a prisoner of their time.

So, Montesquieu was not some sort of a radical espousing republicanism—as were not most of the Framers of the American Constitution, espousing some sort of radical idea that the candidates for rulership should come from "below" or from the commoners, in essence, *We the People*, but from the top of society as signified by property ownership. That is, they should come from the highest social ranks, preferably from the Aristocracy of blood, as was the case in Europe, or in the case of the United States, from an Aristocracy of merit/property. That is, a key reason the Framers of the American Constitution were drawn to Montesquieu's model of

[21] Montesquieu (1949), p. 12; here is how Montesquieu regarded democracy: "The people's suffrages ought doubtless to be public; and this should be considered as a fundamental law of democracy. The lower classes ought to be directed by those of higher rank and restrained within bounds by the gravity of eminent personages."

Aristocratic government—it was because it allowed the "better sort" to rule America, not *We the People*.

The Founders, like all elites, want their own kind to lead and rule their society—that is, set the example and standard for the rest of the populace. The Founding Fathers, in making sure that the "best" ruled America, did so by making property ownership the *sine qua non* of fitness for political office and rulership. How is the portion of *We the People* capable of rulership to be determined? By property ownership. It was first fully noticed in the North, that class politics can relieve a man of his duty to fight in the American Civil War. That is, the Enrollment Act of 1863 allowed a draftee to pay $300 for someone else to do their fighting in that bloody conflict. The South, too, reached an existential crisis when they were defeated by the North and realized that the Plantation structure was broken, with the defeat and collapse of the Southern plantation aristocracy. The South suddenly came face to face with those that it once enslaved, and those other subsistence farmers and homesteaders living on the edges of the large plantations, as outsiders to the planter class, were going to be neighbors and partners, with equal voting power, was unthinkable to a Pre-Civil War generation. But with the destruction of the South, it became clear that the resurrection of the South would require *de facto* means to control the former slaves and the petty farmers regardless of any *de jure* freedoms granted them by the North and imposed on them with the passage of the Civil War Amendments and Reconstruction. The American Founders were not democrats. Therefore, they could not have drafted a democratic constitution. They were an admixture of Lockeans and Republicans (republicanism traditionally understood). The Constitution they drafted contained and contains many aristocratic provisions. The American Civil War shattered some of the anti-democratic provisions but not all of them. The remainder of those provisions we are dealing with today. It left the South shattered and broken, with its old Planter class left in ruins. This meant that the former Planter Aristocracy needed new legal tools to control the undesirables in its midst.

The Supreme Court serves as a good vehicle, free from facing the voters, to restrain any nascent democratic efforts from swallowing up private property. As the Supreme Court started using the *Due Process Clause of the Fourteenth Amendment*, not as a *procedural* matter, but to make *substantive* changes to economic policy, *it was transforming the Civil War Amendments into new tools in the war of the classes.* It started to become clear, by the close of the Nineteenth century and early Twentieth century America, that the Court was prepared to act as the legislative branch and to use this power in the protection of the new emerging industrial class system.[22] As farmers started transitioning into industrial workers or the proletariat,[23] the Supreme

[22] American class system reference; *See also,* White (1997); *See generally*, Tiger and Levy (1977); Marcus (1972), pp. 260–276 (politicians of both parties did all they could to align themselves with the new elite industrialists).

[23] Lears (2009) (Giantism also leads to imperialism as a regular feature of American foreign policy since the close of the nineteenth century). *See generally*, Sennett (2006); Diner (1998) (Diner presents a cogent social history of the period); *see further*, Link and McCormick (1983).

Court acted as a final arbiter as to the fate of those workers. This usurpation action of acting as legislator and judge said something about the original Constitution boxing in the "unwashed"[24] masses (the emerging proletariat of late Nineteenth century America) via the power of judicial review—with the lawyer class serving as the last arbiter of what is good for the working class. The Legal class became an intermediate body between the property interests and *We the People*.

The *principle* may be stated this way:

> After the American Civil War (with the passage of the Civil War Amendments), the Due Process Clause of one of these Amendments (the 14th) was used by the Supreme Court to wield tremendous power to protect property and dissolve democratic efforts by Progressives and Populists threatening to invade the sacred temple of Property that is the core of the American Constitution. The Supreme Court was very effective in putting down these commoners with the power of judicial review.

1.2 The Role of Judicial Review and Property Protection

During the Economic Due Process era, the Court officially adopted Social Darwinism as to the survival of businesses and an open *laissez-faire*[25] attitude that those businesses that survived are good and strong, and those businesses that go under are weak and worthless, and it is for the good of all that they go down. That is, the markets were performing an essential service for society by thinning out weak businesses, as they succumbed to the pressures of competition that allows only the strong to survive. Such a philosophy adopted by the Supreme Court is not a judicial philosophy, but one of deciding which business lives and which dies. So, if monopolies emerged, so be it. They became the Big Businesses that could eat up the competitors and clearly showed survival power. However, nowhere is it written in the Constitution that Social Darwinism is the law of the land.[26] Yet, the Supreme Court took it upon itself to pass judgment and give its blessings to such enterprise.

---

[24] Any reference to the "unwashed" masses or "mob" rule have been used to denigrate the prospects of democracy and many other such phrases, such as the "multitude", the "commoners", the "general public", "We the People", the "uninformed public" in less harsh terms, have been used throughout American history to denigrate the prospects for democratic rule and democracy, phrases that have been used from time immemorial to refer to those unfit for rulership. Obviously, these phrases have a polemical stance. Here, these references are being used to form the contrast between democratic rule versus aristocratic rule, with phrases like the "best" people, the "strongest" people, the "brightest," etc. being used indicate the fitness for aristocratic rulership. At points in this work a phrase like the "unwashed masses" will stand as equivalents for the commoners and We the People.

[25] Gillman (1993), p. 63. "In all, the last quarter of the nineteenth century witnessed changes that crushed the Lockean state of nature that had inspired many of America's founders and replaced it with a Darwinian social order in which dependence rather than independence was becoming the more common social experience, manifesting most pointedly in a "chronic conflict between employers over the costs of production;" that is, in widespread and violent class conflict."

[26] For a good overall analysis of Social Darwinism in America during this period, see: Hofstadter (1955).

That is, the Supreme Court took a special interest in the protection of property under curious circumstances. It transformed a *procedural* clause in the Constitution into a *substantive* tool to quash any further breach or affront to private property, due to greater and greater numbers of people seeking the vote. Originally mostly the propertied had access to the ballot, as the process unfolded, of allowing more and more of the unpropertied to vote, it became dangerous for this large class of people to hold the levers of power over the propertied class.[27] Or better put, the vote was a "*pro forma*" process or deal for eligible American citizens. It would show the world that America was a democratic country. But it was not believed or expected that "all" eligible Americans were in "reality" going to vote. Otherwise, additional restrictions would have been needed to be put in place, by the Framer's Aristocratic government, to make sure it was not imperiled by commoners or *We the People*. It was not expected that the masses would be eligible to vote without tight restrictions, to be sure that only the "right" property owners ruled America. If the "common" people were eligible to vote too, then this would imperil the whole infrastructure and plumbing system erected by the Framer's Constitution. So, watching the vote was a very critical process from the start to be sure that the "wrong" people did not vote.

The property restrictions were followed up with economic restrictions to protect monopolies and disperse smaller companies. If we take the extension of property protection into commerce, contract, and finance we are building up similar bodies and layers of property protection and restrictions as to market entry. And the number of individuals, from the vast pool of workers and small to midsize businesses, must be restricted or eliminated from the market, if the big players are to build up a wall of protections, and the small players or the leftovers, without bulk and size to enter the market, must survive on their own. Instead of selling stocks and bonds to support the needs of their businesses, simply put, the workers and small businesses must survive on their own. Since government intervention usually favors the big players, the workers and small businesses must do what they must, by pulling themselves up by their own bootstraps, even though small and mid-sized businesses provide most of the jobs in the United States in comparison to those provided by big business or government. Small businesses provide roughly 65–70% of all the jobs in the United States. Large corporations provide roughly 15% of the jobs and government the remaining 15% of jobs. Yet small businesses are treated as the least or last in order of governmental assistance. Why might this be the case, you ask?

---

[27] Class system, American class system based on property ownership, state voting, and electoral college voting versus individual citizens that were unpropertied and unqualified to vote using a plethora of methods over the years to keep them away from the polls. That is, the poor or African-Americans were left outside the democratic system because voting was controlled by the States and each State qualified those voters that it believed would further the property establishment's foundations. So, control of the Federal government was left to property owners, the States, the Electoral College and through appointment, for high offices, with confirmations by the Senate. Originally Senate office was selected by the States, not *We the People*, and the President that makes high office nominations to the Senate is selected by the Electoral College rather than directly by *We the People*.

Big corporations can afford pools of lobbyists and other influencers, small businesses survive on day to day, week to week receipts. Social Darwinism, going under the label *laissez-faire*, found fertile soil in America in which to plant deep roots of its ideology. This philosophy was compatible with property protection and the cleaning out of the "unwashed" masses. This philosophy helped the new capitalist class and deeply wounded the working class from ever establishing deep roots in the United States. Such a philosophy is deadly for the unskilled, unlearned, the feeble, or suffering from any other condition not compatible with the capitalist enterprise.

Antitrust law and policy has its origins in the United States because it became clear that, by mid-nineteenth century and especially by the close of the Nineteenth century, America needed to come to terms with the merging of enterprises, or the consolidation of enterprises or the question of bigness of enterprises, posing a monopoly problem. This is not to say that issues of monopoly only emerged in the Nineteenth century America, but the tremendous growth in manufacturing, railroads, electricity, etc. started to develop and grow so that those that controlled these important and vital enterprises could control large swaths of America.[28]

The fight to develop and bring forth legislation to control monopoly in America was not a straight linear effort, but required continuous visitation to control this problem, and it continues to this day to be a problem.[29] The first major efforts resulted in the passage of the *Sherman Antitrust Act* of 1890.[30] Given that this effort, involving rather loose statutory language, one could understand how a wide range of interpretations could be made of it, along with the Supreme Court being hostile to such legislation at the time. Corporations were under the impression that this was only token regulation of their businesses and could find many holes in the statute to shield their corporations from it. So early in the Twentieth century a renewed effort was made to control monopoly with the passage of the *Clayton Antitrust Act* of 1914.[31] Along with establishing the FTC (Federal Trade Commission),[32] legislators made renewed efforts to hold the tide of corporations seeking monopoly power. What eventually became clear was the government had a fight on its hands with its

---

[28] For further analysis as to the economic and social conditions during this period, see: Morgan (1970); Trachtenberg (2007); Wiebe (1967); McConnell (1970); Beatty (2007); Dobson (1972).

[29] Not to shatter any expectations, or read the future into the past, Antitrust law proved to be a weak candidate to control monopoly in America and an abysmal failure. Therefore, we, living in the twenty-first century, endure under the power of monopoly because, *We the People*, failed to put down the corporation and rule over them. Instead, the corporate form of business rules over us, with government playing second fiddle. This probably would not have been a big surprise to those living in early twentieth century America—the realization that monopoly power will sink *We the People* or democracy if they failed to regulate and control corporate power. So, *We the People* are paying the price and consequences of the State not being able to break the back of monopoly power in the early part of the twentieth century. And so, this leviathan has grown to the point that in fact is the current *de facto* governing or ruling body of the United States today.

[30] *26* Stat. 209, 15 U.S.C. §§ 1–7.

[31] *15 U.S.C. §§ 12–27, 29 U.S.C. §§ 52–53.*

[32] *FTC Act, 15 U.S.C. § 41.*

continuous monitoring and efforts to bring giant companies to heel. With the Supreme Court protecting the property and economic foundation of the American Constitution, with the power of judicial review, the tripartite government broke down.

1.3 The Impact of British History on the American Colonies—Aristocracy and Common Law

One aspect of English jurisprudence adopted by the Americans was the Common law. The common law gave Americans the foundational experience that the British accumulated over many centuries of common law jurisprudence, by trial and error at the local level.[33] Unlike the Continental Europeans that used the formalized Roman law-based system, the Civil law, the English stitched together their law from the ground up, by *ad hoc* local jurisprudence that was judge made and that overtime accumulated into precedents and applied by the local judges to adjudge similar cases. This unsystematic and unformalized, ground up system, gives the judges the discretion to use their judgment in dealing with cases and make allowance for shades of differences between cases, since not all cases are identical, or one size fits all jurisprudence. It also may have given the English judges the idea or belief that if local judges can apply and make law at the local level. That is, the common law imbued with natural justice, is a good source of rule not only for the Commoners but Crown and Parliament. Sir Edward Coke[34] (1552–1634), as we will later see, is one of those judges that reached the heights of English jurisprudence in the Sixteenth and Seventeenth centuries—that was of the opinion of judges holding Parliament and Crown to account by way of judicial review.

The British people's struggle to free themselves from the rule of monarchy was not a linear historical event but a centripetal force of power politics to counter any linearity of motion in a unidirectional manner—in a mix of motions that 'eventually' led to the *Magna Carta*,[35] and finally set the stage of the British people freeing

[33] For good commentaries on the common law, see: Broom (1896).

[34] MacKay (1924), p. 215; *see further*, Friedrich (1963), p. 78. "In Bonham's case (1610) Coke formulated this position with particular sharpness. "It appears in our books [of law] that in many cases the common law will control the Acts of Parliament and sometimes adjudge them utterly void; for when an Act of Parliament is against the common right or repugnant or impossible to be performed, the common law will control it and adjudge such act to be void." And since the common law can become valid only through a decision of the courts, one can see here the clear basis for judicial review of legislative acts as it later became a reality under the written constitution of the United States."

[35] Jones (2015), p. 2. "Famously, John was forced to promise that "no free man is to be arrested, or imprisoned, or disseized, or outlawed, or exiled, or in any other way ruined, nor will go or send against him, except by the legal judgment of his peers or by the law of the land" and that "to no one will we sell, to no one will we deny or delay, right or justice.""

themselves from monarchical rule, starting with the Seventeenth century Civil War and ending the journey with Nineteenth century parliamentarian rule—along a continuum that would eventually reduce the monarchy to a ceremonial role. Let me put the matter better and clear up any misunderstanding. Britain developed like most of the regions in a post-Roman world that collapsed in the fifth century A.D., as did other European peoples, under feudalism with territories being fought over and held by strong men that eventually gave themselves the 'title' of kings. Britain was no different in this matter. But at some point, in British and European history, the serfs and other commoners inched their way up, until they held sufficient power to be able to behead their Kings and Queens, should they prove to be too oppressive.

The *principle* may be stated this way:

> Civilizations pass from the scene. The ancient civilization of Greece and Rome slowly but surely were eclipsed by the march of Christendom. But once a civilization is replaced by another, in this case Greco-Roman, by Christendom, there cannot be going back in historical time. They can only be recalled or remembered in memorial time. How they lived or governed themselves can be deduced from the historical record and other evidence left behind. But no modern human can ever relive these times outside the mental re-enactment, that is by way of Mind.

As mentioned earlier, the key moment that changed the course of British history was the Civil War of the Seventeenth century[36] (1642–1651) and the Long Parliament (1640–1660) that established the precedent that Kings could no longer take Parliament for granted. Parliaments prior to the Civil War were simply lackeys and puppets of the King serving as tax collectors when the Crown needed more money to finance more wars. The Long Parliament finally set the precedent that Parliament was not to be the plaything of the King. And eventually Parliament moved front and center of British society, with Monarchy and Parliament eventually forming a Constitutional Monarchy. The sharing of power between the Crown and Parliament, after the *Glorious Revolution*, characterized Britain well until the Nineteenth century when Parliamentary power or Parliamentary Supremacy was fully embodied into the British way of life. We foreigners, of course need to be careful in characterizing the British power relations based on the Montesquieu model or the division of power. The British seem to have their own way of doing things. Instead of dividing power, the British seem to have the tendency to *fuse* power such as Crown-Lords-Commoners and judiciary into one integrated and entangled ball of wax, which will not allow the foreigner to fully grasp what is happening under the hood of the British system without a great deal of effort in disentangling the mess—even though the Monarchy was ultimately sidelined and consigning to a ceremonial role.[37]

---

[36] For a modern interpretation and history of the English Civil War, see: Purkiss (2006).

[37] From the Long Parliament (1640–1660) forward the relationship between Crown and Parliament was uneven until it stabilized for a couple of centuries by forming a constitutional monarchy. It will take additional fights to push the Crown to the sidelines completely. Of course, when I say "completely," I do not mean it being without influence at all. Many European countries have permanently removed their royalty, but the British people have not done so. This should indicate to

The English Civil War was a major turning point, not only for England but also for her colonies. The drafters of the American Constitution were well aware of British history. The Civil War, along with the *Glorious Revolution*, were well known aspects of recent British history. And the partnership formed between the Crown and Parliament, after the Glorious Revolution, set the political pattern of *shared power* rather than a single entity holding absolute power. And it may have further opened the door that rebellion is an option if either Crown or Parliament trampled on the people's natural rights. The theory that Natural Rights were inviolable by Crown-Parliament. And if the Crown or Parliament trespassed on their natural rights, as they perceived them living out in the colonies or as British subjects, they reserved the right to rebellion and revolution to regain them. Whether in fact the British treated their North American colonies oppressively is a debated matter and will not be treated here. The main point being that certain principles derived from the *Magna Carta*, Natural Law,[38] and the Common Law gave the colonists[39] tools that they could use to defend, excuse, and explain their actions in the battles for their freedom during the American Revolution. Corwin says:

> Thus in 1765 the royal governor of Massachusetts Province wrote his government that the prevailing argument against the Stamp Act was that it contravened "Magna Charta and the natural rights of Englishmen and therefore, according to Lord Coke," was "null and void": and on the eve of the Declaration of Independence Judge William Cushing [c]harged a Massachusetts jury to ignore certain acts of Parliament as "void and inoperative," and was congratulated by John Adams for doing so. In fact, the Cokian doctrine was invoked by the Supreme Court of the United States as late as 1874.[40]

Now, how does the power of judicial review fit into all this?[41] Firstly, the power of judicial review is not simply a creation of the American system of justice. The power

---

us that although the Parliament is the real power behind the throne in England, it should not be interpreted that the Crown has no influence.

[38] Swisher (1946), p. 5. Swisher says that a constitution that negatives or forbids or delimits certain actions falls back on the Natural law as an appeal. He puts the matter this way: "Such beliefs are formulated in many different kinds of statements and are variously related to concepts of natural law, natural justice, and divine law and formulations under still other terms. Suffice it to say that they run back through most of recorded history. The development of the American conviction that certain areas of control were altogether forbidden to government came through out British heritage from at least as far back as Magna Carta."

[39] Rakove (1996), p. 20. "[A]merican constitutional thinking was profoundly shaped by the great disputes between Stuart monarchs and their opponents (in Parliament and out) which reached a momentous climax in the Glorious Revolution of 1688–89. On a host of issues—ranging from the great paradigms of mixed government and separation of powers to the "inestimable" right to trial by jury—the contending positions of the Stuart era were still vividly recalled a full century later."

[40] Corwin (1978), pp. 221–222.

[41] *United States v. Butler*, 297 U.S. 1, 62–63 (1937), I will attempt to consider Justice Robert's procedure for measuring the statute against the Constitution and adjudging whether the statute comports with the Constitution or exceeds its boundaries. I hope to show the absurdity of Justice Robert's view of how the Supreme Court abused this power. I will argue that what Justice Robert's proposes is impossible because the Court was not authorized to do this in the first place. That is, the Supreme Court usurped this power by its own authority—simply by proclaiming that it can adjudge

of the judiciary to review legislation as comporting to ancient law, the common law, or natural justice was proposed for the British system by Edward Coke, long before the American Revolution and Constitution-making. However, it was understood that judges were not to cross the line between ordinary legal interpretation and making law.[42] Secondly, the American power of judicial review is said to comport with written constitutions, unlike the British which have an unwritten Constitution. It has come to be seen as an important feature of written constitutions. Thirdly, what is judicial review exactly? It is the power of the American Supreme Court to overturn the will of the American people, the legislative will, by declaring laws and regulations as unconstitutional because they do not comport with the written specifications of the Constitution. Fourthly, this power of judicial review was firmly formalized into American history with the landmark case of American jurisprudence, *Marbury v. Madison*[43] in 1803.

One probable reason for acquiescing to the use of this power is that the judiciary is well placed to throw a bucket of water on overheated politicians trying to respond to an irritated or inflamed public seeking legislative remedy for their problems. That is, the judiciary will be an important intermediary between the people and legislature—to review and prevent any laws that result from the furnaces of populist fires that might come to control Congress or taking actions imprudent while under the grip of an agitated populace.[44] The need for a non-democratic process to dampen the fire or energy of political will and tell these agitators that their actions exceed the parameters of the Constitution as they see it. If legal interpretation can somehow

---

statutory law and hence acquire the power as the final arbiter of law in the United States. *See further*, Lazer (1967), *see in particular*, Chapter 6: "The Supreme Court and Judicial Review," pp. 182–239.

[42] Broom (1896), pp. 4–5. Broom explains the proper role and scope of the judge to apply the law or interpret it according to accepted cannons of interpretation. Brooms makes it clear that under no circumstance is it the province of the judge to apply the law free from its legislative mornings or render it null and void based on his opinions. "It is the province of the statesman, not the lawyer, to discuss, and of the legislature to determine, what is best for the public good, and to provide for it by proper enactments. It is the province of the Judge to expound the law only: the written, from the statutes; the unwritten law, from the decisions of his predecessors and of the existing Courts, or from text-writers of acknowledged authority, and upon the principles to be clearly deduced from them by sound reason and just inference; it is not, however, the duty of a Judge to speculate upon what may be most in his opinion for the advantage of the community."

[43] 5 U.S. 137 (1803), the *Marbury v. Madison* case involved one William Marbury seeking to obtain his commission as a justice of the peace that was signed by John Adams and sealed as the outgoing administration of John Adams was leaving office in 1801 but never delivered to Marbury. Marbury filed an affidavit that required the Secretary of State, James Madison, to show cause as to why a *mandamus* should not be issued to compel the Secretary of State to deliver Mr. Marbury's commission, under the Judicial Act of 1789. Chief Justice Marshall writing for the Court claimed that the Supreme Court could not issue a *mandamus* to the Secretary of State because the Court lacked original jurisdiction and would violate the Constitution to issue such a *mandamus*. And the Congress, through the passage of the Judicial Act of 1789, lacked the power to pass such legislation granting the Supreme Court such authority if the Constitution itself did not enumerate such a power for the Court.

[44] Hamilton, Federalist # 78.

break the fiery passions of the People, the result will be pragmatic laws rather than revolts and revolutions.

The Supreme Court, for example, can simply quash any legislative activity that in its opinion damages the interests of private property. If the legislative body is simply equal to the judicial body, then a case could be made as to the judicial meddling in lawmaking. By placing the Legislative branch first in the Constitution, the Founders were aiming to give the Legislative branch *Primus inter pares*, and hence was placed ahead of the other bodies. However, the legislative body was understood, not exactly as in the British model of being the prime mover of English law. Parliamentary supremacy was not achieved overnight in Great Britain but had to be fought over every step of the way. That is, Parliamentary supremacy did not simply emerge after the English Civil War or the Glorious Revolution. The King always managed to have his hands in the pie making of law and policy. The British having an unwritten constitution allows them great flexibility in the making of the law. However, the United States with a fixed written Constitution that flexibility is gone. Nevertheless, even though Parliament lost prestige by the time of the American revolution, it still was believed that the legislative branch should get first place in the Constitution—it should be the prime mover as long as it could be checked by the Executive and Judicial branches of government. By giving the Legislative branch primary position because it has the greatest representational range over the other two bodies, the executive and the judiciary—the Executive delimited by the Electoral College and the Judiciary being delimited by appointment. It was "presumed" that each branch was to stay in its own lane under a divided theory of government as laid out by Montesquieu.

That is, each branch of government was supposedly co-equal to each other, but in the course of American history, each branch attempted to grab more power for itself. The judiciary did its power grab before the ink was dry on the Constitution, the Executive branch attempted to overreach during times of danger. But also, during periods of legislative deadlock—by way of the overuse of the pardon power and other executive prerogatives, such as the overuse of executive orders and powers to fight wars or other military conflicts under less than emergency conditions, in order to bypass Congress. This has been a well understood disorder that continues to plague the well-ordered and designed constitutional government and well embroidered tripartite structure.[45] Even though it was clear to the Founders that no single branch should rule supreme over the other branches. It could not help but shape the American Congress to look like the British Parliament but with checks and balances—a tamed Parliament, in the case of Britain tamed by the Monarch and in the case of America tamed by the Presidency and the Judiciary. Of course, the

[45] Of current events, the abuse of the pardon power and the abuse of the use of executive orders to circumvent Congress were not front and center consideration at the Convention. Of course, this is not the fault of the Founders since they could not anticipate in what manner the Constitution would be abused by its posterity.

Founders could not envision the type of administrative state that will emerge to fill out or put substance to the few lines of direction given in the Constitution.

The American Founders were not going to establish a parliamentary system of government. But the Founders at the Constitutional Convention of 1787 were aware of English history and the English Civil War fought more than a century earlier. That is, the Framers of the American system were not ignorant men designing a new system from scratch. Although the Montesquieu tripartite model won out, it also resembled quite a bit the English system. Nevertheless, it placed its most trust with the Legislature, being directly closest to the People. However, given the British Parliament's tendency to use taxation to finance its wars, nothing unusual about using the power of taxation for wars in the aggrandizement of Crown and country, but it also taught the colonists not to give exclusive power to a single entity—the lessons learned by the colonists is that if Parliament can use its power of taxation to bleed the colonists, why could not Congress do the same if it was given absolute power in tax matters. One reason Parliament was able to topple the Monarch—Charles I—in the Seventeenth century English Civil War was the monarch's constant need for more money to finance more wars. Now, during the mid-eighteenth century, when Britain was an established Constitutional monarchy, Parliament also needed to raise money for defense and wars.

What became clear to the American Founding Fathers was that they could appeal to the *Magna Carta*, in the drafting of their *Declaration of Independence* in 1776, to break with the British using the *Magna Carta* and John Locke's natural law philosophy as a way of saying: "No Taxation Without Representation." Before Britain became a Constitutional Monarchy in the Eighteenth century, one means that Monarchs used to finance their wars was through taxation, by using makeshift Parliaments to collect those taxes. And once the taxes were collected, the Crown promptly dissolved Parliament until another installment of cash was needed. It is suggested here that one reason the United States did not become a Parliamentary democracy was because the Framers saw that a Parliamentary government could just as easily trample on their natural rights as a Monarchy. Of course, the original *Magna Carta* said nothing about *We the People* or democracy being a dispute between the Barons and King John in the Thirteenth century. Nevertheless, by the time of the American Revolution, the *Magna Carta* was the NorthStar for colonists. Simply because, by the Eighteenth century, the *Magna Carta* acquired a *symbolic* status for freedom. The great British jurist of the Eighteenth century, William Blackstone, interpreted the *Magna Carta* to comport with the needs of the British people of their era.

The *principle* may be stated this way:

> The Magna Carta was the NorthStar of America's push for freedom and liberty from British colonialism. As Blackstone saw the matter, this document was not a dead letter law—what power could a document of the 13th century possibly have in application toward the direction of Freedom for the American colonies of the 18th century? The Magna Carta had become a symbol of Freedom and Liberty, according to Blackstone.

The Founders were able to use the slogan with great effect in mustering up the courage and resources to fight the British empire: *"No Taxation Without Representation."* Since the colonists lacked parliamentary representation then parliament should not impose the *Stamp Act* on them without their say so.[46] So, when America started drafting its Constitution, they knew that Parliament, just as much as a Monarch, could circumscribe their freedom or property interests if the legislature was not properly boxed in and checked. Even though the American Congress was to have the broadest representational reach and placed first in the Constitution, it did not mean that it was to be trusted to do the right thing. Because it could just as easily trample on the sacred rights of property as any monarch or dictator. The complexities of the regulatory and administrative state, needed to carry forward the constitutional word or mandate, were in the future. However, given the independence of each state and the replication and compounding of the Federal model would be suggestive that entanglements and ensnarements were not too much off into the distant future. Noticeably clear to the Founders, but no alternative solution for the time, was the creation of a "compound republic" was going to lead to many disputes and entanglements.

The Founder's solution was to go for a mixed government with checks and balances—Montesquieu style. An Aristocratic Constitution that would save property from *We the People* and check Congress via the other branches of government. A very clever scheme that could make it look like America was all about *We the People*, but at the same time fearing the People, attempted to design a constitutional system with numerous poison pills to halt any property transfer or property confiscation. Unlike the case of Congress and the Presidency, Alexander Hamilton proclaimed that the Supreme Court was going to be the "least dangerous" branch.[47] It became important that the executive power not be able to grab absolute power by way of a strong leader with 'unrepublican' inclinations. So, they boxed in the presidency using the electoral college vote rather than the popular vote. Ackerman says that when it came to the Presidency at the Convention that they "feared a

[46] Of course, the scope of representation is a rather tricky matter and argument, in that the British could counterclaim the American grievance of lack of representation, with the reply that a portion of Englishmen also lacked representation in England too. I will not fight nor relitigate the matter here. However, it should be clear that the principle of "representation" took hold by the close of the eighteenth century. And whether it be the British at home or the colonists, it could use it to great effect regardless as to the range of this power during the period.

[47] Bickel (1986). The fact that a pro-monarchist or pseudo-republican was signaling that the Supreme Court was the weaker of the three branches should signal caution signs; *see*, Alexander Hamilton, *Federalist* # 78. The fact that Supreme Court justices are appointed for life might signal independence to pursue political ideologies that are far removed from *We the People*. Hamilton must have known that giving these Brahmin of law life appointment will shield and protect them from democracy and the voters. So, it gave them wide latitude to opine from up high, under the assumption that these justices would somehow be "neutral" arbiters of the law. That is, they were Beings that could not be biased, bribable, subject to corruptions, or suffer any other ills that plagued the human animal from time immemorial. They were the immortal beings from up high ready to pass judgement on the "unwashed" masses, the "common" people, or *We the People*.

demagogue" could emerge. So, they used the Electoral College technique to prevent that from happening.[48]

Ackerman is correct as far as it goes. The Founders did not anticipate the formation of political parties. But at the same time, using the filtration of the Electoral College, would further ensure that a radical President could also be kept out. The Electoral College is tied into the idea that a President elected directly by *We the People* could pose a threat to property interests. By having the President filtered through State selected electors it could free him to protect the rights of property without too much blowback from the populace. We can clearly see that under the American Aristocratic Constitution, the principle of "one person, one vote" falls dead on arrival. Why might that be the case? Because the Founders did not trust *We the People* to elect our leaders. It is a winner take all system. Those that did not get a majority are wiped out rather than apportioning the votes. But if protection of property is the goal, mechanisms such as these, become essential in filtering out the wrong candidate for President. And, therefore, we have several instances where the candidate for president won the popular vote but lost the Electoral College vote.[49]

The *principle* may be stated this way:

> The Founders were able to use "checks and balances" very effectively in the Constitution. They needed to add these poison pills in case the "commoners" or We the People attempted to democratically override the Aristocratic republican system they put in place. Also, Judicial Review and the Electoral College served the Aristocratic system well.

The interest in property and singling out property for special protection in the American scheme, the Founding Fathers were showing their class interests. Political parties, for the drafters of the Constitution, were equivalent to factions or factionalism since the rise of political parties did not exist at the drafting of the Constitution. Eventually these political parties will emerge and come to dominate the political agenda of America. That is, America or *We the People* have no political agenda unless it is blessed by the political parties' infrastructure and adoption. They increased the division of society and the strongest party that is well financed, either by the backing of the landed interests in early America or finance-capital in later generations, is going to set the rules for participation in American politics. There can only exist one democracy in America, and that is the democracy of money-interests.

The *principle* may be stated this way:

> It is not possible to have a "pragmatic" democracy and uncontrolled (unlimited acquisition) of private property. Either democratic interests will set the rules or private property interests. It cannot be both because it is a contravention of historical experience.

[48] Ackerman (2005), pp. 5–6; *see further*, Ackerman (2013).

[49] The most recent event is the 2016 election between Hilary Clinton and Donald Trump. Hilary Clinton won the popular vote but lost the Electoral College vote. What matters is Electoral College victory, not popular vote victory. So, Donald Trump became President of the United States.

Property accumulation in a few hands cannot provide the ground conditions or fundamental principles for democratic rule. Without proper control of private property accumulation, there is no possibility for democracy anywhere in the world. That is, any possibility for pragmatic democracy rather than democracy in "name" only. Should such controls be weak or non-existent, then no one should be surprised that the property interests will quash the People like a bug—and render any semblance of pragmatic democracy just as metaphysical or utopian as the ideal forms of democracy. Because the power of private property will always defeat the power of democracy. The concentration of property power versus the diffusion of democratic power spells the end of democracy. However, the matter may be rendered moot on the proposition that democracy is not possible at all. But assuming that some modified form of democracy is possible, it is incompatible with the acquisition of unlimited private property. The main issue is what type of relationship a republic stands to a democracy. Is there any connection or overlap between a republican state and a democratic state? The Founders rejected the establishment of a Democratic State in favor of a Republican State. So, then the question arises as to why the United States is considered a democracy if the Founders created something other than a democracy?

It could be argued, and it has been argued, that although the Framers did not create a democratic state, at its point of origin, it became so over time. It shed its republican/aristocratic model post-Civil War, and as the Nineteenth century ended, America has been transformed into a democracy. If democracy means that a set of people cast a ballot for a set of competing candidates for office, and the candidate that can claim a majority of the votes upon tabulation, then this tool of counting votes becomes the definition of democracy.[50] However, even after this loose and basic notion of democracy, the United States would still not qualify because it is not a majority of the votes that win, but a threshold reached in the casting of electoral votes. That is, for the highest office in the land, the Presidency, is not determined by majority rule but by Electoral College rule.[51]

---

[50] Analysis of democracy—majoritarian democracy; pure "majoritarian democracy" is feared as a system of government by most countries around the world. Each country places its own delimitation on the concept via constitutional democracy—be it a bill of rights, rules, and regulations as to voting, etc. the popular idea is that majority rule can lead to the "tyranny of the majority." So, anti-majoritarian democrats or constitutional democrats usually provide provisos to keep We the People at bay. Other ways to control pure majoritarian rule involve adding an upper house to Congress to quell any wild ideas that were voted in by the bottom House of Congress and of course the use of electoral votes and the Electoral College to be sure that majorities can be defeated if they are too wild for the establishment to absorb. New Zealand is usually taken in as a country able to live without an upper house of Congress. This type of majoritarianism is usually frowned upon by other so-called democracies as too radical. *See further*, Levinson (2006), pp. 201–210.

[51] Electoral college, specific constitutional reference; Levinson (2006), pp. 81–97 "It is an embarrassing fact that the American system that American citizens do not cast their ballots directly for their favorite candidates for the presidency. Instead, they vote for electors ostensibly (but not always) committed to a given candidate. The Byzantine procedures by which we elect our presidents are spelled out in clause 2 and 3 of Article II, section 1, and in the Twelfth Amendment

Given the shaky foundational groundwork already discussed in the construction and building of the American Constitution, would it not compound the problem, the anti-democratic problem, by adding to it the power of judicial review to a Supreme Court that exists by appointment rather than by election? And, given that Supreme Court justices are appointed for life, should the power of judicial review be taken away from the Supreme Court? If so, why? Yes. Because it is a vestige of aristocratic rule. It functions as a check on democracy. It is a mechanism for the protection of property. It elevates the lawyer class[52] as the gatekeepers of democracy. It gives first of place to property ownership and corporations over and above citizenship. And the Supreme Court becomes the prime mover of the American government rather than its legislative body.

> A Court committed by its tradition to the cause of property rights, composed of judges who were inevitably drawn largely from the ranks of the "haves" and who were of course by definition lawyers and thus imbued with the conservative bias that has always characterized the American legal fraternity—such a Court was almost certain to throw its weight against the regulatory movement and on the side of the business community.[53]

It took a major effort for the government to bring regulatory, tax, antitrust and other tools to control monopoly and control unhinged capitalism. A *laissez-faire* capitalism that has become the *sine qua non* of the American way of life. The less government, the better. Now, who will tell the People or *We the People* that have been under the thumb of monopolists the past hundred plus years that taxation is theft? Who will tell the People that they do not matter unless they are big stakeholders in their country? If they happen to be small business owners, small scale

(which modified the original clause 3, which I omit below." p. 83; *see further*, Longley and Braun (1996).

[52] Elevation of the lawyer class; *see also*, Horwitz (1977), Chapter 5, "The Relation Between the Bar and Commercial Interests," pp. 140–159. The differences and conflicts between the legal profession and commercial interests during the eighteenth century, according to Horwitz, were mended and strengthened by the 1st quarter of the nineteenth century. Rather than remain antagonists, they partnered to promote economic development in nineteenth century America. Furthermore, there appears to be a certain relation that will eventually be build up between property, commercial, and corporate interests that would negative the small-time lawyer or country lawyer as the law profession grew up along with commercial interests, one hand helping the other hand, in amassing tremendous power together. Therefore, the idea that the law and lawyers ought to serve as servants, advisors, and guides to the established interests would serve the profession well in the end by using their professional status for the good of the community—the moneyed community. Of course, interest outside the established interests, were for renegade or radical lawyers to soil their hand with. Similarly, the judiciary could be "neutral" as long as it involved establishment interests—the money interests in short. Of course, the impoverished and dispossessed of society were left on their own under the assumption that the law served the money interests, not the middle class or poverty stricken. And, so, during the Gilded Age, the judiciary became the handmaidens to corporations that will eventually rule America by the start of the twentieth century; *see further*, Skouras (2011), p. 37.

[53] McCloskey (1994), p. 69 (reference to post-Civil War Courts that attempted to hold back the regulatory deluge during the rise of American industry at the close of the nineteenth century America).

farmers, 9 to 5 workers, or others with little or no money, that they do not count in the American system of government. Who will tell the People?

The *principle* may be stated this way:

> Western civilization endorsed the proposition that the "best," the "strong," and the "wealthy," should serve as the rulers of the masses. This translates into property ownership as the foundational principle of constitutional government. The Founding Fathers were prisoners of their time as we all are. No one can escape their time, culture, or civilizational horizon.

Compounding the property protections originally established by land ownership, there also need to be protections for the emerging industrial base and corporations, as they displaced and replaced landed property as the new rulers. That is, finance capital needed protection with the rise of the Industrial Age—with the corporations serving as the spearhead to render the "nightwatchman" state even weaker byway of the propagation of false economic theories conducive to establishing a *laissez-faire* ideology. The late Nineteenth century and early Twentieth century expansion of the corporate form of business,[54] under the corporation as a "person" idea, will eventually replace landed property rulership of America with finance-capital rulership. The corporation was defined as a "person" by the Supreme Court. In short, early efforts to control monopoly was hindered by the Court at the expense of *We the People.*[55]

Of course, the scope of the power of judicial review is wide and ranges well beyond the property and economic sphere. And many works have explored the total range of this power.[56] Here, however, it is of critical importance to focus on how this power has altered and affected the People of the United States with respect to property and economic interests. How has the Supreme Court defanged Antitrust law?[57] How did the Court center the Constitution around the protection of property? That is, the Court used the Due Process Clause[58] to invalidate threats to private property. The Court deemed it necessary to protect property and big business

[54] Corporate "person"; the corporation becoming the "new" tool to spearhead capital accumulation and property protection under the newly added Civil War Amendments meant to protect the emerging African Americans as they emerged from the bondage of slavery to freedom—the Fourteenth Amendment.

[55] Horwitz (1977), p. 211. "The triumph of contractarian ideology by the middle of the nineteenth century enabled mercantile and entrepreneurial groups to broadly advance their own interests through a transformed system of private law. Having destroyed or neutralized earlier protective or regulatory doctrines at the same time as they limited the power of juries to mete out rough and discretionary communal standards of justice, a newly established precommercial legal elite was able to align itself with aggressive business interest."

[56] The total literature on the topic of judicial review is voluminous to say the least. Since this power was acquired by the Court, its critics and supporters debated the matter endlessly, and, so, it is important to post some delimitations and guideposts for our analysis and review of this power.

[57] Antitrust (The Sherman Act).

[58] Berman (1983), p. 12. ""Due Process of law" is, in fact, a fourteenth century English phrase meaning natural law. Thus natural-law theory is written into the positive law of the United States. This does not, however, prevent one from giving a political ("positivist") explanation of it. It is easy

under the theory that any regulatory interference into a person's business was a violation of their property, as corporations acquired the status of 'persons.'[59] Freedom of contract became the cry of the day. This is code for the commoners are not "proper" citizens in America to the extent that the wants and needs of the many do not comport with the interests of the few; so, to the working class or middle class is of any interest to the Establishment, it is so to the degree it can furnish the labor power needed to run the economy and system. Once these laborers are used up by the economy and system, they have nothing else to offer—so they are best disposed of once the workers lose their power to serve as industrial tools; they can be disposed as industrial waste, once they have been stripped of their labor power and nothing else left to offer the system.[60]

As we asked earlier, should the Legislative branch be given Supreme power in the United States?[61] If the Supreme Court is stripped of the power of judicial review and Congress becomes the final arbiter of the law, would this benefit or hurt *We the People*? Woodrow Wilson thought it would benefit democracy. If so, then the judiciary cannot be its equal, in the determination of all legal matters as final. As indicated earlier, although the Framers assumed that the Legislative branch, like the British Parliament would be front and center in lawmaking, the Framers also fell under the spell of the French model set forth by Montesquieu.[62]

The Montesquieu model envisaged three co-equal branches of government. What has become clear over time is that the theory of co-equal branches of government sounds good on paper or in theory but becomes an unworkable and impractical model. How so? It compounds bureaucracy, not just by redundancy, or duplication of tasks, but the entanglement of crisscrossing departmental responsibilities and

enough to show that the state, or the powers that be, or the ruling class, benefits from the due process clause and "wills" it to be."

[59] Corporation as "person": "Thus, for example, in *Northwestern Nat Life Ins. Co. v. Riggs,* 203 U.S. 243 (1906), the Court accepted that corporations are for legal purposes "persons," but still ruled that the Fourteenth Amendment was not a bar to many state laws which effectively limited a corporation's right to contract business as it pleased. However, this was not because corporations were not protected under the Fourteenth Amendment—rather, the Court's ruling was that the Fourteenth Amendment did not prohibit the type of regulation at issue, whether of a corporation or of sole proprietorship or partnership." *See further*, Bakan (2005) a critical examination of corporate pursuit of power and profits under personhood protections.

[60] For a review and analysis of the victory of money and property during this period: see, Beatty (2007).

[61] Wilson (2002) (argued for Congressional Supremacy).

[62] It is interesting to note that the new regime after the French Revolution did not see fit to give the power of judicial review to their judiciary. The 1st written Constitution of France in 1791 prohibited the judiciary from reviewing legislative and administrative acts. Rousseau and Montesquieu were not supporters of the judicial review power within and in light of French history. Cappelletti (1970), p. 1026. "Largely because of these abuses of the judicial function, the ideology of the Revolution, enshrined in the works of Rousseau and Montesquieu, stressed the omnipotence of statutory law, the equality of man before the law, and the rigid separation of powers in which the judge, the passive *bouche de la loi*, performed the sole task of applying the letter of the law to individual cases—a task conceived as purely mechanical and in no way creative."

agency layering unnecessarily to serve the people. So, to simplify this process and maintain some sort of democracy for the People, there must be a cutting off and disposing of the Senate,[63] as an unnecessary appendage and a vestige of an aristocratic era. The Senate is simply an anachronism. It is the vestige of privilege and class system—which privileges the few. Sanford Levinson characterized the Senate this way: "[T]he Senate was the importance of offering guaranteed representation to America's financial elites as a way of protecting private property."[64]

Montesquieu, on the other hand, finds the need for a Senate as essential to any properly balanced government. He writes:

> If a permanent body be established to serve as a rule and pattern of manners; a senate, to which years, virtue, gravity, and eminent services procure admittance; the senators, by being exposed to public view like statues of the gods, must naturally inspire every family with sentiments of virtue.
>
> Above all, the senate must steadily adhere to the ancient institutions, and mind that the people and the magistrates never swerve from them.
>
> The preservation of the ancient customs is a very considerable point in respect to manners.[65]

Montesquieu's conception of the Senate is an Aristocratic one; that is, that a higher chamber is needed to provide guidance, education, manners, traditions, etc. to the masses or render disciple and oversight over the "democratic mobs" that may have

---

[63] Vestige from an aristocratic era of politics, during Montesquieu's time such hierarchical institutions offered balance against the irrationalism forces of democracy and the "unwashed masses." Currently, there is no need for such an institution other than a reminder of a time when the opposition to the rise of democracy was complete; *see further*, Levinson (2006). Levenson makes the point that two legislative bodies (bicameralism) versus a single legislative body (unicameralism) are usually not of equal power. That is, "of the eight European countries that have two legislative houses, six are described as only "weakly" bicameral, because, in effect, one house can almost certainly prevail against the opposition of the other." (p. 30) He only finds Switzerland and Germany to have "strong" bicameralism. "It is no coincidence that Germany and Switzerland are also strongly *federal*, as, of course, are the United States and other such bicameral countries as Canada and Australia. Bicameralism to some extent may be a proxy for the degree that one is committed to preferring the dispersion of loyalties and identities attached to federalism as against focusing more strongly on a single *national* identity. In any event, it is exceptional to see two legislative houses that are equal in power. The British may have their House of Lords to complement the House of Commons. Not since 1911, though, has the House of Lords enjoyed any real parity of power with the House of Commons, and it has become ever weaker in the almost full century since." (p. 30) The point being that this bicameralism is additional control where the upper chamber can check the lower chamber, the upper chamber usually drawn from the better sorts. Currently in the United States, as I suspect other countries that have similar control mechanisms in place, it simply draws people of money as the most common denominator, but under two centuries of class warfare it is letting in some of the "commoners" as well. This upper chamber should have been gotten rid of two centuries ago. The fact that it has not, regardless of whether it involves the weaker or stronger version of bicameralism, is a testament to the power of the money interests trying to hold back the tide of the propertyless and "unwashed" classes knocking at the door or simply ramming at the door until this upper chamber body one day meets its end.

[64] Levinson (2006), p. 32.

[65] Montesquieu (1949), p. 47.

elected imprudent persons to the lower House. For our times, we simply need to ask the question as to the feasibility of democracy. If democracy is not a feasible system, then whatever appendages are placed on the "democratic" system are irrelevant because democracy becomes an abstraction without substance. However, if democracy can be a viable pragmatic system, then there is no need for such an appendage as a Senate.

British historiography points to a Parliamentary Supremacy,[66] as to the making of laws for the public. If there is no such thing as a "general public," but discrete units, then the concept of State must be reformulated to account for the will of the discrete public rather than just one centralized and generalized public. The modern concept of the Nation-State with a known geographic location in which the State/King is the *de facto* ruler under that geography needs to be re-conceptualized as alternative spaces open-up. But, also, the traditional walls of a City/Town also need re-conceptualization as the border limits become fused with hyper-reality. As technology becomes fused into political systems, the borderlands that indicate territorial integrity also cross over into cyberspace.

In summary, for this study, I will focus on the economic damage done by the practice of judicial review—the Supreme Court using this power for the protection of property, monopoly, and corporations, from the Gilded Age to the New Deal. However, I hope to impugn the practice of judicial review and such power should be withdrawn from the judicial branch. The British were right not to grant the courts such a power. The British have come under fire in recent times for withholding such a power. As post Second World War countries started adding judicial review to their constitutions, and with post-colonial countries also seeing fit to add judicial review and, finally, the fall of the Soviet Union seeing Eastern European countries add the practice to their constitutions, the British stand against such practices. Nobody seems to give the British any credit for their steadfast stand against this tidal wave of judicial review popping up all over the globe. Rather than being condemned as some sort of holdout, they should be praised for not giving this power to non-elected officials that have not gone through the fires of elections.

Unfortunately, because America emerged during a particular time and age that found democracy suspect, experimental, or even dangerous, the Founders neglected to include an explicit restriction of the power of judicial review in the text of the Constitution, and therefore creative interpretations, by such a clever Chief Justice John Marshall, was able to incorporate and fold such a power within the duties of the Supreme Court. The Court was able to pilfer such a power even under the noses of such notables as Jefferson and Madison. What does the Supreme Court, having the power of judicial review, express about the structure and function of the American government? This power allows for the continuous monitoring and policing of the Constitution by the judicial branch. By examining Supreme Court cases, we have the

[66] Currently, Parliamentary Supremacy finds itself on the defensive with the British model being one of the few still standing with the post-Second War rush to adopt judicial review in many countries around the globe. Schor (2007), p. 259.

basis of observing how the judicial branch functioned in overseeing the other branches of government.

How can the discourse of constitutionalism warp the manner and conditions of institution building? America did not build new institutions after the new Constitution was adopted. It had British institutions already in place.[67] It simply modified the existing institutions. The rights of citizens were not a novel concept, John Locke already spelled them out in the Seventeenth century; those natural rights[68] that could not be infringed upon either by Crown or positive law, found their way in the American *Bill of Rights*. The American colonies were birthed within the context of the British experience and the dueling between Crown and Parliament.[69] The result of those duels was ultimately the victorious Parliamentarians over the Monarchy. And a hybrid model of *constitutional monarchy* won the day by the time of the American Revolution. So, sharing power between different branches of government was not a novel thing. And just like the British experience moving from monarchy to constitutional monarchy to eventually Parliamentarianism, in the course of the Nineteenth century (whereby the Crown now only serves as a ceremonial role, but still serving as a powerful *symbol* of British unity) the British consolidated power within Parliament, with King and Queen serving simply as figureheads; so too America moved in a similar direction starting with features of an Aristocratic Republicanism to greater participatory trajectory of *We the People*, by giving access to the propertyless the vote and finally opening up the system to wider body of voter participation.

The principle may be stated this way:

> The Parliamentarians' defeat of the Crown in the 17th century English Civil War was a major world event. It will eventually consolidate the power of Parliament and foreshadowed the power of the gentry and bourgeoisie to first bring the Crown to heel and second to

---

[67] Berman (1983), p. 12. "Similarly, historical jurisprudence—the theory that the law derives its meaning and authority from the past history of the people whose law it is, from their customs, from the genius of their institutions, from their historic values, from precedents—has been built into the English legal *system* since the English Revolution of the seventeenth century; yet English legal *philosophy* has swung between positivism and natural-law theory, and historical jurisprudence has had relatively few adherents, at least in the twentieth century."

[68] The nature of and status of natural rights has become a rather controversial matter in the world of jurisprudence, if not a somewhat antiquated debate in modern jurisprudence due to the emergence of utilitarianism and positivism in the nineteenth and twentieth centuries to contest if not to bury this old and medieval idea of natural rights stemming from a deity. However, these modern versions of jurisprudence depend on a philosophy of individualism rather than traditional communal or community rights. A modern attack on this utilitarianism and positivistic jurisprudence is by Ronald Dworkin. *See*, Dworkin (1978).

[69] British institutions—British Constitutional history—Ackerman (2005), p. 11. "The Philadelphia Convention of 1787 saw itself as a proud successor of the Whig tradition, and when it looked to the future, it naturally supposed that assemblies would once again take the lead in speaking for the People."

> eventually lead the bourgeoisie to gain political power. Unfortunately, in later centuries it will be uncovered that capital power can be just as oppressive as Crown power.[70]

Since the British have an "unwritten" constitution, it is easier for them to incorporate political changes to their system. America, on the other hand, having a "written" constitution makes incorporating change to the system much more difficult because of the hurdles that need to be overcome to change the Constitution. So, the problem that has been debated in Twentieth century America is: whether America has a "living" constitution, like the British style of incorporating change with time, or a "dead and fixed" constitution, without room for change unless a supermajority consents to changing it. This amounts to institution building that becomes frozen over time because changes are not forthcoming as needed. Just like parts of an automobile that need repair, if the owner does not make those repairs, it will ultimately end up with a non-operational automobile. The debate as to whether it is better to have a fixed mechanical constitution that does not change with time or a living organic constitution that is fluid and in flux has not been settled in American history—put more succinctly, whether a Newtonian Constitution (the Founding Fathers model) or a Darwinian Constitution (the Progressive model) is the best?

As noted earlier, the Supreme Court took the initiative to snag the power of judicial review from the other branches of government.[71] The Court took this power under the flimsiest of excuses. Although it cited historical precedent, logical analysis, and practicality,[72] none of the reasons are sufficient for the substantive power grab it had undertaken, with *We the People* not being a bit the wiser for it.[73] I intend to focus on the property and economic damage. Of course, this is not to say that the Court only confined the damage to the property and economic domains,[74] but a case can be made for damage it brought across the social and political spectrum as well. Hence, I hope to present a coherent argument as to why the power of judicial review must be withdrawn from the Court.

---

[70] The principle as stated here is neither clear cut nor without need further qualification as far as the British is concerned. That is, the propositions are a debatable matter as to "who" these Parliamentarians really were. The poison of anachronism assumes that these Parliamentarism were progressives and fighting the Crown for the right reasons. Unfortunately, the ground level historian of whatever variety or stripe could find fault with the somewhat clear cut, rosy, and positive picture of reality on the ground as painted here as opposed to those in the midst of the "nowness" of the historical moment. So, this principle needs to be looked at in the context of seventeenth century England and not the Britain of the nineteenth century. So, the reader has been cautioned.

[71] Jeffersonian-Madisonian alternative conceptions of judicial review versus the Hamilton-Marshall vision of the power; *see also*, McCloskey (1994), p. 6.

[72] Marbury v. Madison, 5 U.S. 137 (1803).

[73] McCloskey (1994), p. 10. "Historical accident and bad logic may explain the inception of judicial review, but by now the American nation has lived with the consequences for more than 150 years.", p. 10.

[74] Miller (1968), p. 71. "For true it is that the modern corporation, as economist Gardner C. Means has said, "has undermined the preconceptions of classical economic theory as effectively as the quantum undermined classical physics at the beginning of the twentieth century.""

Tocqueville noticed early in American history that the power of judicial review was a special property of the American system of government.[75] The political dimension of this power is rooted in the Framers' distrust of democracy. This initial distrust makes democratic change to the document an extremely difficult process. The Founders put in sufficient amounts of poison pills to be sure to kill off any democratic overthrow of the Constitution and its aristocratic foundations. It was designed to serve aristocracy rather than democracy.[76] The French, with the coming and passing of the French Revolution, which was to transform all of Europe to one degree or another—dare I say the whole globe in time—were very mindful of the ways of aristocratic rule could overcome the principles on which the French Revolution stands upon.

Of course, this aristocratic dimension has philosophical and jurisprudential consequences as to its foundations and consequences for institution building. If justice is based on aristocratic institutions, it will look very different than if based on democratic institutions. That is, the jurisprudence of justice rolled out from aristocratic institutions will be different than if rolled out from democratic institutions. Let us put the matter this way: since the Constitution of the United States has a foundation of the protection of private property, the justice system that will stand on such a foundation will give, by definition, preferential treatment to property owners over the dispossessed.

The power of judicial review and the natural law did not drop into the American scene out of nowhere. And, the British system, in particular John Locke, served as a key figure and an important source of political philosophy for the Framers of the American Constitution. Locke was to the American Founding Fathers what Aristotle was to the Medieval period. So, the power of judicial review has historical components in natural law and stratified social institutions.

---

[75] Dunn (2005), p. 73. Dunn suggests that Tocqueville noticed that the coming of democracy to the New World was a sign of the historical moment for democracy's return, in Dunn's words, "Second Coming." Dunn goes on to says, "In Tocqueville's book *Democracy in America*, we find for the first time the recognition that democracy is the key to the distinctiveness of modern political experience and that anyone who hopes to grasp the character of that experience must focus on and take in just what it is that democracy implies."), p. 73. Of course, today, the use of the word "democracy" covers and adorns just about anything and everything under the sun. It could be used by dictators, despots, and tyrants just as well as egalitarians in the legitimation of their regimes, even though the "concept" of democracy has been detached from the word.

[76] *See*, Storing (1985); *see further*, the secret meeting to consider the new constitution in Philadelphia; *see further*, the removal of *We the People* from playing a direct role in the selection of officials; *see further*, the property qualification and numerous hoops each citizen must jump to get to the voting booth; *see further*, the need for a second and upper chamber of representation similar to the House of Lords or based on the Aristocratic principle of wise and propertied men needed to steady the ship of state; *see further*, the role of the Electoral College in the American political system; what does all this amount to? Democracy as an experimental model was not to be trusted and safety mechanisms needed to be in place to halt or stop the "commoners" from moving forward towards political power. The need for centralized power and centralized systems to disperse troublemakers to the periphery and make the average voter as peripheral as possible and away from the centers of power.

References

Ackerman B (1991) We the people: foundations. Harvard University, Cambridge
Ackerman B (1998) We the people: transformations. Harvard University, Cambridge
Ackerman B (2005) The failure of the founding fathers: Jefferson, Marshall, and the rise of presidential democracy. The Belknap Press of Harvard University, Cambridge
Ackerman B (2013) The decline and fall of the American republic. The Belknap Press of Harvard University, Cambridge
Ackerman B (2014) We the people: the civil rights revolution. Harvard University, Cambridge
Areeda P, Hovenkamp H (2013) Antitrust law: an analysis of American principles and their applications. Wolters Kluwer Law & Business, New York
Bakan J (2005) The corporation: the pathological pursuit of profit and power. The Free Press, New York
Beatty J (2007) The triumph of money in America: the age of betrayal 1865-1900. Vintage, New York
Becker CL (1941) Modern democracy. Yale University, New Haven
Berman HJ (1983) Law and revolution: the formation of western legal tradition. Harvard University, Cambridge
Bickel A (1986) The least dangerous branch: the supreme court at the bar of politics. Yale University, New Haven
Broom H (1896) Commentaries on the common law, 9th edn. Sweet & Maxwell, London
Cappelletti M (1970) Judicial review in comparative perspective. Calif Law Rev 57:1017
Cochran TC, Miller W (1942) The age of enterprise: a social history of industrial America. The Macmillan Comp, New York
Cooper JM (1990) Pivotal decades: the United States 1900-1920. W.W. Norton & Comp, New York
Corwin ES (1978) The constitution and what it means today, 14th edn. Princeton University, Princeton
Dahl RA (2003) How democratic is the constitution? 2nd edn. Yale University, New Haven
Dahl RA (2006) Is political equality a reasonable goal? In: On political equality. Yale University, New Haven
Diner SJ (1998) A very different age: Americans of the progressive era. Hill and Wang, New York
Dobson JM (1972) Politics in the gilded age: a new perspective on reform. Praeger, Westport
Dunn J (2005) Democracy: a history. Atlantic Monthly, Washington, DC
Dworkin R (1978) Taking rights seriously. Harvard University, Cambridge
Fishkin JS (1997) The voice of the people: public opinion & democracy. Yale University, New Haven
Friedrich CJ (1963) The philosophy of law in historical perspective. University of Chicago, Chicago
Gillman H (1993) The constitution besieged: the rise and demise of Lochner era police powers jurisprudence. Duke University, Durham
Ginger R (1975) Age of excess: the United States from 1877-1914, 2nd edn. Macmillan Publishing, New York
Hobsbawn EJ (1969) Industry and empire: from 1750 to the present day. Penguin Books, London
Hofstadter R (1955) Social Darwinism in American social thought. Beacon Press, Boston
Horwitz MJ (1977) The transformation of American law 1780-1860. Harvard University, Cambridge
Jones D (2015) Magna carta: the birth of liberty. Penguin, London
Kammen M (1987) A machine that would go of itself: the constitution in American Culture. Vintage Books, New York
Lazer H (1967) The American political system in transition. Crowell, Springfield
Lears J (2009) Rebirth of a nation: the making of modern America 1877-1920. Harper Perennial, New York

Levinson S (2006) Our undemocratic constitution: where the constitution goes wrong (and how we the people can correct it). Oxford University, Oxford

Link AS, McCormick RL (1983) Progressivism. Harlan Davidson Inc., Wheeling

Longley LD, Braun AG (1996) The electoral college primer. Yale University Press, New Haven

MacKay RA (1924) Coke: Parliamentary sovereignty or the supremacy of law? Mich Law Rev 22: 215

Marcus RD (1972) The business of politics: national party structure in the gilded age. In: Gatell FO, Goodman P et al (eds) Readings in American political history. Oxford University, Oxford

McCloskey RG (1994) The American supreme court, 2nd edn. The University of Chicago, Chicago

McConnell G (1970) Private power and American democracy. Vintage Books, New York

Michelman FI (1998) Constitutional authorship. In: Alexander L (ed) Constitutionalism: philosophical foundations. Cambridge University, Cambridge

Miller AS (1968) The supreme court and American capitalism. Vintage Books, New York

Montesquieu CL (1949) The spirit of the laws (trans: Nugent T). MacMillan, New York

Morgan HW (ed) (1970) The gilded age. Syracuse University, Syracuse

Morone JA (1990) The democratic wish: popular participation and the limits of American government. Basic Books, New York

Prakash S, Yoo JC (2003) The origins of judicial review. Univ Chic Law Rev 70(3):887–982

Purcell EA Jr (1973) The crisis of democratic theory: scientific naturalism & the problem of value. The Kentucky of University, Lexington

Purkiss D (2006) The English civil war: priests, gentlewomen, soldiers, and witchfinders in the birth of modern Britain. Basic Books, New York

Rakove JN (1996) Original meaning: politics and ideas in the making of the Constitution. Alfred A. Knopf, New York

Rodgers DT (1987) Contested truths: keywords in American politics since independence. Basic Books, New York

Schor M (2007) Mapping comparative judicial review. Wash Univ Global Stud Law Rev 7:257

Sennett R (2006) The culture of capitalism. Yale University, New Haven

Siegan BH (2001) Property rights: from the magna carta to the Fourteenth Amendment. Transaction Publishers, Piscataway

Skouras G (2011) On the formation of the American corporate state: the Fuller Supreme Court 1888-1910. In: Desuza AP (ed) The journal jurisprudence, vol 9, pp 37–58

Storing HJ (1985) The anti-federalist. The University of Chicago, Chicago

Sunstein C (2004) The Second Bill of Rights: FDR's Unfinished Revolution and Why We Need It More Than Ever, New York

Swisher CB (1946) The growth of constitutional power in the United States. The University of Chicago, Chicago

Symposium (1981) Constitutional adjudication and democratic theory. N Y Univ Law Rev 56:259

Tiger ME, Levy MR (1977) Law and the rise of capitalism. Monthly Review, New York

Trachtenberg A (2007) The incorporation of America: culture and society in the gilded age. Hill and Wang, New York

White GE (1997) Revisiting substantive due process and Holmes's Lochner Dissent. Brooklyn Law Rev 63:87

Wiebe RH (1967) The search for order 1877-1920. Hill and Wang, New York

Wilson W (2002) Congressional government. Routledge, New York

Zunz O (1990) Making America corporate 1870-1920. University of Chicago, IL

Chapter 2
English Constitutional History

2.1 Hobbes, Locke, and Coke (Seventeenth Century)

During Seventeenth century England there emerged some outstanding political and legal minds. Thomas Hobbes the philosopher of absolute sovereignty—supporting the Royalists in the English Civil War. John Locke, the philosopher of natural rights, property rights, and individual rights, supporting the Parliamentarians and opposed absolute sovereignty. And, in the legal domain, Sir Edward Coke attempted to place the rule of law above Crown and Parliament. These three giants of Sixteenth and Seventeenth century England can briefly be characterized thus: The Parliamentarians defeated the Royalists. Thomas Hobbes, a royalist, was against the dispersal of sovereign power. He believed that it should be concentrated in one sovereign, the King. For Hobbes, the law is the command of the Sovereign, and the Sovereign's duty is directed toward maintaining the peace. The common law, for Hobbes, unlike Coke, is not the higher authority to the command of the sovereign. The sovereign must be free to do what must be done to maintain the peace. The command of the sovereign is the key determinant if the citizens will yield their loyalty and lives to live in community with others. If the common law helps toward that end, well and good, but if it hinders the powers of the sovereign then it weakens the King's prerogative from providing the protection necessary for the safety of his subjects.

Hobbes should not be viewed on a canvas stretched out by time but within his own time. His masterpiece, *Leviathan*, is a powerful portrait of the contrast between the state of nature and civil society. With the emergence of modern science, the human animal could be viewed in a new light—so many springs and wheels turning—the laws of motion, the pushing, pulling—the inner body under mechanical forces—heart and muscles serving as springs of motion. Both in geometry and physics, Hobbes tried to set the body in motion under mechanical forces, the muscles serving as the springs to action. Although he was a strong proponent of monarchical power, he was also someone that examined nature and human nature with a cold eye and tried to condense the elements needed for a people to become safe and live in a

G. Skouras, *Constitutionalism and Democracy*,
https://doi.org/10.1007/978-3-031-66906-4_2

safe environment. In the end, he had no permanent home. The church viewed him as dangerous atheist. The Parliamentarians viewed him as a royalist. And even the monarchist would have their doubts about the reliability of an independent thinker.

He was a man that witnessed the comings and goings and the doings of the human being in the society he lived in. Anarchy and disorder bring about fear of all against all. The English Civil War being one of the big turning points in his lifetime. To sum up a man born into the late sixteenth century England, during the closing end of Tudor England, growing up during a time when Shakespear was still alive and living a long life into his 90s before expiring. He obviously was a top scholar in his day and remains so to this day.

John Locke was a supporter of the Parliamentarians. He believed that power should be shared. And, that the concentration of power leads to tyranny. For Locke, natural rights were divine rights that no sovereign could take away from his subjects without causing a revolt or revolution. Locke was inclined to individualism and the rights of the individual. What might be referred today as liberalism or individualism. As a Whig, he saw no need for the concentration of power in the hands of the King or in one sovereign body. He too at some point had to flee England after Lord Shaftsbury's death. His two *Treatises on Government* did not endear him to the British power centers. He believed in limited government, and the primary function of the government was the protection of the individual and property protection. Demanding that the individual have a place in such a system, especially a commoner with natural rights, was tantamount to picking a fight with the aristocracy and those that are the "betters" of others. Regardless of Locke's parliamentarian support, by the time of the seventeenth century the British supported their Royals despite just cutting off the head of one of them. That is, so entrenched was the Crown in fact, that even after they cut off the head of King Charles I, they eventually would recrown a new one.

Although Locke became America's, or should I say the Founding Father's, favorite philosopher, this does not mean that the English had the same love for him as the Americans. As the philosopher of natural rights and as America's first philosopher—Locke enjoyed pride of place with America's Founders. They adopted his revolutionary philosophy when it came time to free themselves from the English. Not only can his philosophy be seen in the American *Declaration of Independence*, in the *Bill of Rights* and along with Montesquieu, in the building of the *American Constitution*. However, Locke's power in the establishment of the American constitutional order did not go unchallenged by republicanism and communitarianism.

Edward Coke, died before the Civil War, found power regardless of origin, Crown or Parliament, can be overruled by the Judicial department because judges not only had "natural reason" but also "artificial reason" (reason available to the legal experts by training in the law) and, along with their experience with the common law, the judges were in the best place to serve as the final interpreters of the law. Therefore, according to Coke, the Judiciary should be able to pass judgment on the law and nullify any actions that contravene the common law. That is, any command or law of the sovereign must comport with the common law and natural reason. Crown and Parliament will reject Coke's view of the matter. Since Coke died before the English Civil War, the Parliaments, summoned during his lifetime, were mostly lackeys or puppets of the Crown, mostly serving, as in previous generations, as tax collectors for the King. Although Parliament starting building it up its own power base, well before the Civil War—as the representatives of the People—it became clear that by the 1620s, Parliament was flexing its muscles and rejecting the Crown's request for money. As the King tried to raise money for wars against Spain and France in 1626, it seemed strange that his requests can go unmet and rob him of his natural inheritance—his prerogative power. But according to Coke whether it be Crown or Parliament, the common law and the rule of law must govern—that neither Crown nor Parliament was above the law. The rule of law must have a final interpreter and the judges are in the best position to tell us what the law is. Of course, such thinking will eventually lead to his replacement as the Chief Justice of the Common Pleas.

Each of these English giants, except for Coke that died before the English Civil War, brought aspects of reality into view either because the Civil War clarified their perspective for what constitutes a secure environment, under the might of a Sovereign or the need for the natural rights of individuals to act free from the command of the sovereign. Security depended on natural justice being measured out properly—that would secure every citizen their life, property, and liberty[1] free from an "absolute" monarch bent on grinding the People down, without some expectation that an individual's "natural rights" meant something more than *pro forma* laws. That is, the rule of law comports with natural reason to establish individual rights inherent in the individual as such and cannot be violated by governing authority without affording that individual all the proper accoutrements for his defense. Locke as a supporter of the Roundheads will espouse a Whig liberal philosophy that would later be referred to as bourgeoisie philosophy or the philosophy of the sturdy middle class. Hobbes, on the other hand, learned the lesson that without a strong sovereign,

[1] Lecky (1899), p. 1. Note that the "natural" rights listed above does not include the right to a vote. Although the Parliamentarians won the English Civil War, this does not mean that the English also secured the right to vote. Then who had the right to vote? According to Lecky, even in the eighteenth century, let alone the seventeenth century, was there some security obtained from the Parliamentarian's victory. Lecky says that according to Burke there was no right to vote established even in the eighteenth century. What was established was not a right to vote but a privilege, or if you will, an accommodation to a vote by grant of State. Lecky says: "It was then [18th century] almost universally held that the right of voting was not a natural right, but a right conferred by legislation on grounds of expediency, or, in other words, for the benefit of the State." So, there should be no rush to the conclusion that the Parliamentarian's victory over the Crown in the seventeenth century somehow transformed England into a democracy. The best way to think of the matter is that the victory opened the door for the commoners and the bourgeoisie an entry point to the halls of power. Parliament broadened the "voice" of the gentry and emerging bourgeoisie, but this was not a democratic revolution. For that to happen, England needed further transformations that would help further break down the British class system. But as of the seventeenth century, the Crown was simply defeated by the Aristocracy with the help of the emerging bourgeoisie. The rise of the Industrial Revolution will help usher in the money interests (non-inherited money interests) and further reduce the power of Crown and Aristocracy of blood in order to make space for the commoners to vote. This was a couple of centuries in the future.

an absolute sovereignty, after all unlike Locke, was a supporter of the Cavaliers, and basically having to flee England, after the Parliamentarians defeated the Royalists, thought that the protection of self was primary—without life, property and liberty are grand illusions that will not follow the dead body to the afterworld.

As I said above Coke died before the English Civil War and lived most of his life under Elizabethan England—that is, Coke lived most of his life in the Sixteenth century (lived both in the Elizabethan Age and into the Stuart Monarchy) and, having died before the Civil War, was, nevertheless, a strong proponent of the common law. The common law and natural reason could serve as a check on both the King and Parliament. Hobbes, as a supporter of the Cavaliers, found Coke's theory to be wrong. That is, Coke's theory of "natural reason"[2] that lawyers use to decide cases was not superior to the King's "reason" in passing legal judgment. All the judges needed to do, according to Hobbes, was to follow the instructions handed down by the King. If judges "made" law, it was under the understanding and consent of the King.[3] The King is sovereign. Obviously for Hobbes, the common law did not provide the clarity, strength, and determination needed to secure the peace. That is, Hobbes directly contested Coke's support of the common law.[4]

Hobbes believed that if the Sovereign was not strong enough to keep the peace, then there cannot be civil society—only anarchy. If the sovereign cannot keep the peace, then by definition he is a weak sovereign. The sovereign must be free to use prerogative power to put down any threats to peace and stability. Work, production and the carrying forward of daily tasks become difficult under conditions of instability, chaos, and anarchy. There can be no worse condition for a society than chaos and instability because each citizen cannot feel safe and hence cannot produce for themselves. With another power center opening up, in addition to the Crown, namely Parliament, can only serve to disperse power and hence weaken the sovereign power to bring the necessary force to establish and maintain civil society and end the ways of the jungle of each against all.

Whether the English people emerge from the Civil War with an intact hierarchy—commoners, nobles, and Crown—similar to the Medieval world[5] or open-up another

[2]MacKay (1924), p. 218. According to Coke, 'natural reason' can be found in all persons, 'artificial reason' is reason comes by study and training in a particular field such as law. Hence, although King James has natural reason, he lacks artificial reason in training and study of law. So, he is in no position to pass judgement on the law, according to Coke. Coke sees natural reason and the common law as the means for grating judges and the judiciary a say of what the law is and if King or Parliament pass laws in contradiction of natural reason, the judges can strike them down as null and void. Also, Coke, after being stripped of his posts on the bench and a member of Parliament, played an important role in the passage of the *Statute of Monopolies*, restricting the King's role in the granting of patents.

[3]According to J.P. Kenyon, Tudor and Stuart kings were not opposed to the common law generally. The issue of whether the king was outside or above the parameters of the common law was not decided at the time of the Civil War, according to Kenyon. *See*, Kenyon (1969), p. 7.

[4]Hexter (1980), pp. 477–479.

[5]Tombs (2016), pp. 49–52; it appears that the English feudal system was modified by the Norman Conquest of England in 1066 to the extent that the hierarchy took on a different and more

power center to the Crown, Parliament, rested on the war's outcome. In the era of the *Magna Carta* (1215) the Barons were able to extract certain rights from King John,[6] in the Thirteenth century, but there still remained in place a hierarchical structure of society[7]—those that tend the land (serfs), those that fight (nobility), those that pray (clergy), and on top of the pyramid, the king himself.[8] The *Great*

---

centralized control over England than the previous generations of kingdoms. "Social, economic and political control of land and its people—what in the eighteenth century would retroactively be termed the "feudal system"—was given a more centralized and rigorous form after the Conquest swept away many existing rights and eliminated English thegns." (p. 51) But, nevertheless, the English feudal system was different from continental Europe to the extent that it was sufficiently flexible to allow the system to accommodate change, the 1st being the accommodation of the Norman Conquest. For better or worse England was transformed forever. Obviously, the Anglo-Saxon heritage of the English was broken with the victory and infiltration of the Normans—some pure-bred Brits and sections of Britain less infiltrated by Norman blood maintained a golden image of England before the invasion for many centuries after the event—sort of retroactively seeking those English freedoms taken away by the conquerors; perhaps, nostalgically looking back to a purer England, as things were before the Conquest. However, the feudal hierarchy, whether in England or continental Europe, existed where everything had its place in the Great Chain of Being. Everyone knew their place. One cannot help assuming the Norman Conquest would forever serve as an itch on the English-backside to recover those imagined pre-Conquest rights—to get back those ancient rights taken by the Normans. Forever itching to finally ink them down lest the next generation of monarchs forget, the *Magna Carta* seems to have satisfied the itch to limit Norman domination of the Anglo-Saxon heritage; *see further*, Trevelyan (1988).

[6]An example of how the 3rd Plantagenet King John operated through the prerogative, similar to modern American presidents using executive powers wrested from the legislature, to operate free from oversight and control from other political bodies. That is, the power to wipe the record clean of people convicted of crimes, the pardon power, executive decrees, and war power authorizations. In the case of King John, he could sell "exemptions" from justice. "A handsome trade was done too in selling exemptions from royal justice: The king could, and did, sell immunity from lawsuits at the shire court[s]." Jones (2015), p. 37.

[7]Pollock and Maitland (1923). "Now we have to speak of the unfree class. Slavery, personal slavery, and not merely serfdom or villeinage consisting mainly in attachment to the soil, existed, and was fully recognized, in England until the twelfth century." (p. 35) These authors are making a distinction as far as the English ranks or class system before the Norman invasion of 1066 England and post-invasion England (pp. 25–63). However, what needs to be kept in mind is that the English, like all the other Europeans, during medieval times in the Western Civilization fell under the grand scale rankings that Christianity also brought to the battle, besides the ranking coming from wars won or lost, battles won or lost that would set the table of class systems. That is, the medieval belief in the Great Chain of Being regardless of the particular rankings of each territory or region as carved up by kings or strongmen of their times. And the Great Chain of Being will carry through well into Modern Times, of course with some ruptures, damaged limbs so to speak, or other beating it might have received from the battering of religion and other forms of spirituality received post-French Revolutionary times. However, even to this day, the Great Chain of being may no longer exist in any concrete form or shape but still goes on in some sort of *symbolic* manner in the classification of people locally and globally.

[8]Tiffany (1903), in England the King owned the land during feudal times and as of Tiffany's publication in 1903. And this feudal system is in place today with the Queen holding "all" English land. ""Tenure" is the term used to designate the specific feudal relation between a feudal lord and his tenant, it being based on a grant by the lord to be held by the tenant on condition of the rendition of certain services. In England, all land was and is held of the king as "lord paramount," either

Chain of Being[9] was well established in medieval England, as well as Western Civilization. And, as it was to be and remain until it was critically wounded and left for dead with the French Revolution of the Eighteenth century. The *English Civil War* of the Seventeenth century was finally able to disrupt this structure, by weakening the king and eventually toppling this structure, as Parliament would eventually triumph under another era. However, it should be noted that the English are a clever people by way of layering their political system in such a way that getting to the bottom of it could be a challenge to the foreigner or the untrained eye. Although the Parliamentarians defeated the Royalists, it should not be taken at face value that the Commoners or the People were victorious. Of course, the emerging bourgeoisie and other aristocratic families were all in the ready to move in to fill any spaces for those that fell or lost favor after the Civil War—as the new gentry tried to move up in the English hierarchical system.

2.2 English History/Long Parliament (Seventeenth Century)

Why did the practice of judicial review, rejected by the British, find a home in the United States? The British Parliament's struggle with the Crown,[10] to gain power based in English society meant that the Crown's prerogatives were going to be encroached upon—that is opening up another power center. The British were not prepared to open up yet another power center to Crown and Parliament—namely the judicial branch. As indicated earlier, the English prefer the *fusion* of power rather than the separation of powers as long as the end result is an orderly society. To disentangle this rolling up of governmental functions may be more complicated or obvious, due to the layering of English society. That is, in the aftermath of the Civil War and the *Glorious Revolution*, with the consolidation of power in a Crown-Parliament partnership, the last thing they wanted or needed was the judiciary to put their hands in the cookie jar, too. That is, a meddlesome judiciary to question their

---

directly, or through the interposition of "mesne" lords." (p. 17) In England, although Parliament reduced the Crown to mostly a ceremonial role, it appears that Parliament has not reduced the Queen to a tenant but as in feudal times, the Crown is the owner of English lands. Just how remarkable is that? That the continuity of tradition, culture, and history remains in place despite the upheavals the British people suffered through the past 1000 years. If Vico was alive today, I am sure he would detect and deconstruct for us the import of symbolism and tradition for the British people.

[9] The *Great Chain of Being* was a Medieval concept that everything in the earthly and heavenly spheres had their proper place with the lowest of the low creatures up to man, and ultimately reaching the very top, the creator at the very top of this pyramid, God.

[10] It should be made clear that although the Parliamentarians moved a step forward, at that time, over monarchical rule, they should not be mistaken as men of We the People or pro-democracy. Sean Wilentz says: "But the revolution's leaders kept radical dissenters on the political margins. At the famous army debate at Putney in 1647, Cromwell and his lieutenants squelched any possibility of popular suffrage." Wilentz (2005), p. 5.

power or their wisdom. The English Civil War[11] will eventually give Parliament the upper hand over the Crown but not immediately. In the early part of the Seventeenth century, Sir Edward Coke in *Bonham's Case*[12] attempted so restrain the power of the King-in-Parliament and failed[13] to establish an independent base for the judiciary. The case angered the Crown, and he was removed from his post as the Chief Justice of the Common Pleas. And as indicated earlier the British having the penchant or rolling things up rather than the division of powers. The more divisions of sovereign power, the more power centers open up and a greater disorder is introduced into society. To excavate the British system, with generations of layering of society, is no simple matter especially for a foreigner trying to pry into the British way of life. What is taken at face value may have a different position or status at the foundational level.

The *principle* may be stated this way:

> Why did the British refuse to grant their Judiciary the power of judicial review? The British rolled up their Judiciary into a single branch of government and did not have a separate division of government with checks and balances like the United States. If they did accept Judicial Review, it would open-up a third power center to Parliamentary and Crown power.

In the Eighteenth century, Sir William Blackstone[14] concluded that Parliament gained sufficient power to guide British direction but was still tied to the Crown in the fusion of Parliamentary power with monarchical power. The power of judicial review was a dead end as far as the British people were concerned.[15] Why did the

[11] For a modern view of the period, see: Purkiss (2006); Braddick (2009); Gaunt (2003); Worden (2009); Russell (1990).

[12] Siegan (2001), p. 12. "Corwin asserts that Coke's statement in *Dr. Bonham's Case* became the most important single source of the notion of judicial review." (Scholars in recent times have become skeptical of the adequacy of Coke's precedent in the *Dr. Bonham* case. That its proposition and use by traditional historical and legal understanding needs revision, at least as understood in the United States. Be that as it may, Stoner (1992), p. 14 says: "To assess the meaning, much less the influence, of *Doctor Bonham's* case for judicial review in the United States, one must delve into Coke's legal thought as a whole."

[13] Wolfe (1986), pp. 90–91. England provided the example of a regime in which first feeble efforts to reestablish a power of judicial review had withered, and where legislative supremacy was established as a basic political principle. In the early seventeenth century, during the resistance to the Stuart Kings, Sir Edward Coke had attempted to establish the principle of judicially enforced constitutional limits on government. In *Bonham's Case* he argued: "And it appears in our books, that in many cases, the common law will control acts of parliament, and sometimes adjudge them to be utterly void, for when an act of parliament is against common law right and reason, or impossible to be performed, the common law will control it and adjudge such act to be void."

[14] William Blackstone (1723–1780), *Commentaries on the Laws of England*, in some sense Blackstone's *Commentaries on the Laws of England* was the Bible of American jurists.

[15] Wolfe (1986), pp. 90–91; "Coke's dictum, however, was not to win out in English constitutional history. Legislative supremacy, the doctrine that the legislature is the ultimate sovereign power and that its acts are unreviewable by any other body, became the basis of English law. Sir William Blackstone stated it in this way, in his *Commentaries on the Laws of England* (1770): the legislature "hath sovereignty and uncontrollable authority in making, confirming, enlarging, restraining, abrogating, repealing, reviving, and expounding of laws. [T]his being the place where that absolute,

English have reservations about judges reviewing Parliamentary statutes? According to Maitland, Coke was mistaken in believing that judges had power to oversee or have judges interpret the law according to natural reason and natural law principles. Maitland goes on to say that: "Coke distinctly claims that the judges may hold a statute void, either because it is against reason and natural law, or because it trenches on the royal prerogative. He alleges precedents for this—cases in which the statutes have been held void. I do not think that they bear him out."[16]

It has been pointed out, perhaps the Americans adopted the power of judicial review because they have a written Constitution while the English have an unwritten Constitution. The structure of the British government versus the structure of the American government as an important factor in dispensing with the power of judicial review.[17] It must have been lack of experience, as to why Americans acquiesced to

---

despotic power which must in all governments reside somewhere, is entrusted by the constitution of these kingdoms. [T]hat it is, that what the parliament doth, no authority upon earth can undo." *see also*, Maitland (2000), Maitland cannot accept Coke's views and understanding of the theory of the power of judicial review. That statute law was unreviewable by judges to accord with natural reason (pp. 297–311); *See further*, Coke (2005) (3 volumes).

[16] Maitland (2000), p. 301; *See further*, Hallam (1881), pp. 1–2, *See in particular*, Vol. I. Chapter I. Hallam claims that the English experience was different from the eastern and southern European governments with the British being based on the Celtic and Gothic tribal traditions and kingships that would makes them different from those governments that were willing to accept absolute monarchy. In other words, the British inherited a mixed government. So, there is no need to have judges declare laws contrary to royal decree, prerogative, or statute because of this mixed government. However, over the course of history after tribal conflicts and contests, those tribes that survived took additional powers for themselves and the tribal and communal decision-making was being walled off from the commons, especially during the Middle Ages. After the Norman Conquest, England would be transformed forever with investment in the usual trappings of the Crown being above the people. The old Celtic and Angels traditions supplanted by outsiders. With the common law no longer able to restrain the king's prerogative. Even though Coke hoped that the law could restrain royal prerogative and statute. Maitland maintains that Coke was mistaken in thinking that the power of judicial review could restrain the king's prerogatives or parliamentary statute (pp. 300–301).

[17] Maitland (2000). Where does sovereignty lie in England? According to Maitland this question should not be asked as far as Middle Ages England goes. Because there is no clear answer for it. One might have assumed that it lies with the Crown. However, the progression and maintenance of power and succession issues could make questions about English sovereignty a bit dicey. Over much struggle and bloodshed, Maitland sees sovereignty emerging with the Crown. During the seventeenth century Maitland says sovereignty was: "Now I think that at the onset of our period there were three claimants for sovereignty, (1) the king, (2) the king in parliament, (3) the law." (pp. 297–298) If Maitland means that the King and the King-in-Parliament were one and the same thing, then his theory makes sense. However, Maitland wants to maintain the distinction between political theory of sovereignty versus the constitutional matter of English rulership. I for one cannot see the distinction as Maitland proposed it. The seventeenth century settled the matter of sovereignty according to Maitland. Sovereignty is to be found in king and parliament (p. 302) That is, the king-in-parliament is no different than the king because the king-controlled parliament during the Tudor and Stuart periods to the extent that it could call them forth when he needed to collect taxes for wars and other spending habits of kings and queens and dismiss them should they fail to please him. The Tudors and less so with the Stuarts sought absolute rulership for England. Now, the degree of success of their desires, with the impediments confronted, for acquiring such power are obvious

the Supreme Court's usurpation of judicial review power. That is, America lacked historical experience in institution building when the Supreme Court usurped this power.[18] Perhaps, the American Framers, most of the important ones still alive at the turn of the Nineteenth century, when the Supreme Court decided the landmark case of *Marbury v. Madison*, were not fully conscious of the enormous power it was letting go into the hands of the judiciary. Perhaps, unlike the British Parliamentarians,[19] they were suspect of concentrated power, and the judiciary opening up a third power center was proper because of the American division of power and the judiciary receiving its own status within the American Constitution. The problem is that although the judiciary has an important role to play, the Founders did not explicitly know just how much power to grant it other than its traditional role of settling cases. That is, its scope is tied to the individuality of the case rather than having the scope and range of legislative policy. So, although the Founding Fathers were not naïve men, but well versed in history, politics, and the ways of the world, it is not clear why they did not outright reject the additional power grab by the Judicial branch. It took a lot of bloodshed for the Crown to give up the power in having the ultimate say in British affairs.[20] Of course, I am simplifying, to the extent that it was not an immediate or instantaneous process of transferring control from Crown to Parliament. Obviously, the Crown continued to have an important say in British affairs, and continues up to today, even though the modern Crown is mainly a ceremonial role and office. The Crown, nevertheless, serves a *symbolic* role of the unity of the British people.

---

to any student of English history (pp. 297–311). The problems of succession and sovereignty were much clearer with Americans having a written Constitution and clearer specificity with the three equal branches of government. However, this does not preclude serious difficulty should each of these equal branches of government begin jostling (which they engaged in before the ink was dry on the Constitution) for more power than they are assigned by the Constitution. Just because a nation has a written constitution it does not mean that the power struggles over sovereignty and rulership cease to exist. Similarly, in seventeenth century England after the bloodshed of the English Civil War, with the victorious Parliamentarians, it did not mean that the Crown was on its knees and the power struggles between Crown and Parliament will continue well into the nineteenth century. Even though an opponent might be defeated on the battlefield, it does not mean that they remain defeated in the backdoors and alleys of history. By forming a so-called constitutional monarchy, it might have stabilized the British system, but it should not be taken as settled in the backdoors of power.

[18] *Marbury v. Madison, 1 Cranch 137 (1803)*.

[19] Smith (1965), p. 68. "In making the judges independent of the King, Parliament had no intention of leaving them free to exercise irresponsible powers. To have made them really independent would have been to create a new political power of essentially the same character and no less dangerous than the power of the King which they were seeking to circumvent."

[20] The English Civil War (1641–1651) and the Glorious Revolution of 1688 generated and still generates the fight of political and historical interpretations surrounding the events; Christopher Hill, Marxist interpretation versus Whig interpretation; Christopher Hill, *The World Turned Upside Down: Radical Ideas in the English Revolution* ; Austin Woolrych, *Britain in Revolution, 1625-1660* (a counter view to Christopher Hill); *see further*, G.M. Trevelyan, *The English Revolution 1688-1689*; E.P. Thompson, *The Poverty of Theory and Other Essays*.

The Long Parliament sat from 1640 to 1660.[21] In 1648 Parliament was purged of a portion of its members by the New Model Army. Those members that remained after the purge, were referred to as the *Rump Parliament*. After a series of events that disrupted the whole Parliament from being in attendance, the portion of the Parliament that remained put Charles I on trial and beheaded him on January 1649. In 1658, after the death of Oliver Cromwell, those members that were purged in 1648,

---

[21] Hexter (1981); *see in particular*, Hexter's Chapter Seven: "Power, Parliament and Liberty in Early Stuart England," (pp. 163–218). Hexter makes the case, in response to earlier historians and his contemporaries that espoused class or parliament as the opponents of the Crown in Stuart England may need to reconsider some of their views or re-think the matter. That is, the Parliamentarians were not strong enough to challenge the king at that time because Parliament operated at the King's pleasure. What about the House of Commons? Hexter again challenges convention as to the power of this Chamber of Parliament during the Stuart period. He claims that the House of Commons members were too weak and cowed by the Crown to show enough courage, let alone challenge Charles I. "The notion that a body [Parliament] so feeble, so ephemeral, so incapable of getting what it wanted was struggling to wretch sovereignty from the hands of the king is simply absurd. In the first quarter-century of Stuart rule such a notion could scarcely have entered the mind of a member of the House of Commons, much less passed his lips. Neither the institutional structure of the House of Commons nor the ideology of the day favored the emergence of an opposition party in the House, seeking political battle with the king. [T]he only way to serve the commonwealth, the people of England, was as governor, officer, or magistrate; and in England all governors, officers, and magistrates held office by the king's appointment or commission. The government of England was the king's government both in state and in church. If the House of Commons did not stand in corporate opposition to the king and did not lead the opposition in the country against the court, neither did the individual members of the House." (pp. 170–171) So then the question must be asked: if Parliament did not challenge the Crown during the English Civil War, then who did? Clearly, Hexter does not believe the Whig or Marxist-'tinged' Whig tradition is the explanation. He points out the dangers of historians "refracting" nineteenth century Parliament into the seventeenth century Parliament. He warns that such a process will result in the re-interpretation of the English Civil War (p. 189). We are not going to resolve in this footnote the "causes" of the English Civil War other than point out some of the traditional explanations such as: the Irish Insurrection, the Bishops War, the abuse of the prerogative, the need for the Crown to raise money to keep fighting wars, King Charles I natural disposition and arrogance against the commoners and lower ranks of society, cultural changes from the early Stuart period of James I to the later Stuart period of Charles I, the persistence of religiosity—the fact that proper Protestantism was unable to consolidate its hold of society, so that even a minority of Catholics could be seen as a threat to Anglicanism and of course the Puritanism not being satisfied as to the purity of Anglicanism, with Catholics still posing a threat to water down pure Puritanism with an admixture of Catholicism and Anglicanism, and so forth. These are some of the standard explanations as to the English troubles leading to the Civil War. Nevertheless, Hexter's research makes some valid points regarding the House of Commons not fully in a position to lead the charge against Charles I. My view is that it was not simply the House of Commons itself but Parliament as a whole, with Charles I, treating members of the House of Lords, regardless of their rank, poorly—that it was a cross-current of dislike cutting across class status, religious affiliation, or inclinations, and so forth that consolidated the opposition called the "Parliamentarians" versus Crown in the Civil War. That the Marxist interpretation of class and economics being the cause of the English Civil War is too simplistic. British Marxists of course continue to put up a fight on this matter. Economics is an important force in historical change, but in the case of the English Civil War, religion too is a very potent drug in causing trouble. So, it is safe to put down economics and religion as the chief troublemakers in the history of the human animal.

were allowed to return and to take their seats, in order to make way for the Restoration and to dissolve the Long Parliament which occurred in 1660. After the Protectorate—Oliver Cromwell[22]—came to an end, preparations were made to restore the Monarchy under Charles II. The new Convention Parliament then opened negotiations for the Restoration of Charles II.[23] However, the Long Parliament, although interfered with, during its twenty years of continuous sitting in session, ultimately prevailed because it established the principle that: *Parliament cannot be dissolved without its consent.* In other words, Parliament gained the power to seat itself or dismiss itself at its own will, not the Crown's will. This power was not easily going to be shared with the Judiciary, by letting them have a final say in Parliamentary/Crown policy.

The *principle* may be stated this way:

> The king is dead. If the king rises again or is resurrected, the king will never be the same again. Parliament is here to stay. Many nations got rid of their Kings and Queens. Britain continues to believe that symbols matter in the balancing of institutions—with the Crown serving as the unity of the British people.

2.3 Parliamentary Supremacy

The English, having been invaded again and again from those northern tribal regions by Celts, Vikings, Danes, Angels, Saxons, etc. seemed to have developed a fierce internal constitution and fortitude, derived from those northern European tribal cultures, which made them almost immune to submission of "absolute" rulership. In short, an extremely difficult people to domesticate under a central power nor allow a king to achieve "absolute"[24] power over them. In their early history (pre-Norman Conquest) only a few kings could attempt to domesticate them. They tolerated and needed their kings but refused to worship them as gods. What is clear is that the English people could never tolerate "absolute" kingship.[25] Even during the days

---

[22] Oliver Cromwell (1599–1658), the role of Cromwell has become controversial over the generations. One of those on the ground level and contemporaneous observer and supporter gave Cromwell an early defense. *See*, an early defense of Cromwell offered by John Milton, "God's Kingdom on Earth," pp. 1–5.

[23] Restoration of the Monarchy under Charles the II (1660–1685).

[24] "Some of James's pronouncements are notorious. In *The Trew Law of Free Monarchies* he asserted that kings were God's vice-regents on earth, that there were no legal limits to their power, and that the sole function of elected assemblies was to give advice." Kenyon (1969), p. 8.

[25] Green (1892); Tombs (2016); *See further*, the *Magna Carta* set the stage to delimit kingly power or absolute authority. As said earlier, kings that could control property, could control life itself. In the case of King John, he could designate land as forest land which prevented the commoners from using, taking, removing, hunting, etc. on that property to feed themselves, heat their homes, graze their livestock, among lots of other activities necessary for living in that society and era. Jones (2015), pp. 37–38. "During John's reign and the reigns of Henry II and Richard before him new swaths of the countryside had been designated as forest—which could mean moorland and agricultural land as well as thick patches of trees. On forest land hunting deer and boar was

before the Long Parliament was established, English Kings needed Parliament to raise and collect taxes. Unlike France, which in fact, at one point in its history, reached "absolute"[26] monarchy, there was something in British history and character that could not tolerate absolute rule or divine rule. The emerging bourgeoisie[27] and aristocracy[28] were never too far away from the reign of power. The bourgeoisie being the "new" incoming power as market and industry started taking off. As to America, it lacked the institutional experience and historical maturity to build independent institutions outside of those they inherited from the British. And, when it was time to make a fresh start, the American colonies were suspicious of both Crown and Parliamentary rule. The Americans instead opted out of mirroring

forbidden, as was collecting firewood, felling trees to clear land, or erecting buildings. Harsh fines and corporal punishment could be levied on those who transgressed. The forest was the king's personal property and lay outside the normal scope of the law." *See further*, How King John closed off lands for his own personal use is similar activity that the English would undertake over centuries with enclosure or enclosing of more and more land until finally in the nineteenth century the Commons was killed off. Slowly but surely century after century of enclosure movement left the Commoners out in the cold. Skouras (2020).

[26]The French Sun King—Louis XIV (1638–1715).

[27]The birthing of the money-making class in Britain has not been without controversy. Some historians believe that the Tudors were very hospitable to the middle classes. So, it was assumed that Elizabethan England gave these classes a strong push forward as far back as the sixteenth century. J.H. Hexter, however, disputes this matter and disputes the evidence pointed out to support such as claim, *see further*: Hexter (1981), see chapter 5 "The Myth of the Middle Class in Tudor England," pp. 71–116. However, by the time of the Stuarts, seventeenth century Britain, the middle-classes had built sufficient power along with the landed owners to be able to bring down the British Crown and behead Charles I. So, even if we assume that the middle classes, both in Tudor and even Stuart England, lacked the power of the landed classes, it would be safe to assume this this new class of people was going to be a disruptive force for class and hierarchical system of the British empire. Again, Hexter makes clear that the gentry Puritan Parliamentarians of the seventeenth century should not be taken to be similar to the Whig Liberal Parliamentarians of the nineteenth century. He warns of the error of anachronism in wanting to see our favorites of a particular century comport to our standards and ideals of another century or historical era (pp. 171–179). "By contrast R.H. Tawney identified the 'rising gentry' of the seventeenth century with the revolutionary bourgeoisie, intentionally and explicitly. In the dialectic of history their role was precisely that of the often ascribed to the middle classes in the French Revolution: seizing from the enfeebled hands of the feudal orders the power to which, by the process of history, they were the due heirs. Having arrived at that point in economic development which prepared them for the seizure of power, they liquidated by political action a feudal social regime prepared for collapse by its inherent economic contradictions. The upheaval in England was the precursor of the market economy, of possessive individualism, and of the bourgeoisie triumphant." (p. 173)

[28]G.M. Trevelyan has lined up the gentry both Tory and Whig as the twin inheritors of the Glorious Revolution, the byproduct of the Cavaliers and Roundheads, the Anglican and the Puritan that will end civil strife in England since the close of the seventeenth century. *See*, Trevelyan (1965). However, it should be noted that Trevelyan's view of the revolution is a debated matter and hotly contested at times by the Marxist British historians. Nevertheless, Trevelyan is a competent and excellent historian for the Whig version of British history.

the British system,[29] in that it was establishing an 'experimental democracy' or better put: a "republican" form of government.

In sum, the English Civil War of the Seventeenth century was a watershed moment, not only for the direction of Great Britain but also for her colonies. Should the Parliamentarians have lost the battle, and the Monarchy continued to maintain its power, free from Parliamentary check or oversight, is at this point speculative history.[30] As said earlier, the British simply could not accept the French model of Absolute monarchy. The emergence of the first steps taken by the "commoners-bourgeoisie"[31] was simply the attempt to disrupt and break with the Medieval hierarchy. But the road turned out to be a long one. The road to 'republicanism' or 'democracy' might have been delayed or postponed for another era to break.[32] We, living in the former British colonies, owe a debt of gratitude to the Parliamentarians of the Seventeenth century that would eventually lead to a Commoners' Parliamentary system. And, ultimately, give *We the People* the potential for greater representation—be it in the House of Commons or the American Congress.

2.4 Philosophy of History

British-American historiography takes off as an outpost along the eastern coast of North America. Its colonial location serving as trading posts. However, sharing a common history, law, culture, and language, despite the Atlantic separation, was

[29] Although Americans did not want to mirror the British political system, at the end of the day there remained a strong resemblance of it. Maybe, shedding a heritage, tradition, and folk ways is not as easy as may be imagined by those that fought the American Revolutionary War.

[30] This optimistic tale should be read with caution due to the dangers of anachronism. We may be attributing something more modern to the Parliamentarians than was the real case.

[31] Again, a note of caution, the composition of the Parliamentarians included many sections of the population and not simply a class war in the Marxist sense. Within family members, between neighbors, and all ranks of society did not neatly line up for Crown or Parliament in a straightforward and clearly aligned as Marxist or economics class-based theory would suggest. These Parliamentarians included both reactionaries as well as progressives and emerging bourgeoisie.

[32] Bailyn (1970) (Based on the Charles K. Colver Lectures at Brown University given in 1965), from "Sources of Political Culture," chapter. Bailyn makes clear that the English King even after the English Civil War and the Glorious Revolution of the seventeenth century still maintained considerable power in the running of the government, but still held considerable power even after the Civil War and the Glorious Revolution. "[A]t least after 1707, that the King would not veto acts of Parliament; he had given up any claim to the right to create courts by his own fiat or to dismiss judges without formal impeachment; he had agreed to convene Parliament at least once in every three years and to call for general elections at least once every seven; not to leavy taxes save by Parliamentary grant; not to maintain an army in peace time; and not to wage war for alien territories without the consent of Parliament." (pp. 24–25) [quote shortened here check pages] Bailyn clearly presents the factual summary of the King's predicament, but the symbolic role of the King, under the push and pull of Parliament, in the settlement agreement stung the King in particular and the prestige of the Monarchy as a whole.

sufficient to provide these colonies a grounding of the ways of Britain in particular, and the ways of Western civilization, in general. Although there was a transmission of cultural artifacts from across the Atlantic, had to be either suspended or exceptions made as the battle of civilizations eventually came to a head. British historiography and historicity could not provide them a place/ground or the natural world of the Europeans. That is, as newcomers to a new land, their ways of being and doings clashed with the native peoples of North America on this side of the Atlantic. As the newcomers were clearing land and peoples, on this side of the Atlantic, the rule of law and Natural law could not dictate the ground being of where the plough/gun meets the bow and arrow.

The native peoples of North America on this side of the Atlantic proved that their ways of being were incompatible with the Europeans.[33] So, there had to be a break, at some point between the history transmitted via culture to the New World, with the facticity and confrontation of another peoples, whose history was tribal and nature worship. The new-comer's history being based on Western-Christian metaphysical world of their British kin. The clash of civilizations,[34] left the Native Americans almost dead or on life-support for those lucky few that survived the encounter or exterminated altogether for the unlucky ones. If they were not killed outright in battle, the diseases brought over by the newcomers, were sufficient to finish off the Native American populations for which they had no immunity.[35]

The *principle* may be stated this way:

> The implant of Western Civilization on this side of the Atlantic was going to be a problem for the native peoples of North America. Lacking guns, organization, and European germ immunity will leave them vulnerable to bloodshed and only a thin line between life and death for their posterity.

As the British Civil War raged back in England, the rule of Oliver Cromwell and finally the *Glorious Revolution* ending with a new crowning. Both Hobbes and Locke, writing their masterpieces, *Leviathan* and *The Second Treatise on Government,* were busy developing their political philosophies while British-Americans were clearing the land and surviving. It will not be long before, less than hundred years after the *English Glorious Revolution*, that the Americans will break from the British empire. The Americans were not fighting a Civil War but laying the foundations for a Civilizational War. What is clear is that the British common law would travel with these Americans, even as they rejected the whole monarchy-nobility-church setup. So, the triumph of Parliament, the establishment of a constitutional monarchy, and the adoption of the common law, are contexts to locate the American

---

[33] Bailyn (2013), p. 56. "A captured workman accompanying Smith on his journey to the Chickahominies was tortured to death in ways familiar to the Indians but not to Englishmen, despite their knowledge of terror-inducing public executions. At a leisurely pace, his extremities were cut off with mussel shells and tossed into the fire before him; he was flayed—the skin torn from his face and head—then disemboweled while still alive; and finally burned to ashes."

[34] For a popular and rather controversial work on the subject matter, see: Huntington (1997).

[35] The role of diseases in wiping out populations, see: Diamond (1997).

experience in the New World. The common law will have a powerful hold on the colonists because it came from below and was seen as organic in nature—bottom-up law and experience. This would eventually give American judges the notion that they were not only to interpret statutory law but also make and apply common law as the situation required. That is, judge made law might give the impression to the British-American judges that they could make law as well as interpret it. That is, eventually the Americans would tolerate allowing their judges to make and interpret law, under the belief judges were "objective" and "neutral" in dispensing justice. The British were not so trusting, their judges British judges not be given the power of judicial review of legislation. Despite Edward Coke's high praise of natural reason and the common law, in *Dr. Bonham's Case*, the British held the line. In other words, the British judiciary was not an independent entity serving as the "final arbiter" of British law. In the United States, the courts would be co-equal to the legislative and executive; once the judiciary usurped the power of judicial review, it would serve as the "final arbiter" of what the law means and what the law is. For the British, the Supremacy of Parliament means that the courts are to follow parliamentary laws, and these take precedence over the common law.

Americans inherited from the British a history and historiography that favored pragmatic-empirical philosophy to that of rationalistic-idealistic Continental philosophy. This biased the American philosophic and jurisprudential systems towards the pragmatic over the speculative. Eventually, starting with the Eighteenth and Nineteenth century British empirical-utilitarian philosophy crossed swords with continental rationalistic-idealistic philosophy. That is, David Hume and Jeremy Bentham encountered Immanuel Kant and G.W.F Hegel. And so, the debate and battle were joined as to whether "empirical" data will serve as the grounding or "rational" ideas will be the foundation? For the rationalists-idealists the philosophy of history cannot be based on the empirical series of facts, but as facts filtered and interpreted by the mind,[36] simple "causal" connections, or better put, "constant conjunctions" as per Hume,[37] may have a place in the natural world of Newtonian natural science, describing the motion of billiard balls, but hardly adequate for the mental reconstruction of factual events. And the use of a philosophy of history that brings these events under a more comprehensive pattern, as "reenactment" or better put, as per Hegel, mental re-enactment. Any attempt to grasp British history, solely from geographical and natural environmental ground conditions may accumulate data for natural science purposes but leaves out one important element as far as history is concerned, the mental phenomena that orders and makes sense of the data. The natural conditions influenced the shape of British historiography—the fact that it is an island gave it additional protections from enemies not found in the European terrain where states or tribes are contiguous to each other. However, history is

[36] Collingwood (1945, 1946); *see further*, "Robin George Collingwood," *Stanford Encyclopedia of Philosophy*, Jan. 11, 2006 (revised May 13, 2015), pp. 1–33.

[37] For a comprehensive view of Hume's analysis of the concept of "causation," *see*, Hume (1978); *see further*, for a comprehensive approach/differences between sciences based on the physics/mathematical/quantitative model verses the historical/social science model based on qualitative/understanding/explanation/meaning model.

nothing without the mental power to connect facts and find their meaning, not in a metaphysical universe, but in a mental universe.

The *principle* may be stated this way:

> Along with the Common law, Americans took a pragmatic and empirical philosophy from the British. That is Hume and Bentham over Kant and Hegel—empiricism over rationalism.

How history unfolds is not simply a matter of historiography, but the historicity of events germinating new events, or better put, sparking new events; it is unknowable to the spectator of historical moments what will be birthed during each event. The natural sciences require that its knowledge/data be tested by prediction confirmation. History is not a predictive science. The levels of contingency in the historical record go beyond the mental rearrangement of mind to make accurate predictions before the event occurs rather than *post hoc* analysis of the event. That is, history, unlike the natural sciences stresses the understanding/meaning of events over and above the quantification of events in time.

People often look to history for examples, patterns, and other markers to help explain events in the present and even sally forth as to make predictions about the future. This is a useless enterprise given the contingency of the moment. Every point in time and space is a contingent account of the event. Whether an event emerges similar to past events is a matter of giving mental comfort for those existing in the present, in the hope of bringing some familiar pattern or order to a chaotic world of events. History can only speak to human behavior and not the ordering of the natural world. History has explanatory value in explaining our behavior to ourselves, not so with the world of nature or the natural world.

The New World, pre-American Revolution and post-Revolutionary is not a continuation of British historiography. Its location, place-in-time, and encounter with new peoples break the continuum of the facticity of events, in a place-location very different from the European context, even with the continuous flow of culture and people from one side of the Atlantic to the other. The point being the cultural artifacts transferred from Britain to America must be discontinuous along the dimensions of time-place. That being the case, the American "rule of law" must be specific to the American context, regardless of British jurisprudence. The law dealt out within the American context might resemble the law of the British, but this is a starting point not an end point. The mental re-arrangement of facts on this side of the Atlantic could not be an exact duplicate of the European context. Thus, the role of contingency in historical events becomes discontinuous with time-place and historical facticity becomes context bound to the location-geography that the event is produced and generated thereof.

References

Bailyn B (1970) The origin of American politics. Vintage, New York

Bailyn B (2013) The barbarous years: the peopling of British North America: the conflict of civilizations 1600-1675. Vintage, New York

Blackstone W (1766–1770) Commentaries on the laws of England. Boston

Braddick M (2009) God's fury, England's fire: a new history of the English civil war. New Haven, Phoenix
Coke E (2005) The selected writings of Sir Edward Coke. Liberty Fund, Carmel
Collingwood RG (1945) The idea of nature. Oxford University, Oxford
Collingwood RG (1946) The idea of history. Oxford University, Oxford
Diamond J (1997) Guns, germs, and steel: the fates of human societies. W.W. Norton & Comp., New York
Gaunt P (2003) The English civil wars 1642-1651. Osprey, Oxford
Green JR (1892) A short history of the English people. George Newnes Limited, Southapton Street Strand W.C.
Hallam H (1881) The constitutional history of England. John Murray, Albemarle Street
Hexter JT (1980) Thomas Hobbes and the law. Cornell Law Rev 65:471
Hexter JH (1981) Reappraisals in history: new views on history and society in early modern Europe. University of Chicago, Chicago
Hume D (1978) A treatise of human nature, 2nd edn. Oxford University, Oxford
Huntington SP (1997) The clash of civilizations and the remaking of world order. Simon & Schuster, A Touchstone Book, Chicago
Jones D (2015) Magna carta. Penguin Books, London
Kenyon JP (1969) The Stuart constitution: documents and commentary. Cambridge University, Cambridge
Lecky WEH (1899) Democracy and liberty. Longmans, Green, and Comp., New York
MacKay RA (1924) Coke: parliamentary sovereignty or the supremacy of law? Mich Law Rev 22: 215
Maitland FW (2000) The constitutional history of England. Cambridge University, Cambridge
Pollock F, Maitland FW (1923) The history of English law. Cambridge University, Cambridge
Purkiss D (2006) The English civil war: papists, gentlewomen, soldiers, and witchfinders in the birth of modern Britain. Basic Books, New York
Russell C (1990) The causes of the English civil war. Oxford University, Oxford
Siegan BH (2001) Property rights: from magna carta to the fourteenth amendment. Transaction Books, Piscataway
Skouras G (2020) Modernity, the commons and capitalism. Br J Am Leg Stud 9:2
Smith JA (1965) The spirit of American government. The Belknap Press of Harvard University, Cambridge
Stoner JS Jr (1992) Common law & liberal theory: Coke, Hobbes, & the origins of American constitutionalism. University Press of Kansas, Lawrence
Tiffany HT (1903) The law of real property. Keefe-Davidson Comp., St. Paul
Tombs R (2016) The English and their history. Vintage, New York
Trevelyan GM (1965) The English revolution 1688-1689. Oxford University, Oxford
Trevelyan GM (1988) A shortened history of England. Penguin, London
Wilentz S (2005) The rise of American democracy: Jefferson to Lincoln. W.W. Norton, New York
Wolfe C (1986) The rise of modern judicial review: from constitutional interpretation to judge-made law. Basic Books, New York
Worden B (2009) The English civil wars 1640-1660. New Haven, Phoenix

Chapter 3
Early American Constitutionalism and the Supreme Court Usurpation of Judicial Review Power

3.1 Founding Myths

As with all Founding's, be it ancient or modern, there is a mixture of myth and history in the founding of new states. The discourse that perpetuates that Founding serve as the foundational myths or principles that will bind, *We the People*, as a collection of individuals into a common identity with a collective history passed on from generation to generation.[1]

The differentiator between fact and myth is of little importance in laying the foundations of a new state. The myth may enhance the facts. That is, the edifice of a state is built up by the weaving of the two into a cohesive whole. As we saw previously, Giovan Battista Vico was able to deconstruct myths from ancient Greece and Rome, philological clues were providing valuable information of how their foundational myths told us many facts about those peoples that would have been missed by simply following the facticity of the evidence left behind, and that some sort of phenomenology was essential in the unweaving of the tales or stories these ancient societies and peoples told themselves if they were to remain one people, one identified collective. To the natural scientist myths are fictions. To the human animal myths are symbols of meaning.

The *principle* may be stated this way:

> The symbolic can be as important as the facticity of the matter, entity, or substance. Without the symbolic, the entity loses its identity. Symbol and myth weave a reality just as strong as the weaving of theories and facts.

Tocqueville (1805–1859), too, told some myths about the America he encountered in his classic book, *Democracy in America*,[2] despite him being a French Aristocrat

[1] Wolin (1990), pp. 8–31.

[2] Morone (1990), p. 3. "Recent scholarship significantly qualifies Tocqueville's egalitarian picture of early America. In many ways, Puritan and planter elites carried old world hierarchy across the Atlantic."

G. Skouras, *Constitutionalism and Democracy*,
https://doi.org/10.1007/978-3-031-66906-4_3

visiting America almost half a century after its founding, and in no way considered a Founding Father. Nevertheless, he managed to come to America, close enough to the Founding, that the myths and facts he weaved together contributed to the story of America. This aristocratic foreigner came during America's infancy and managed to tell a story of the America he found that Giambattista Vico (1668–1744) would consider a foundational myth, of a people he found here even though he only spent about nine months (1831–1832) touring the country. He certainly was a very observant tourist,[3] but he also came with baggage from the Old World (Europe) with a predisposed idea of what America must be like as a follower of Rousseau[4] and Montesquieu. But he came early enough to observe the country in its infancy before it achieved commercial success and became an industrial powerhouse that was to follow the American Civil War.

Even though he was a latecomer to be at the original Founding of America, he managed through the publication of his, two volumes,[5] book on American democracy to continue to solidify the American myth. The myth that Tocqueville told was about the interweaving of New England small town democracy and the burgeoning of new territory, as the country was expanding westward under the Jackson presidency. He found Jacksonian America to be as the tales of Rousseau suggested; yet the facts on the ground also suggested issues and problems the new state will face in the future, serving as a sort of prognosticator of the future state—serving a similar function that the Greeks and Romans would use in antiquity by their consultation of their oracles and augers to predict fortune or disaster, and only undertake the action under favorable circumstances and the making of appropriate sacrifices to the appropriate gods—for favorable winds or calm waters in their journeying or whatever big undertaking they embarked upon.

His dream about America, and the facticity as he found America, had to be reconciled with his belief that democracy was here to stay, and that America will lead the way, or better put, all the world will be a democracy eventually. The acorn of democracy planted in North America was one day going to dominate the world. There was no going back to Aristocracy and Royalty (Monarchy). What is clear is that Tocqueville fell between two worlds. The French Revolution would eventually lead to the ending of Old-World Europe (royalty & aristocratic systems) and a New

---

[3] He purportedly came to study the American penitentiary system. So, the use of the word 'tourist' might suggest he came as a vacationer. He had an unpaid fellowship of sorts and official French authorization to study the prison system here. However, his interests and travels in America went very well beyond the scope of the French authorization—in his digging into the American political, social, economic, and cultural systems he encountered here—into the spirit, culture, work, church, and many other institutions as he passed through America in 1831–1832. He was able to weave his notes and observation into a masterpiece of how this new experimental project called 'democracy' was moving along in the New World.

[4] Jacques Rousseau (1712–1778), *The Social Contract* (1762) and *Discourses on the Origins of Inequality* (1755); the degree to which Rousseau's state of nature thesis and imagination influenced Tocqueville's outlook will not be explored here with any depth.

[5] *Democracy in America* publication dates, volume I (1835) and volume II (1840).

World (USA) that held the promise of an emerging democracy. Yet after writing on democracy, *he could not be taken as a true believer in democracy*—maybe in the abstract but not in reality. And he could not bring himself to believe in the democracy of the New World, even though he thought that democracy was coming to Europe and the world. Even in his day, the New England model was fading as the vastness of the West was being opened up for settlement and commercialization. Nevertheless, the appeal of the New England town model held his fascination as it did for others that came to visit the New England area. Unfortunately, a country the size of the United States could not model itself on the New England model as it was evident as Jacksonian America was clearing the way for Western Civilization to settle all parts of North America. He also found a plethora of civic associations and clubs Americans joined—that is Americans as joiners. He posited that this was a good indicator that the human animal was being well tamed in America by this civic association motion.

Of course, since he visited an Agricultural America, his prognostication and analysis had one major flaw—what if under an Industrialized and Corporate America this willingness to join civic organizations dropped off? Would that still be a good indicator or index of American democracy? It appears that he missed an important aspect of human nature. He assumed the perfectibility of man. And, reasoned that by joining civic associations man was becoming less brutal and less deadly than previous generations. Of course, this was a serious mistake on Tocqueville's part because human nature does not change overnight, over the centuries, dare I say, over the millennia, at least according to Darwin. So, he was seriously mistaken as to the fundamental properties of human nature—which is that the human animal is a very dangerous animal. It has always been assumed by all the great philosophers and great teachings of the world that the human animal is a "peaceful" animal unless provoked or feared for his life, in which case, he could become a deadly animal. But the truth of the matter it is the reverse case: *firstly, the human animal is by nature a "deadly" animal, and only secondarily, under certain circumstances or conditions can be viewed as a "peaceful" animal.*[6] Why all the philosophers and men of learning seemed to miss this fact or justify its behavior externally (outside factors) impinging

[6] I already discussed this issue in a paper of mine recently. See, Skouras (2020) There you will find an evolutionary explanation for the deadly nature of the human animal. In short it has to do with the evolutionary layering of the human brain—from the amphibian to the reptilian to the mammalian—in that the mammalian brain sits on top of a reptilian brain. Another philosopher has also expressed a view as to the deadliness of the human animal, see: Smith (2007), p. xiii. He balances the culture into the animal is placed and the natural genetic makeup of the animal. In that culture can moderate the biologism of the animal. I certainly agree with his analysis there. However, as I expressed in my article above, I do not believe that culture has been sufficient a deterrent to the extent that historical experience suggests—that the human animals have never lived in an era free from spilling rivers of blood of its own kind nor any other creature is safe on planet earth from the rapaciousness of this animal. Here is how Smith starts his book in the Preface section: "Almost 200 million human beings, mostly civilians, have died in wars over the last century." The culture-biologism matrix should be throw out as not a productive index of the threat that such a human animal poses on earth.

on the animal's behavior than as "internal" to the animal—esp. since some of the most brilliant minds in history dissected human nature in whichever way possible.

The *principle* may be stated this way:

> Ancient and Medieval philosophers have mischaracterized the human animal. Although these philosophers were well aware the dangers this animal poses, they severely underestimated the degree of harm it is capable of. These philosophers were justified in their views because they lived pre-20th century and could never imagine that by marrying this animal with modern technology what it was capable of—that is, marrying of this animal with modern technology will explode in a world conflagration—in a blood bath the world has never seen before. And, further, philosophers of the past made the mistake of mischaracterizing the force of evolution and biologisms would play in the makeup of such animal. That is, it was assumed to be a spiritual creature in the form of a flesh and blood body and that such an animal was capable of being domesticated under civilizational conditions. They had no proper understanding of its evolutionary and biological determinants. That is, these philosophers made the mistake in thinking that the human animal is capable of leaving behind its biological determinants and free itself through the constraints and benefits of civilizational life. Once the human animal leaves the jungle, it can be reformed, pacified, and upgraded to a higher existence than that of the life in the jungle as a beast or brute. The philosophers of the past made a serious mistake in holding out the hope that the human animal can let go of its biological determinants and necessities and enjoy the freedom and liberty of living a peaceful life within civilization. As for modern analytic philosophers, that lived through the 20th century, they were too busy studying the nature of the "proposition" in their academic hives. As to the existentialist philosophers of the mid-20th century, they may have been too busy pulling their hair out wherever they might find themselves.

Further, as Tocqueville continued to examine America, he noticed early on that there was a particular uniqueness with the judicial system of the United States. So, he stopped to consider the matter as to why Americans grant their judiciary the power to overturn legislation considered and passed by the more representative branches of government. So, he asked a question that goes something like this: Why has the United States become the only country that grants the power of judicial review?[7] This was a very good question for his time as it was when the Founding Fathers considered the matter. Why is it only in America, the People enjoy the power of judicial review, yet his own France and other parts of the globe ignored it?

The power of judicial review has taken hold in the American political system.[8] Yet, this power is withheld by many countries around the world. At least up to the

[7]Tocqueville (2003a, b), On the Power of Judicial Review in the USA, pp. 116–124. "Confederations have existed in other countries besides America; republics found elsewhere than on the shores of the New World. The representative system of government has been adopted in several European states, but I do not think, up until now, any nation in the world has constructed judicial power in the same way as the Americans.", p. 116; *see further*, as the United States grew in power and became a super-power in the twentieth century, other countries looking at it for leadership became more amenable in copying its practice of judicial review. For a current listing of countries following the practice of judicial review in whole or in part or not following altogether under different types of government and constitutional structures, *see*, Wikipedia: https://en.wikipedia.org/wiki/Judicial_review.

[8]McCloskey (1994), p. xi. "Historians still disagree over what powers the Founding Fathers intended to give these judges. Certainly, the Founding Fathers had no blueprint for such as court.

Second World War, with an explosion of countries adopting the American model of judicial review after the war. Why is this so? It might have come to be perceived from the three co-equal branches of government that the judiciary is the best branch to utilize this power—better than the executive or legislative branches. It might have been perceived that such a branch is "the least dangerous"[9] and less political than the other two branches. There may be some truth to this perception, but the matter only treats surface ground rather than substance. What does this mean? It hides more than it reveals. Under current times and conditions, it might be helpful if a new nation or an older nation rewriting its constitutions to add a judicial review clause. This will provide that nation with the "color" of law and appearance as a modern democratic state. If a nation wants to be perceived as a modern democracy, it might do well to disperse power across several branches of government. But, again, we are still operating at the perceptual level rather than the substance of the matter which may not accord with such perceptions.

Judicial review power was able to be established in the United States because divided government meant that any branch of government can snatch more power for itself and keep it, and any attempt of dislodging it after the fact would be a very difficult task. This is not to only single out the judicial branch. Other branches are not immune to power grabs regardless of any perceived specification in the Constitution—with the Executive adding executive powers to its portfolio with the Legislative, assumed to be the strongest branch, trying to defend itself from any further erosion of its power. Ackerman points out how the United States has turned from a congressional democracy into a presidential prerogative state.

3.2 Montesquieu's Model of Government, the Constitutional Convention and Natural Rights

The Framers of the American Constitution were learned men and some even had familiarity with Greek-Roman history, but they were also well familiar with the history of their mother country. Even though they were fighting a revolutionary war to free themselves from British rule, they could not help but think of themselves as rebellious British. The British tradition and way of life allowed them to design a political system remarkably similar to the British with a few American features.[10]

Many of them would be astonished and most might be shocked that any branch of the central government had attained such power."

[9]Ward and Castillo (2005), p. 1. "Alexander Bickel is perhaps the most influential constitutional theorist of the last half century. He sought to explain how judicial review, a nondemocratic institution, could be justified in a government that derives its legitimacy from the majority rule."

[10]The fact that England generated a rather unique form of government for the eighteenth century—being a mixed government between the powers of the monarch with the powers of parliament; such a mixed governmental structure was well in place throughout the eighteenth century, not only in England but the American colonies tinkering with their version of mixed government—the

And, further, they could draw many lessons from British history and tradition.[11] However, at the same time they did not want to mirror the British in the layout of their government. Instead of giving primacy to Parliament (the Legislature), they opted for Montesquieu's model of government.

The American Constitution was drafted on a tripartite model that removed the royalty and nobility from the equation. That is not to say, there were no monarchists at the Constitutional Convention. One suspect was Alexander Hamilton. Hamilton admired the powers of royalty and nobility in stabilizing political systems and that an 'experimental' system such as 'democracy' needed many non-democratic elements and hedges in place before letting the 'common' people take power. The center needed to hold. So, what better way than a King or strongman? For Hamilton, a person like George Washington gave him the assurance that the center will hold, as long as Washington, remained the leader. Hamilton thought he could give the American system similar powers to that of a monarchy but under republican labels.[12] However, the American revolutionary fighters or patriots would not tolerate a Hamilton re-Crowning a central leader or re-establishing the monarchy in American clothing.[13] It settled on a tripartite co-equal system of government, with checks and balances. And the Framers, reading ancient history and especially admiring the Roman 'republic' model, used it to separate power rather than have an entangled system of Crown-Parliament. One central point of interest, and differentiation from the British model, deals with the power of judicial review.

Governor, Colonial Councils, and some form of House of Delegates or Assemblies or version of the House of Commons. See, Bailyn (1970), Chapter II, pp. 59–105.

[11] Siegan (2001), p. 2. "To be sure, the Americans had severed their political bonds with England but not their reliance on the English common law."

[12] Hamilton on judicial review, *Federalist # 78*; *see further*, Smith (1965), pp. 79–80. Hamilton's proposal placed the Executive office beyond democratic control. Smith says: "He was an uncompromising opponent of democracy and considered the English government of that day, with its hereditary monarchy and aristocracy, the best form of government ever devised." *See also*, Madison (1985), pp. 129–139, Madison reporting on the Hamilton Plan. *See further*, The Documentary History of the Ratification of the Constitution Digital Edition, ed. John P. Kaminski, et al., *https://csac.history.wisc.edu/wp-content/uploads/sites/281/2017/07/4.-HAMILTON-PLAN.pdf.*

[13] Bryce (1909), pp. 38–52. Bryce mentions the point of Hamilton looking for a substitute King in an American president. However, due to the contingency of the timing of the American Constitution drafting, the idea of crowning a new monarch was not a viable option. Bryce however makes the case that a King George with reduced or constrained powers, along with improved form, could be the perfect candidate for office, by simply stripping out the title King and replacing it with the title President. "Assuming that there was to be such a magistrate, the statesmen of the Convention, like the solid practical men they were, did not construct him [the new position of Executive/President of the United States] out of their own brains, but looked to some existing models. They therefore made an enlarged copy of the State Governor, or to put the same thing differently, a reduced and improved copy of the English king. He is George III, shorn of a part of his prerogative by the invention of the Senate in treaties and appointments, of another part by the restriction of his action to Federal affairs, while his dignity as well as his influence are diminished but his holding office for four years instead of for life." Bryce, p. 39.

Again, as noted earlier, why did the British withhold such power and the Americans eventually came to accept it? According to Edward Corwin, there are several indications pointing to the judiciary as the proper body to interpret the Constitution.

> Cases "arising under this Constitution" are cases in which the validity of an act of Congress or a treaty or a legislative act or constitutional provision of a State, or of any official act whatsoever which purports to stem directly from the Constitution, is challenged with reference to it. This clause, in alliance with the Supremacy Clause (Article VI), furnishes the constitutional warrant for that highly distinctive feature of American Government, judicial review.[14]

Let us leave aside for a minute the indirect point that the Constitution contains references pointing to the judiciary as the proper authority for its interpretation.[15] What is known and clear is that the American Founders knew very well of this power called 'judicial review.' During the Constitutional Convention,[16] this power received some airing, but there seems to be confusion, indecision, or fuzziness as to whether the Founders wanted to incorporate such a power into the Constitution.[17] However, Corwin wants to assume that such a power was already implied or baked into the drafting of the American Constitution, into the fabric of the would be American legal system, as part and parcel of the acceptance of the doctrine of *vested rights* and the *separation of powers* and acknowledged as being a part of the fabric of American law, or better put, a consequence and resolved acceptance of the English Common Law heritage.[18]

The Founders at the Convention were not dealing with an unfamiliar power called "judicial review." It has a history of British attempts of appealing to "natural rights" or "common reason" to circumvent or modify laws deemed detrimental to society, as fundamental rights that no executive or legislative body could withdraw from the people. Let me state the process this way: British common law gave common law courts the impression of gathering local rules and traditions and forming workable principles called "common" law rules, in which they developed and applied to the local population. And in due time, and especially under the jurisprudence of Sir Edward Coke, judges concluded that they are the proper people to hold Crown-Parliament to account as being in violation of the common law and natural rights. However, Coke and his jurisprudence was unsuccessful, in this regard, because the Crown-Parliament retained the right to rule free from meddling judges and passing judgment on Crown-Parliamentary business.

---

[14] Corwin (1978), pp. 221–222.

[15] Corwin (1964), *see in particular*, Chapter 2, "The Basic Doctrine of American Constitutional Law," pp. 25–45.

[16] For the official records of the Constitutional Convention of 1787, see: Farrand (1966–7) (3 volumes).

[17] Farber (1989), p. 1089. "The difficulty of determining the plausibility of a historical interpretation is increased by the need to interpret the collective views of a diverse group of individuals. These individuals may not have agreed with each other on the interpretation of a provision."

[18] Corwin (1964), pp. 25–45.

However, Coke believed in such a thing as "artificial" reason, which Thomas Hobbes found unacceptable—which gave judges and other legal specialists superior power in legal determinations. That is, parliamentary law, not in accord with natural reason or the common law, could be rendered void by judges that also possessed artificial reason—on top of natural reason. Parliament thought otherwise, and eventually Parliament's laws were positive and primary, an appeal to natural law and natural rights were not foundational[19] nor left to judges to pass judgment on. The judges were to stick to the traditional methods of legal interpretation and not interfere nor pass judgment or hold veto power over Crown-Parliament. Of course, I am compressing the time scales here since full independence from the Crown was not to be. Even since the nineteenth century when Parliament consigned the Crown to a symbolic role, it still plays the role of informing the Crown of its actions even today. Regardless of what Coke thought about the power of "natural reason," the judiciary should know its place within the British system and be sure it stays there. There was no "higher law"[20] that was unalterable.

Since the British never rejected God, it is hard to say the exact role of God's law in the nation-state, except to have God's law banished to ecclesiastical courts. But this does not say anything about how appeal to "natural" law would affect the day-to-day ground floor level of common law application. Experience and the common law were all that was required, and there was no reason the common law or parliamentary or royal action could not be altered by new experiences. But the fact that British society and people never cast off or threw out the Deity should also remind us that what ground forces determine must also be consistent and generally approved by a particular culture.

[19]Natural Law and Natural Rights, especially after the French Revolution, lost their appeal, they were still a potent force as long as a Deity centered universe continued to be believed by the general populace. So, an appeal to natural law was not necessarily eliminated, even though what 'officially' counted was positive law. In other words, there was a spectrum across the use and utility of Natural law depending on the type of society one lived in. One could appeal to God's law or Nature's law as long as it did not violate positive law directly or contaminate the law. If such a law could sort of run parallel to the positive law, it could directly or indirectly be appealed to in a pinch. So, 'officially' a judge or a court was applying 'positive' law, he might also resort to 'natural' law 'unofficially' of course. However, even if appeal to Natural law should be exposed, it most likely would not bring the masses to the barricades because most likely the masses were religious folks with strong belief in a powerful Deity.

[20]Corwin (1967), Entreves (1970), Finnis (1980), Strauss (1953) and Purcell (1973) Chapter 2: Scientific Naturalism in American Thought, pp. 3–12. Purcell argues that the concept of "natural rights" was dead upon arrival in the twentieth century. This work also maintains that the concept of "natural rights" was dead upon the arrival of the nineteenth century. Once the Age of Reason and the Enlightenment fell into disrepute, the metaphysical philosophy of natural rights also tumbled. Purcell goes further in pointing out that by the early part of the twentieth century Darwinian thinking and Darwinism had well established itself in American academia. The establishments of the new Social Science disciples (Psychology, Political Science, Economics, Sociology, Anthropology) were infused with naturalistic scientific principles as their foundations. So, there was no need for reason or rationalism to establish any metaphysical natural law rights. These sciences were to be based on empiricism, not rationalism.

The myths that a society tells its people, and accommodating their need for spiritual being, cannot become irrelevant at a Founding that will be interwoven with facts as foundational truths for *We the People*. For example, a people or a society that believes in the existence of a God with divine powers is not likely to eliminate such a power completely from its positive laws. Even though at some point it may become unpopular to appeal to divine law. That is to say, the ground myth or religious belief cannot be stripped from a legal system unless the culture, norms, and people of that society also want the deity removed from their system. Otherwise, if a particular society believes that, if the laws are not consistent with God's laws, there may be no way for a society or polity to establish the "rule of law" that is applicable to the whole society. Secular law may fall dead on arrival if the culture is God-based. So that man-made law must comport with a particular culture's beliefs about divine law or its spiritual belief system. Otherwise, the law will never receive legitimacy by the public. Man-made law must comport with God's law. Locke being one major example, worshiped by the American Founders, had a very strong philosophy of the existence of God and natural law.

The *principle* may be stated this way:

> The doctrine and practice of judicial review was not an alien philosophy at the drafting of the American Constitution. It was considered, debated somewhat, and then the participants moved on without "explicitly" setting it into the Constitution. We can speculate all day as to why it was not included. The Founders were unsure, perhaps puzzled, or perhaps a bit fuzzy about how this power would operate within the new Constitution.

As indicated by Corwin, the Constitution draws a few points suggesting the Supreme Court should pass judgment over legislative laws. However, the Founding Fathers never 'explicitly' inserted this power in the Constitution, inference aside. That is, the text of the Constitution does not contain a specific or explicit language granting the Supreme Court the power of judicial review, but it has been argued by scholars and others that the power of judicial review can be inferred. *The Federalist Papers* contain a defense of this power as espoused by Hamilton in *Federalist # 78*.[21] The Federalist papers provide background in defense of the need for a constitution and, also, provide a response to the Anti-Federalists[22] and their propaganda and pamphlets attacking the need for a new Constitution.[23]

---

[21] *The Federalist* # 78.

[22] Jensen (1981) (revising the traditional understanding of the period between the end of the Revolutionary war and the adoption on the Constitution); Kammen (1986a, b), pp. 251–360. See, Part 4: "Selected Anti-Federalist Writings, 1787–1788. *See further*, Strong (1985). The Anti-Federalists claimed not to be fighting against Federalists, but against the "nationalists" that won the propaganda campaign, in confusing the public, of being Federalist but their program and ideology was nationalist. That is, the Articles of Confederation were closer to the principles of "democracy" than the new constitutionalism scheme of the consolidation and dispersal of powers under the new Constitution. Main (1974), p. 13. Main put it this way: "The Antifederalists, like most Americans, believed that if the government were truly to represent the people, the principal power should rest in the popular branch."

[23] Wood (1969), pp. 485–492.

This brings us to the American colonies living under British rule in North America. And as the Eighteenth century rolled on, they came to believe that their liberty, under British rule, was under threat and so moved to revolt against them. Whether the Americans had good justification for taking this revolutionary action, we will not take up here. The debate even to this date has not been settled by historians. And certainly, we will not resolve or serve as mediator here. The Americans prevailed in this battle and opened up the opportunity to govern themselves under their own Constitution.

3.3 Chief Justice John Marshall & Private Property

The Supreme Court of the late Eighteenth century and early Nineteenth century America, although purportedly decides only positive law, was not immune to the use of natural law.[24] Justices such as John Marshall always claimed to be interpreting positive law, however, he and some of his Supreme Court colleagues had the natural law[25] as a backdrop and in a pinch appeal to it. State court justices, too, could resort to natural law to protect rights, and especially property rights, from violation or insufficient protections provided by positive law. Justice Kent, for example, has appealed to natural rights to secure property protections when positive law was insufficient to do the job, including his condemnation of granting suffrage to the "common" people.[26] Wood citing the *Calder v. Bull* (1798) case explains that republican principles prevent the taking of property from one person to give to another under the common law doctrine of "vested" rights. So, the legislature is powerless to interfere with such rights. Wood says: "The judges called these protections "vested rights"—a notion that the great constitutional historian, Edward S. Corwin, called "the basic doctrine of American constitutional law.""[27] In other words, these "vested" rights did not stand on a democratic platform but a theological or natural law foundation. And the Legislature could never touch or change them.

Similarly, Justice Story[28] was a huge proponent of property protection: unlimited support for corporations, linking freedom with the protection of property, use of the power of judicial review to protect private property, almost at all costs—*Dartmouth*

---

[24] *Calder v. Bull*, 3 U.S. 365 (1798).

[25] For a historical and comprehensive understanding of Natural Law and Natural Right, *see*, Leo Strauss, *Natural Right and History*.

[26] James Kent (1763–1847). Wikipedia: *https://en.wikipedia.org/wiki/James_Kent*; he was a strong proponent of property rights.

[27] Paul and Dickman (1989), see, Wood (1989), p. xiii.

[28] Joseph Story (1779–1845); *see further*, Wikipedia: *https://en.wikipedia.org/wiki/Joseph_Story*.

College,[29] *Charles River*,[30] *Boston Water Power Co. v. Boston & Worcester R.R.*,[31] and *Fuller v. Dame*.[32] The taking of property that has been vested amounts to a gross violation of the common law, natural law, and we might even add divine law in the American system. Wolfe quotes the case of *Vanhorne's Lessee v. Dorrance* (1795) to indicated the sacredness of property protection in America and the judiciary serving on the front line of its protection. "The legislature, therefore, had no authority to make an act divesting one citizen of his freehold, and vesting it in another, without a just compensation. It is inconsistent with the principles of reason, justice, and moral rectitude; it is incompatible with the comfort, peace, and happiness of mankind; it is contrary to the principles of social alliance in every free government; and lastly, it is contrary to both the letter and spirit of the constitution."[33]

John Marshall was no exception of men of his generation seeing natural law and natural justice as an appeal to God's laws.[34] If positive law failed to protect property, why not appeal to God's natural law?[35] The Founders were not positivists. They believed in the role of natural rights and natural justice plays in society. That is, they left an open road within the American Constitution for the Deity to play a role, not an exclusive role. America was not designed as a theocracy, although there were theocratic elements in its making. Equally true is also the fact that America was not an atheistic project. Although some of the founders might have given up on a personal God, they still retained the Enlightenment view, of the existence of an impersonal Deity, that set the world in motion—perhaps you might say a Newtonian god that set the world in motion and then left it alone. So, the belief in natural rights arising outside of positive law was a strong element in constitution-making. However, since the Constitution was drafted for: *We the People*, by the Aristocratic[36]

---

[29] *Dartmouth College v. Woodward*, 17 U.S. 518 (1819).

[30] *Charles River Bridge v. Warren Bridge*, 36 U.S. 420 (1837).

[31] *Boston Water Power Co. v. Boston & Worcester R.R.*, 40 Mass. (23 Pick.) 360 (1839).

[32] *Fuller v. Dame*, 35 Mass. 472 (Mass. 1836).

[33] Wolfe (1986), p. 109; *See*, *Vanhorne's Lessee v. Dorrance*. 2 U.S. (2 Dall.) 311 (1795).

[34] McCloskey (1994), p. 33. "But he (Marshall) surely realized that the Court's future lay with the tangible Constitution itself rather than its invisible and most disputable higher-law background, that a Court which claimed the power to go beyond the Constitution would be dispensing with its most valuable support and might end by possessing no power at all."

[35] Officially, John Marshall proclaimed to be following the law, and in only one opinion fell back on natural rights, Fletcher v. Peck. Wolfe (1986), p. 109. "The only opinion in which John Marshall explicitly relied on natural justice as opposed to constitutional provisions was *Fletcher v. Peck* (1810). The case concerned a Georgia repeal of an earlier corrupt land grant (the legislators had been bribed). [T]hese principles, said Marshall, might set limits to the legislative power, ensuring, for instance, that an individual's property cannot be seized without compensation. Marshall went on to discuss the contract clause, but ended ambiguously, in this way."

[36] Wood (1969), pp. 485–492, what Wood refers to as a "natural" aristocracy. Aristocratic not in the sense of titled nobility but as the cream of the crop and America's men of property, or better said, a natural aristocracy. Federalists defending the "better sort of people, according to Wood. Smith (1965), p. 3. Smith says that American constitutional government contains elements of monarchy

privileged, it could not appeal to the gods only. The writers of the Constitution assumed that the common man, with limited talents, could go so far and no further even under an Aristocracy of merit.

The *principle* may be stated this way:

> John Marshall and Supreme Court Justices of his era proclaimed to be interpreting and following the Constitution. It was positive law all the way down. This could not be the case. Why not? Because the U.S. Constitution embedded the principles of Natural Law at its core. Those living in that era were god-fearing men or Newtonian deists under the belief in the mechanical regularity of nature. So, no matter how loudly John Marshall or other Justices protested about the use of Natural Law, they were wrong in thinking only positive law was their guide. As I indicated earlier, the mythology of a People is just as important as the facticity of the event.

Chief Justice John Marshall firmly registered the power of judicial review in the landmark Supreme Court case, *Marbury v. Madison*. Although the Court broached the power of judicial review prior to this case,[37] it nevertheless became firmly established case in American legal history. Of course, Chief Justice John Marshall, being a man shaped by the Eighteenth and Nineteenth centuries, adopted certain beliefs of most gentlemen of his age. A few key beliefs held by John Marshall, might shed light, regarding his devotion to the protection of property—that is, the sacredness of property and its protection, also a belief in the self-interest and acquisitiveness of man, which of course led to his doubts about the Commons domain—individualism over community, property over the general will. Property could secure for the individual their safety and dignity.

Although Marshall gave preference to positive law, some leeway was needed in the appeal to "natural rights."[38] Of course, he shared the mindset of many of the Framers of the Constitution as to the problems of democracy or what might then be called "mob" rule. The tug of war between democracy and fundamental rights, carved out from the democratic process has been a contested proposition especially during depression and other economic upheavals. That is, how to reconcile

---

and aristocracy within it. That it, is a compromised document to the extent that democracy is not pure but entangled with monarch and aristocracy. Chapter 3: "The Constitution as a Reactionary Document" (pp. 27–39) "In the United States at the present time we are trying to make an undemocratic Constitution the vehicle of democratic rule." (p. 31) "It is difficult to understand how anyone who has read the proceedings of the Federal Convention can believe that it was the intention of that body to establish a democratic government. The evidence is overwhelming that the men who sat in that convention had no faith in the wisdom or capacity of the people. Their aim and purpose was not to secure a larger measure of democracy, but to eliminate as far as possible the direct influence of the people on legislation and public policy." (pp. 31–32)

[37] Judicial Review Cases before *Marbury v. Madison*: *Hayburn's Case*, 2 U.S. (2 Dall.) 408 (1792); *United States v. Yale Todd,* (1784) (unreported case); *Hylton v. United States*, 3 U.S. (3 Dall.) 171 (1796); *Ware v. Hylton,* 3 U.S. (3 Dall.) 199 (1796); *Hollingsworth v. Virginia*, 3 U.S. (3 Dall.) 378 (1798); *Cooper v. Telfour,* 4 U.S. (4 Dall.) 14 (1800); *see further*, Snowiss (1987), pp. 1–8. Snowiss says that the *pre-Marshall and Pre-Marbury* court decisions were already preparing or establishing the way for the process of judicial review.

[38] Marshall's decision in using natural rights as law, *Fletcher v. Peck*, 10 U.S. 87 (1810).

democracy with property interests or, more generally, fundamental rights immune to the democratic process or ballot box? The protection of property has been the central force in the making of the American constitutional and political system.[39] That is, the protection of property is the Newtonian force that bends the ark of American history, and for property to have this extraordinary protection, it became necessary to be classified as a fundamental right, which could not be touched by majoritarian democracy or better put, by the 'commoners.' This dualism between democracy and fundamental rights is the centerpiece of constitutional law. Other rights such as 'liberty' are too abstract, and although often mentioned along with the protection of property, do not have the immediacy, tangibility, and concreteness of property ownership.

Why is the Supreme Court especially qualified to serve as the final arbiter of the law? Why is it the job and duty of the Court to oversee these limits? According to the Constitution each branch of government was given its principal domain of duty. The question then becomes what are the consequences if one or more of these branches of government overreaches into the business of the other domains, not granted to them by the Constitution?

The *principle* may be stated this way:

> Natural Rights are God made rights. Natural justice is God-determined justice. Natural law is the grace that God grants the human animal. This natural law protects life, liberty, and property. Any human violation of these god given rights is to be expunged from society. From these God given rights, the "right to property" is the central and all- encompassing right, even above the protection of life and liberty. The American Constitution is god's way and gift to the American people to protect property at all costs.[40]

The solution, to this power grab by the Supreme Court, is not to diminish the Court in its daily duties of providing finality to cases but add the following stipulation: *The Supreme Court, being an unelected body, should never have final say as to what the law means in a democracy.* If the legislature is to be the final arbiter, as to the meaning of the Constitution, it will be a clear danger to those people unrepresented in the polity. So, it is imperative that if Congress is granted the power of judicial review, additional safety measures must be implemented, so that the Congress does not become absolute, as the Founders feared absolute rule regardless of its point of

[39] Strauss (1953) Leo Strauss and the Straussians emphasize the centrality of the protection of property within the natural law and natural right universe; *see in particular*, Chapter Five, "Modern Natural Right," pp. 165–251. Strauss and the Straussians are known to present a Chicago School view of natural rights based on a rather traditional and conservative leaning.

[40] Although Natural Law in its theological mode made an important impact in American Constitution-making, the Founders had closer in mind the natural law and rights as viewed by Hobbes and Locke, and therefore naturalized as inalienable and hence fundamental to the building of any constitutional system. The protection of self and the protection of property seen as intertwined and entangled with one another, with the right to self-preservation and the right to property might as well be one and the same thing.

origin. By granting more power to institutions from below[41]—by local institutions that can serve as a hedge and provide the necessary accountability. That is, the use of the Tenth Amendment points in the direction that the States matter, and some power must devolve to them. The Tenth Amendment to the Constitution of the United States reads: "The powers not delegated to the United States by the Constitution, nor prohibited by it to the States, are reserved to the States respectively, or to the People."[42] Therefore, the supreme law of the land must allow some latitude for the States to determine their way. Otherwise, all final power stays with the determinations of the United States Supreme Court. If the States can have no input, as to what the final and supreme law of the land is, under the theory that only the Supreme Court can have such power, the States and the People of the United States are diminished because the Supreme Court has appointed itself as the final arbiter as to what the Constitution means.

Only a body of representatives standing for election every few years should be given the power of Judicial Review. Again, there is no need to cut down the Supreme Court itself, and the Court can continue in its day-to-day business of providing finality to the cases that come before it. However, having been stripped of its power of judicial review, if a case comes before it that the legislative branch disagrees with the Court's ruling/interpretation—as to its constitutionality—then the case is to be referred-back to the legislative body with the Court's objections and reasons as to why it finds the law objectionable or unconstitutional. Here, the legislature is to re-consider the matter and re-vote on it. If a majority once again finds the law constitutional, then it is the end of the matter. The legislature has spoken, and the law is final. Should the law be a problem for the general-public or voters, then the public has the ultimate right to remove those congressmen and congresswomen that supported the law and vote them out of office and a new Congress can re-take up the matter if it so chooses to do so. That is democracy at work. But as a security blanket or as a countervailing force, some institution, or institutions, from below, with closer

[41] State & local institutions/worker committees representing every profession and industry; the need to eliminate institutions from *above*, like the Senate. There is a need that a Congress, once the power of judicial review resides in their hands and the elimination of a Senate from *above*, that such a Congress be better grounded on *We the People* from *below*. What does that mean? That the Workers of any given society be given a place at the table. How the Workers get a seat at the table is important. And Worker's Unions or Worker's Councils or other body capable of speaking to the life of the workers and working conditions becomes critical that democracy is not only for *We the People*, but also a Worker's Democracy and not simply an Aristocratic Democracy (if that is not a contradiction of terms) that the Framers *originally* setup and left us with basically an Aristocratic Constitution. And such a constitution does not fit modern day democratic parameters. Therefore, it becomes imperative that the Constitution be changed from an *Aristocratic Constitution* of the Founding Fathers to a *Democratic Constitution* to meet the expectations and challenges of the twenty-first century. All Civic institutions, along with the establishment of the unionization of America, with broad representational appeal, have a seat at the table in the balancing and counter-balancing the modern Congress with *We the People* from below rather than the Aristocratic people from above. That is, the New Congress be anchored to *We the People*, if any form of "real" democracy is to be viable and true to its name, not only in theory but in practice.

[42] Tenth Amendment to the United States Constitution.

contact with the general public, might serve as a filter to be sure that any legislation is truly and broadly in the public interests rather than special interests. That is, worker's unions and other civic centers of power—with broad public support and appeal—serve as a countervailing force in case a particular Congress demands "absolute" fealty. That is, large civic institutions, with broad representational capacity, be consulted and allowed a greater voice before major or life changing laws come into effect.

Similar conclusions are also reached by other scholars:

> Professor Tushnet is not alone among prominent constitutional scholars in making this argument. For example, Larry Kramer, former dean of the Stanford Law School, wrote a well-received book espousing what he also terms popular constitutionalism...the people can be trusted, and he defends the deliberative processes of Congress as at least equal to those of the judiciary. He rightly points out that if Congress makes a mistake, it can be changed by that or the next or a future Congress. The change can be based on public pressure or election returns. But if the Court makes a mistake, the only way to overturn it is a constitutional amendment or to wait until the Supreme Court changes its mind.[43]

Larry Kramer, gives a close dissection of the power of judicial review, in his book: *The People Themselves: Popular Constitutionalism and Judicial Review*.[44] His views pretty much tracks the conventional historical analysis from the Notes at the Constitutional Convention with various members making proposals, counterproposals and voting to decide matters as to what stands or falls between the cracks at the end of the day. Kramer at the end of the day reaches the conclusion that at the federalist level the matter remained undecided as to whether the federal courts should have the power to review legislation. Kramer says: "No similar decision was made to endorse judicial review of federal legislation. [Y]et whatever one's views on the former point, even the most sanguine proponent of a judicial check presumably would have recognized the uncertain status of the practice. This is why it made sense to include the Supremacy Clause as a way to ensure judicial review of state laws. No similar proposal was made, or even suggested, when it came to review of federal legislation, a failure made all the more striking by the fact that the Supremacy Clause had been added."[45] Kramer dissects the matter from numerous angles, but at the end of the day, there was no decision by the delegates of placing in the Constitution a clause allowing the Supreme Court to overrule federal legislation.

One scholar that has done an admirable job in following the unfolding of the power of judicial review up to the mid-1980s is Christopher Wolfe. His book, *The Rise of Modern Judicial Review: From Constitutional Interpretation to Judge-Made Law*,[46] presents his tripartite model of judicial progression from the Convention until the book's publication in the mid-1980s. He demarcated the process by establishing three different eras of judicial review: (1) The Traditional Era: From 1789 to 1890s,

---

[43] Chemerinsky (1987), pp. 16–17.

[44] Kramer (2004), pp. 35–91.

[45] Kramer (2004), pp. 75–76.

[46] Wolfe (1986).

(2) The Transitional Era: From 1890 to 1937, and (3) The Modern Era: From 1938 to 1986.

This tripartite model does a fairly good job explaining the Court's interpretive skills in adjusting the Constitution to their eras. I will not focus on all three of these eras in this work nor update Christopher Wolfe's book from the mid-1980s. The judicial review field is bursting with all sorts of commentary and never a lack of scholarly interest from the first day the Supreme Court usurped this power, in the landmark case of *Marbury v. Madison*. So, the examination of this power is never in lack of attention and updates of this sort can be found elsewhere. I will give my attention to what Wolfe calls the Transitional Era (1890–1937). I believe a close review and analysis will be sufficient to make my case and arguments as to why the power of judicial review should be stripped from the Court.

Let me close this subsection with the following observation: John Marshall, a Federalist Justice, assumed by the passage and validation of the American Constitution that central power could be used to consolidate the newly created Federal government's power. It might not have occurred to Federalists such as himself, that the basic and organic organization of American society, at the local level, rested with State governments. By not showing due respect for Local and State governments, the Chief Justice was laying the groundwork for future battles between the States and the Federal government.

3.4 Hamilton v. Jefferson-Madison Vision of Judicial Review

Alexander Hamilton, Thomas Jefferson, and John Madison were powerhouses in the establishment of the early American system. They were in essence central Founding Fathers, among others, they were there when the foundation of America was laid down. Both Hamilton and Madison were active in the Constitutional Convention of 1787. Jefferson was serving as the American ambassador (1785–1789) to France.

Jefferson[47] appears to hold a more democratic idea regarding the power of judicial review to Hamilton's view which is more aristocratic. The power of judicial review does not appear to square with the principle of universal suffrage.[48] Why

[47] Jeffersonian small 'd' democracy and small-scale republicanism political philosophy; he was at first ambivalent about the power of judicial review but turned against it once established by Chief Justice Marshall.

[48] Smith (1965), p. 1. "In the eighteenth century the majority was outside the pale of political rights. Government as a matter of course was the expression of the will of a minority. Even in the United States, where hereditary rule was overthrown by the Revolution, an effective and recognized minority control still survived through the property qualifications for the suffrage and for office-holding, which excluded a large portion of the people from participation in political affairs. Under such conditions there could be but little of what is now known as democracy.", p. 1. Let me put the matter this way: the "commoners" were in no position to make demands as to their political rights.

should non-elected officials hold such a power? It invites the People in the front door but, at the same time, also, opens a back door for the judicial branch to countermand the People's voice, by safely having the lawyering class serve the establishment interests. "Judicial review is basically an American contribution to the practice of government. There were a few steps in that direction in England, but with little difficulty the principles of legislative supremacy won out decisively: courts were not to have a right to pronounce legislative acts unconstitutional."[49]

It has been argued that judicial review is not in contrast or opponent of the People but serves as an aid in the protection of natural and civil rights. That is, the judiciary being free from political pressures is more likely to preserve and safe keep the rights of citizens better than the legislative or presidential bodies. That the rights of the People are safe and protected by a strong judiciary that will not enforce laws that threaten the rights of the People[50]—and are not subject to the will or the winds of elections as one set of politicians come and go. The theory being that the judiciary is really not usurping political power from the legislature in the making of the laws but only supervising the administrative state from carrying forward laws and regulations that will take away the People's rights.

Of course, to the untrained eye, the argument holds water. But if we dig deeper into the matter, we find things are not as they seem. That is, the Administrative State or the modern emergence of the administrative state and administrative law do not spring from the washed fountain of neutrality and comportment, with institutional safety and stability far removed from the turbulence of everyday politics. The fact of the matter is that the Administrative State stands or falls with the other institutions that are the primary players in any system, be it the American system, the British system, the French, etc. That is the dirty secret that the modern Industrial and

---

The "limited" rights they inherited by way of being British men were the result of previous British battles and especially the fighting during the English Civil War and the Glorious Revolution that gave them some recognition and rights. The American Revolution simply carried forward that process, but it did not grant them "unlimited" rights and freedoms. That is, the *Magna Carta* and future British Constitutional additions fought over every step of the way, by way of the Parliamentarians defeating the Royalists, that the British citizen obtained certain "limited" rights. This was an unfolding process of more than 800 years. History is not quantum field theory where particles pop up and die within yoctosecond or on Planck's time scale.

[49] Wolfe (1986), p. 74.

[50] We are currently witnessing this action of a Prime Minister of Israel trying to curtail the power of the judicial branch. That is, the judiciary is becoming very active in the protection of "human rights" which may not comport with the best interests of the Israeli state. Given a weak checks and balances within the Israeli system, Parliament/Knesset is a weak check on the Executive, the Israeli judiciary has served as a check on the executive. By this move and efforts to curtail this judicial power, many groups in Israel fear that basic rights will be curtailed by the executive power. Hence the daily and weekly protests sparked there. The 2023 Israeli reform act will curtail the "reasonableness" standard—that is, it will no longer be possible to use the "reasonableness" standard to review executive actions.

https://www.cfr.org/article/israel-and-debate-over-role-judiciary-democratic-government.

For a comparative of the judicial review systems of Israel, Canada, and the United States, see: Posner (2010), pp. 2394–2456.

Corporate State follows the money. As we all know, advertisers do not spend billions of dollars on advertisements that do not work or fail to achieve their goals. Of course, textbooks in describing the modern administrative state might neglect to point that out since the Executive, Legislative and Judiciary get all the glory and the headlines as the administrative officials skirting back and forth in the background play with the dials.

The British model, with the fusion of the monarchy, lords and commoners avoids the sharp delineation obvious in the American system with its written Constitution. The power of the Courts to overrule Parliament was a contradiction in terms since the House of Lords served as the final entity for judicial appeals. Which means that the British had the legal branch serving as an appendage of the legislative branch rather than as an independent branch of government. Some of the States followed this model prior to the ratification of the American Constitution. But ultimately, the Federalists won the day, and the judiciary was not rolled into the legislative branch in the United States but given a co-equal and independent status.[51]

What has in effect become the power of judicial review is an open door for the Supreme Court to serve as legislator and final judge at the same time. It is a backdoor control mechanism to control the masses. The Court transformed it, during the start of the Industrial Age, as a powerful tool to thrash the masses and protect property, corporations, and contracts at all costs. It became an insurance policy, in case the legislature faltered, by supporting the People, rather than the property interests. Hamilton was prescient in wanting to include such a power in the Constitution if the protection of property is the central organizing principle of the Constitution. In other words, the protection of lives and people are expendable and non-primary if those lives are propertyless people.[52] In other words, the American Constitution exists to protect property, not life. If you happen to be in the propertied class, then you have a friend in the Constitution. However, if you are propertyless, then the best of luck to you.

A Supreme Court empowered to serve as final arbiter and interpreter of legislation, holds the keys to the American way of government. Why should the Court or judges be the sole domain of legal interpretation? Are other bodies lacking or unqualified to "interpret" legal texts? Why is it the judiciary's role to 'interpret' the law rather than read or 'apply' the law? What is "interpretation"? Hamilton was one of the few Founding Fathers that was sympathetic to a pro-monarchy and pro-aristocracy system. So, what did he care about the People? One would assume

---

[51] Wolfe (1986), p. 74. "Among those who spoke to the issue at all at the Constitutional Convention of 1787, only two clearly rejected the power of judicial review, while a large number (about seven) supported it at least in some form. (If statements outside the Convention are included, a much larger number supported it.) The Constitution does not explicitly provide for judicial review. (That in itself is worthy of note.) The great debate is whether the Constitution provides for it implicitly, and if so, in what form."

[52] John Dunn (2000), p. 31. Dunn quoting Adam Smith: "'Civil government, so far as it is instituted for the security of property, is in reality instituted for the defense of the rich against the poor, or those who have some property against those who have none at all.'"

that *We the People* would be the least of his concerns. Even though he came from a commoner's background, he had monarchical and imperial aspirations. Given his status as a poor immigrant, he managed to climb the heights of American society in a relatively short period of time. This was made possible to some extent due to natural talent, but mostly in serving as George Washington's protégé, trusted advisor and sponsorship. Otherwise, he might just have only reached middling heights rather than soar to the top of society simply on his natural talents.[53]

The *principle* may be stated this way:

> Hamilton was a monarchist. This should not single him out in a sea of democrats. No. The other men drafting the Constitution at the Convention were mostly men of substance and of British heritage. In some sense they were "all" monarchists until the troubles with Britain began. So, although they were interested in going in a different direction from the British monarchical system, they created something looking remarkably like the British system albeit with the removal of British titles replaced with republican/democratic titles. So, although Hamilton usually comes in as a monarchist sympathizer, the same could be said about most of the men attending the Constitutional Convention. Let us put it this way: the Founders shook off monachism only a short time before the drafting of the new Constitution. They bore their monarchism lightly on their clothing. And one man alone, Hamilton, would never have had the influence he did, even as Washington's protégé, had he not been swimming in a sea not very hostile to monarchism.

Alexander Hamilton thought that judicial review is needed to serve as a counter-democracy or counter-majoritarian stop gap of the majority violating the rights of minorities. Which minorities might he have been thinking of? Well, the property-owning minorities. Since the 'unwashed masses'[54] or the "commoners" or *We the People* will always form the greater part of any democracy, then there is a need for a power like judicial review, to be given to an unelected and unaccountable branch of government, in order to stop the elected official from taking or interfering with the of the property owners—not to be relieved of their property based on the democratic vote. "Judicial review, he (Alexander Hamilton) added, is necessary in order to guard the Constitution and the rights of individuals when a majority oppresses a minority."[55]

Since the property owners were going to be a minority of the voters, and the unpropertied were to be a majority of the voters, if the system were left on a majoritarian rule basis, it would become necessary to control the majority of voters.

[53] Chernow (2005). Hamilton and other pro-monarchists were always pushing pro-commerce policies and the consolidation of the money interests over the commoner's interest; the Anti-Federalists were not unaware and suspicious of Federalists, like Hamilton, to reform the Articles of Confederation.

[54] As indicated earlier, the Federalists were suspicious that a system of democracy and the "unwashed" masses or commoners were the proper people to run the government and serve as leaders. The rabble had to be held down if the "proper" people were to establish a union of money and property interests. By allowing the Supreme Court to hold the power of judicial review, it could only serve additional protections of property and as a poison pill for those that disrespected property rights.

[55] Wolfe (1986), p. 76.

Hamilton feared that the sacred right of property would be trampled on by the propertyless voters. So, any trick in the book that could be used to stop such a travesty would be a good thing, according to the Hamiltonian mind set. Well, do we want majority rule or not? How does a majority oppress a minority? If democracy means majority rule, then the majority rules that society. A minority that lives in that society can either stay and convince the majority to support them or leave. If democracy means something more than a procedural majority vote, such as a substantive embodiment of certain values, then those values will triumph in that society. Once we deal with majoritarian democracy, we let into the equation the creation of majority-minority schemes. And the only way democracy can work is that people that are in the minority today have a fair and open chance of being in the majority tomorrow. Otherwise, the system breaks down into factionalism. This was a key concern of Madison.[56] The final result being the further division of factions or political parties until there remains only anarchy and chaos.

Hamilton, however, would rather place the security of property in the hands of the legal system (by placing constitutional constraints on the majority from violating the fundamental rights of property owners, or by confiscating their property, or more properly said, a "taking"[57] their property) rather than put it to a vote by the representatives of *We the People*. Nevertheless, Congress seemed to be the proper repository of the People's will in a pre-Federalist constitutional America. "The American revolution encouraged the appeal to a higher law; this might have helped to suggest judicial review as an institutional principle, but it also suggested the sovereignty of the people, which, in turn, suggested legislative supremacy. Indeed, during the years 1776 to 1787, when eleven state constitutions were written, it was the power of the legislature that was exalted (leading to something of a reaction at the constitutional convention)."[58]

The principle was acknowledged by the Founding Fathers that the legislative branch was closest to the People. As laid out by John Mercer, but his exposition did not carry the day.[59] Further, Pennsylvania Chief Justice Gibson made a strong case for the need for legislative supremacy, with his distinction between "civil" powers and "political" powers. Gibson makes the distinction that "civil" power is ordinary power, based on the common law, and could be left to the courts to act as arbiters of finality as to the law. But cases outside the common law, that were "political" cases, the judges had no businesses serving as the final arbiters in those cases. He makes

[56] Madison on factionalism, special interests and Madisonian democracy, Federalist # 10.

[57] Skouras (2000).

[58] Wolfe (1986), p. 91.

[59] Wolfe (1986), p. 91. Wolfe says that John Mercer disapproved of the power of judicial review be given to the judiciary. He put it this way: "The notion of legislative supremacy was defended at the Constitutional Convention of 1787 by John Mercer of Maryland: "He disapproved of the Doctrine that the Judges as expositors of the Constitution should have authority to declare a law void. He thought laws ought to be well and cautiously made, and then to be uncontrollable." This was not the position of most delegates who spoke, but of course the issue of judicial review was never dealt with directly and explicitly by the convention as a whole."

this point in the case of *Eakin v. Raub*.[60] Wolfe says: "On what grounds does the judiciary undertake to revise the proceedings of the legislature? If judicial review is a legislative act overturning a judicial decision on the grounds that it misinterpreted the Constitution? Such a legislative act would be regarded by all as a usurpation of judicial power, and thus judicial review may be regarded as usurpation of legislative power.[61]

Jefferson, in contrast to Hamilton, made it clear that the power of judicial review should not be in the hands of the Supreme Court. In short, one branch of government does not have the exclusive monopoly to tell another branch of government how to interpret the law. Wolfe quoting Jefferson as saying: "That instrument meant that its coordinate branches should be checked on each other. But the opinion which gives to the judges the right to decide what laws are constitutional, and whatnot, not only for themselves in their own sphere of action, but for the legislative and executive also, in their spheres, would make the judiciary a despotic branch."[62] Jefferson gave preference to Congress rather than the judiciary to have the ultimate say. "Jefferson also respectfully acknowledged the position of legislative supremacy. Whatever its limits, this opinion "merits respect for its safety," since it provided for popular control through elections."[63]

Madison shared Jefferson's view that the Judiciary should not have the exclusive power of judicial review. But, unlike Jefferson, he thought the States should not control any lawmaking in contradiction to the federal law because he wanted the power of uniformity of law applied equally across states. But what is clear is that both Jefferson and Madison did not want the Judiciary to have the exclusive and final say on legal matters. In other words, if a coordinate branch of government took an action that another branch disapproved of, there was no need to follow the opinion of that other branch of government. One co-equal branch should not dictate the actions of another branch. However, Madison differed with Jefferson in allowing for the Federal courts to have the power of judicial review regarding state law and state cases but not having the power of judicial review involved at the federal level with co-equal branches of government.[64] Wolfe goes on to quote Madison as to the

---

[60] Wolfe (1986), p. 91. "The best exposition of the doctrine of legislative supremacy in early American history is generally thought to be Pennsylvania chief justice John Gibson's dissent in *Eakin v. Raub*, a case that dealt with judicial review in Pennsylvania state courts but addressed itself to federal power and *Marbury v. Madison* as well."

[61] Wolfe (1986), p. 92.

[62] Wolfe (1986), p. 94 (Wolfe quoting Jefferson's letter to Abigail Adams September 11, 1804).

[63] Wolfe (1986), p. 95.

[64] Wolfe (1986), p. 95. "James Madison seems to have shared Jefferson's views regarding judicial review of acts of coordinate branches, while disagreeing with him on federal review of state court decisions. Madison stated his views on the former question in the removal power debate on June 17, 1789. He acknowledged that "in the ordinary course of Government. . .the exposition of the laws and Constitution devolves upon the Judiciary." But, he asked, "upon what principle it can be contended, that any one department draws from the Constitution greater powers than another, in making out the limits of the powers of the several departments?""

judiciary passing judgement on legislation: "This makes the Judiciary Dept. paramount in fact to the Legislature, which was never intended and can never be proper." From this Wolfe conclude that: "The authoritativeness of Court opinions of constitutionality, according to Madison, is due to the accident of their being the final branch, usually, to consider such questions, but that was neither intended nor proper: other branches, in matters before them, are not bound by judicial opinions of constitutionality."[65] To be clear: just because the judiciary is the final branch to review the legislation, it should not have the power of judicial review to overturn that legislation.

This raises the question of how judicial review established itself in the United States, given two of the most powerful Founding Fathers had negative reactions towards it or were skeptical of giving the Supreme Court such a power? With Federalists already embedded into the system and appointed prior to the establishment of the party system—could the Jeffersonians, just arriving to contest the Federalist agenda, get a fair shake? Can the Federalists have a fair fight with the Jeffersonians if the bench is loaded with Federalist judges? What appears to be the case is that Jefferson and Madison were out flanked by Hamilton and Chief Justice Marshall. "Jefferson, Madison and many other almost equally illustrious statesmen were later to argue that the Congress, the President, and even individual states were, no less than the courts, guardians of the Constitution and coequal interpreters of its meaning."[66] Although this power usurped by the judiciary had been challenged from day one, and has never ceased to be challenged, in the history of the United States, yet it has prevailed and thrived. So, it is peculiar that a monarchist sympathizer, like Hamilton, outsmarted and outdid two of the most powerful Founding Fathers.

What appears to be happening is that during the Revolutionary War and the period of Confederation, the State has had great fear of monarchy (executive) domination. So, they gave great power to the legislative body to counter the executive. But, by the time of the drafting of the Constitution, they seemed to be unsure who should check whom, but by positing three co-equal branches of government, each could check the others. According to McCloskey: "But James Madison, the highest possible authority on the Constitution's intent, though apparently expecting the Supreme Court to disallow laws that *clearly* contravened the Constitution, by no means conceded that the Court could apply its negative judgment to more debatable points or that the judicial pronouncements were intended to be final and binding on the other branches of government."[67]

The *principle* may be stated this way:

> Jefferson and Madison were equally concerned about the power of judicial review residing in the judicial branch. Each had different strategies in either removing this power or

---

[65] Wolfe (1986), p. 96.

[66] McCloskey (1994), p. 6.

[67] McCloskey (1994), p. 5.

curtailing it from doing damage to the Republic. However, Hamilton and Chief Justice Marshall bested the two of them.

3.5 Fragmentation and Democratic Containment

Originally, according to Bruce Ackerman, faction was not a good thing. However, Madison had a plan to address the evil of factions in *Federalist # 10*. Those factions, if concentrated at the local level, were more dangerous than if they could be dissolved in a larger pool of the public. What better way to protect property, other than dispersing concentrations of like-minded people in a sea of an enlarged public? "The Constitution was basically an instrument for the protection of private property and property rights, above all else."[68] What is clear is that if the main driver of the Constitution is protection of property, then the people should be spread out; so that they do not concentrate in towns or cities that could pose a danger to the owners of property. What if these factions could somehow be diluted or dispersed over the whole of America rather than have them concentrated in towns and cities? What if they could be dispersed across state lines, so that each state could curtail them in their own way and, also, keep them in the dark as to what unites them?[69] Ackerman points to Madison's plan in dealing with factions: "In the context of this argument Madison mentioned the chief source of political factions, "the various and unequal distributions of property," and praised the Constitution on the grounds that it could inhibit the success of a "rage for paper money, for abolition of debts, for an equal division of property, or for any other improper or wicked project.""[70]

Similarly, the use of judicial review by the Supreme Court could ultimately dissolve any concentration of labor or unions that threaten property. Of course, Hamilton's view on the matter was not left unchallenged. It became clear to Jefferson that: "In 1820, Thomas Jefferson expressed his opposition to the doctrine of judicial review: "You seem. . .to consider the judges as the ultimate arbiters of all constitutional questions; a very dangerous doctrine indeed, and one which would place us under the despotism of an oligarchy." [T]he Constitution has erected no such single tribunal, knowing that to whatever hands confided, with the corruption of time and party, its members would become despots. It has more wisely made all the departments co-equal and co-sovereign within themselves.""[71]

Later in the Nineteenth century, Lincoln weighed on this power:

---

[68] Wood (1969), p. 111.

[69] Ackerman (2005), p. 18. "According to him [Madison], the creation of a big republic would multiply the number of factions and make it easier for large-spirited notables like Washington and himself to dominate the electoral competition over petty factional leaders. The clever design of the separation of powers would further diffuse factional strife and enhance the capacities of the elite to reason together with relative dispassion about the public good."

[70] Ackerman (2005), p. 111.

[71] Jefferson's opposition to judicial review expressed in a letter, *see*, Jefferson (1905).

> In 1861, Abraham Lincoln touched upon the same subject, during his first inaugural address: "[T]he candid citizen must confess that if the policy of Government upon vital questions affecting the whole people is to be irrevocably fixed by decisions of the Supreme Court, the instant they are made in ordinary litigation between parties in personal actions the people will have ceased to be their own rulers, having to that extent practically resigned their Government into the hands of that eminent tribunal."[72]

This privileged position of being the final constitutional interpreter has set up the Supreme Court, not as a 'co-equal' branch of government, but as the ultimate power of the land. That is, other countries never give such power to their judicial branch as does the United States.[73] Why? Because the idea and practice of 'democracy' is as much distrusted today as it was distrusted by the Framers. Any mechanism that can check democracy is and was welcomed in the United States. The principle of "checks and balances" is code for checking democracy[74] and the protection of property interests.

The *principle* may be stated this way:

> Democracy is an experimental system. Practicality dictates that it be restrained unless it brings down the whole Constitution. Checks and balances are one way to do it. The power of judicial review is another way, or any other method deemed appropriate could be used to pull off this subterfuge of giving political power to We the People but at the same time restraining the People. The important thing is to make it look like the People are the Rulers and the government is the Servant of the People.

So, what does all this mean? It means that those Founders, which discussed the matter of judicial review in the Federal Convention and outside the Convention or

[72] Lincoln's opposition to grating the Supreme Court the power of Judicial Review, *see*, Lincoln's 1st inaugural speech: *https://avalon.law.yale.edu/19th_century/lincoln1.asp*.

[73] Montesquieu (1949). Later with the explosion of countries calling themselves "democracies" after the Second World War and adopting the American model of judicial review to one extent of another—even the Commonwealth countries would find the need to modify their constitutions to include judicial review—and even if the mother country or head to the commonwealth—Britain—refuses and holds steadfast against such practice, it must have seemed to them to better align with American practices rather than the British on this matter. The French and English have their misgivings about such a practice, but the other new "democracies" ploughed forth to show that "human" rights or "civil" rights or the "rule of law" are the ways of the future. Also, former colonies of England such as India, South Africa, and Hong Kong departed from the British way. Hong Kong now under Chinese control is a more complex matter, even though the British relinquished Hong Kong to the Chinese under the understanding that Hong Kong would be free from Chinese interference under the theory one nation two systems track. India gaining independence in 1947. African colonies gaining their independence between the 1950s and 1980s. And Hong Kong returned to China in 1997. Calabresi (2020), p. 403 "In 1945 only three countries in the world—the United States, Canada, and Australia—had judicial review of the constitutionality of national legislation and a working system of checks and balances.", p. 403.

[74] Smith (1965), p. 69. "[I]t is hardly necessary to observe that the courts in England do not exercise legislative functions. The power to decide upon the wisdom or expediency of legislation is vested exclusively in Parliament. The courts cannot disregard a statute on the ground that it conflicts with the Constitution but, must enforce whatever Parliament declares the law. As the judiciary under the English system has no voice in the general policy of the state, the tenure of judges during good behavior carries with it no power to thwart the popular will."

wrote about the power in the *Federalist*, were afraid of democracy, given the 'experimental' concept it was for their times. That is, such a system as rule by *We the People* or commoners was untested and 'experimental' by trying to establish such a democracy was a risky business without proper guardrails or should we say: "checks and balances." It became clear to the men of the Eighteenth century that "checks and balances" was a proper action to take to help mitigate any dangers that might be posed by *We the People*. Given that there were few and far in between examples of successful democracies lasting very long, it dawned upon the Framers of the American Constitution that they should add features and protections to secure the values that they inherited as the progeny of the British Empire. This mentality of the participants, at the Constitutional Convention, made them cautious men in the design of the American Constitution. And, they may not have wanted to open-up another power center within the Constitution by granting the Supreme Court the final verdict.[75] That is, by bringing in the judicial branch to negative legislation, some were clearly fearful that the branch of government, with the largest representative capacity, might sink the ship of state without oversight either by the Executive or the Judiciary or both. But regardless of Wilson's proposal, veto power was not given to the judiciary. It would have to grab such a power itself later.

The Founders were simply the recipients of Western Civilization that prized property above all, and its protection an absolute necessity in the governance of a people. The core is property; everything else is secondary or tertiary or epiphenomenal. Hence, if you are lucky enough to be drafting a constitution, and, you leave out property protection as the core value, the sun that bends space-time which the planets revolve around, you have made a very serious and critical mistake and best fix it right away, before the whole edifice collapses around your ears.

The *principle* may be stated this way:

> Western Civilization demands this: property is all that is the case: life, freedom, and liberty are addendums to the case.

This process of protecting property has the additional advantage of keeping the commoners from becoming too uppity. So, the best thing you can do to avoid such a tragic collapse of the system is to "appear" to create a democracy but in "reality" serve up property as your god. This was especially true for Hamilton, but all the Framers of the American Constitution feared the American people encroaching on the sacred rights of property.[76]

---

[75] Madison (1985), p. 61. "Mr. Wilson thinks neither the original proposition nor the amendment to go far enough. If the Legislative, Executive & Judiciary ought to be distinct & independent. The Executive ought to have an absolute negative. Without such a self-defense the Legislature can at any moment sink it into non-existence. He was for varying the proposition in such a manner as to give the Executive & Judiciary jointly an absolute negative."

[76] Lerner (1957).

3.6 Tocqueville & Civilization

The American Founding Fathers saw the protection of property as key to any civilized society. All they had to do was look, and not look far, to see how the native peoples of North America lived. These Europeans occupying a new land, on a new continent, could not understand nor abide living alongside a tribal people—that they considered uncivilized, by European standards.[77] How could these Native Americans, live a proper life, without the ownership of land and demarcation and enclosures necessary to separate one's own property from another, and why could not these native tribes see the superiority of the European way of life? What was the matter with these people? The new settlers understood the principle: *that he who controls the land, controls the political system.* Most native peoples of North America had no conception of the relation between land ownership and political domination. For the Native Americans, the land was just there. For the Europeans, the land was for profits and domination.[78]

Tocqueville understood very well in *Democracy in America* the value of property and why its protection was a must for the settled Europeans here. The power of judicial review, as acquired by the courts, could provide the necessary discipline for the masses to properly respect property ownership. Going further, according to the German philosopher G.W.F Hegel, property ownership is a key component for a person to be rational. According to this logic, since the "primitives" or Natives of North America lack control and ownership of property, they must be beasts of nature or savages. And as savages was exactly how they were treated, by the arriving hordes of Europeans.

> He (Hegel) accepted that there can be no question but that private property is necessary. 'In order that a person be a fully accepted and independent organism, it is necessary that he find or make some external sphere for his freedom'. This is achieved by possession, which objectifies the individual society. 'The rationality of property does not lie in its satisfaction of wants, but in its abrogation of the mere subjectivity of personality. It is in property that person primarily exists as reason'.[79]

The America that Tocqueville found was passing from the scene. Property ownership in the form of land was going to be replaced by property in the form of financial capital in the next generation. The America of *Democracy in America* was being replaced by a Commercial and Industrial America—a powerhouse that will dominate world history in the fullness of time. And along with the "uncivilized" Native

---

[77] Tocqueville (2003a, b), pp. 875–927 (on the American Indians/Native Americans).

[78] Damrosch (2010), p. 87. "Yet the more Tocqueville and Beaumont saw of Indians, the more impressed they were. "I sometimes wonder," Beaumont wrote, "whether these Indians, whom Europeans despise, deserve to be called savages. The ones I saw on the way to Saginaw live peacefully, in their forest. Everyone who has any contact with them agrees in praising their honesty, their good faith, and their magnanimity. The Europeans who trade with them do have one great superiority, it's true, which is to cheat them constantly."

[79] Hawthorn (1976), p. 47.

Americans of North America, eventually farmers, workers, small craft trades and small businesses—in short, the multitude or masses of the working classes will become *We the People* of America—a majority of the American public. Workers that worked with their hands for their bread.

The *principle* may be stated this way:

> Tocqueville landed on the North American continent as the Clash of Civilizations was unfolding. The Europeans settling North America needed to clear the land of native peoples that held a different value systems regarding property ownership and property laws from the incoming Europeans—esp. Protestant Europeans of a Calvinistic bent with property ownership as an indicia of being among God's Elect. The battle was joined during Tocqueville's visit to the United States. Will the settlers be able to clear the lands—first in the Eastern coast and later more inland—from the Native American people. For President Jackson, the answer was simple. The native peoples needed to be relocated further into the interior of North America. It was clear to the newcomers that the native way of life and being was incompatible with the European way of life. The Europeans placed great value in land and property ownership. The confrontation between Europeans and Native Americans was joined. The fight was not only about the property component. North America was large enough to absorb the native peoples and Europeans. It also was a battle over culture, religion, and ways of being that placed the native peoples on a different Civilizational timeline from the Europeans timeline horizon. The question to be settled: Was America to replace the ways and ideologies of the Native peoples by way of the European way of life or were the native peoples strong enough to either push back on the Europeans, if not expel them from North America altogether. The answer was final. One Civilization defeated the other. That is all.

If the new American government was to bring Western Civilization to North America, it must have a government strong enough to tame and discipline, not just the natives of North America, but the workers as well, and in general, *We the People*. The constitutional tools were ready to confront the workers and contain them, just as a generation earlier the Native Americans needed their own containment—the reservation system. The classes of the disposed workers, only with their labor power to sell, confronting the class of finance capital, was not going to end any better than the confrontation of the Native Americans aligned across civilizational lines.

References

Ackerman B (2005) The failure of the founding fathers: Jefferson, Marshall, and the rise of presidential democracy. Harvard University, Cambridge

Bailyn B (1970) The structure of colonial politics. In: The origins of American politics. Vintage Books, New York

Bryce J (1909) The American commonwealth, 3rd edn. The Macmillan Comp., New York

Calabresi SG (2020) The global rise of judicial review since 1945. Cath Univ Law Rev 69(3):401

Chemerinsky E (1987) Interpreting the constitution. Praeger, CT

Chernow R (2005) Alexander Hamilton. Penguin Books, New York

Corwin ES (1964) In: Mason AT, Garvey G (eds) American constitutional history. Harper Torchbooks, New York

Corwin ES (1967) The "higher law" background of American constitutional law. Cornell University, Ithaca

Corwin ES (1978) The constitution and what it means today, 14th edn. Princeton University, Princeton
Damrosch L (2010) Tocqueville's discovery of America. Farrar, Straus and Giroux, New York
Dunn J (2000) The cunning of unreason: making sense of politics. Basic Books, New York
Entreves AP (1970) Natural law, 2nd edn. Hutchinson & Co., London
Farber DA (1989) The originalism debate: a guide to the perplexed. Ohio State Law J 49:1084
Farrand M (1966–7) The records of the federal convention of 1787. Yale University, New Haven
Finnis J (1980) Natural law and natural rights, 2nd edn. Oxford University, Oxford
Hawthorn G (1976) Enlightment & despair. Cambridge University, Cambridge
Jefferson T (1905) In: Ford PL (ed) The works of Thomas Jefferson, vol 12. G. P. Putnam's Sons, New York, pp 365–368
Jensen M (1981) The new nation: a history of the United States during the confederation 1781-1789. Northwestern University, Evanston
Kammen M (1986a) Selected anti-federalist writings 1787-1788. In: The origins of the constitution: a documentary history. Penguin Books, New York
Kammen M (ed) (1986b) The origins of the constitution: a documentary history. Penguin Books, New York
Kramer L (2004) The people themselves: popular constitutionalism and judicial review. Oxford University Press, Oxford, UK
Lerner M (1957) The supreme court and American capitalism. In: McCloskey RG (ed) Essays in constitutional law. Vintage Books, New York
Madison J (1985) Notes of debates in the federal convention of 1787 reported by James Madison. Ohio University, Athens
Madison J (The Federalist) # 10
Main JT (1974) The anti-federalists: critics of the constitution 1781-1788. W.W. Norton & Comp., New York
McCloskey RG (1994) In: Levinson S (ed) The American supreme court, 4th edn. University of Chicago, Chicago
Montesquieu CL (1949) The spirit of the laws. (trans: Nugent T). MacMillan Publishing, New York, NY
Morone JA (1990) The democratic wish: popular participation and the limits of American government. Basic Books, New York
Paul EF, Dickman H (eds) (1989) Liberty, property, & the foundations of the American constitution. SUNY, Albany
Posner RA (2010) Judicial review, a comparative: Israel, Canada, and the United State. Cardozo Law Rev 31:2393
Purcell EA Jr (1973) The crisis of democratic theory: scientific naturalism & the problem of value. University of Kentucky, Lexington
Siegan BH (2001) Property rights: from Magna Carta to the fourteenth amendment. Transaction Publishers, Piscataway
Skouras G (2000) Takings law and the supreme court. Peter Lang Pub., New York
Skouras G (2020) Modernity, the Commons and Capitalism. Br J Am Leg Stud 9(2):368
Smith JA (1965) The spirit of American government. The Belknap Press of Harvard University, Cambridge
Smith DL (2007) The most dangerous animal: human nature and the origins of war. St. Martin's Press, New York
Snowiss S (1987) From fundamental law to the supreme law of the land: a reinterpretation of the origins of judicial review. Stud Am Polit Dev 2:1
Strauss L (1953) Natural right and history. University of Chicago, Chicago
Strong H (ed) (1985) The anti-federalists: writings by the opponents of the constitution. University of Chicago, Chicago
Tocqueville A (2003a) Two weeks in the wilderness. In: Democracy in America. Penguin Books, London

Tocqueville A (2003b) Democracy in America. Penguin Books, London
Ward KD, Castillo CR (eds) (2005) The judiciary and American democracy: Alexander Bickel, the countermajoritarian difficulty, and contemporary constitutional theory. SUNY, Albany
Wolfe C (1986) The rise of modern judicial review: from constitutional interpretation to judge-made law. Basic Books, New York
Wolin SS (1990) The presence of the past: essays on the state and the constitution. John Hopkins University, Baltimore
Wood GS (1969) The creation of the American republic 1776-1787. Norton Comp., New York
Wood GS (1989) Preface. In: Paul EF, Dickman H (eds) Liberty, property, & the foundations of the American constitution. SUNY, Albany

Chapter 4
The Era of Economic Due Process—Social Darwinism (Property, Monopoly, Corporatism)

4.1 Social Darwinism & The Law of the Jungle

The struggle for survival in the United States reached a new height in American history as agricultural workers started becoming factory workers in mass, during the closing decades of the Nineteenth and early Twentieth centuries. This struggle for survival pitted the unskilled workers with capitalists. The struggle did not end well for the unskilled workers. "In the years between the collapse of Reconstruction and World War I, virtually every man, woman, and child in America had to face the unsettling consequences of industrialization. [T]heir opportunities, their pains, and their choices can be guessed at only from aggregate statistics and an occasional diary or letter."[1] Reporters and social workers had a front row view of the unfolding Industrial Revolution on the lives of the unskilled, agricultural and immigrant workers pouring into the urban centers of America.[2]

Abraham Lincoln noticed during his presidency major changes underfoot in the 1860s, that eventually any appeasement of Southern Aristocracy was going to pose a serious problem, in adapting the Newtonian model of the Constitution, to the dangers and forces gathering to topple the American system by the Southern States seceding from the Union. Lincoln also, noticed the early formation and accumulation of capital was going to pose a danger to the workers. That is, the workers will be seriously disadvantaged as the formation of capital interests consolidates.

[1] McCormick (1997), p. 107.

[2] Here are some of the Muckrakers of the period: Lincoln Steffens, *The Shame of the Cities* (1957); Upton Sinclair, *The Jungle*, Jacob Riis (1997), *How the Other Half Lives: Studies Among the Tenements of New York*; sometimes referred to as "muckraking" reporting or journalism, they had a window seat of witnessing the American turnover from an Agricultural society to an Industrial society.

G. Skouras, *Constitutionalism and Democracy*,
https://doi.org/10.1007/978-3-031-66906-4_4

The killing of more than 600,000[3] Americans during the Civil War and the countless millions that subsequently succumbed to the coming of the Industrial Revolution can to some degree be attributed to the rigidity of the American Constitution. And the dangers that were about to sweep the next generation of workers out of historical time as they became irrelevant to the Industrial Age. Of course, this is not to suggest that Lincoln was some sort of fortune teller, but only to point to the emerging evidence that American society and people were going to be in a battle for their lives and livelihoods. "He [Lincoln] feared that certain basic principles of democracy were in danger. He believed that the Confederates' main purpose was to perpetuate aristocracy and to deny the people all right to participate in the selection of public officers other than legislators. He likewise sensed that wage workers were headed for trouble, that danger was threatening them. He foresaw the possibility that capital might be achieving dominance over labor."[4]

The struggle for survival was exacerbated during this period in American history because outside of factory work there were few mass scale opportunities to absorb all those coming off the farms—that is, alternative opportunities for farmers transitioning to industrial workers. And the institutions in place, with an emphasis on minimal government or the "nightwatchman"[5] state, were inadequate to address mass scale transplantation. Nor was the government sufficient to properly oversee the expansion of the United States, from a country east of the Mississippi River, to one that ranged from the Atlantic to the Pacific oceans. Nor was the American government capable of planning for the immigration of millions of people coming to the United States from Eastern and Southern Europe—that is, how to incorporate the millions of European immigrants pouring in, both impoverished and unskilled, for work outside the factory system. All that could be done is to dump most farmers and immigrants into factory systems, or, hopefully, they will somehow be absorbed in the vastness of open space that is North America. And, further, these same unskilled workers were most likely locked out of the political system for one reason or another.

The struggle for survival, under altering economic landscapes must have been like surviving jungle conditions—the strong and lucky survive, the rest are left to nature. Upton Sinclair's book *The Jungle*[6] confronts the observer with the industrial horrors of surviving in an urban/industrial jungle. With a 'nightwatchmen" state in place, it became clear that each was on their own to survive the jungle. Would it then be any surprise that the Constitution grants rights, *abstract rights*, which may contain many pretty words, strung together signifying nothingness, for the workers?

The *principle* may be stated this way:

[3]The old numbers calculated for Civil War dead was about 618,000. However, recent research shows that the number could have been as high as 750,000; *see further*, New York Times article, Guy Gugliotta, "New Estimate Raises Civil War Death Toll," *https://www.nytimes.com/2012/04/03/science/civil-war-toll-up-by-20-percent-in-new-estimate.html.*

[4]Nichols (1963), p. 249.

[5]Robert Nozick (2013), *Anarchy, State and Utopia* (the minimalist state as the best state ideology).

[6]Sinclair (1985).

> In America, the Industrial jungle reduced each person to a statistic. Like Nature's jungle, the survivors are fed, and the dead can rest in peace.

Who could or should survive such a jungle experience and conditions? According to the popular philosophy of the time, Social Darwinism, the strong, the healthy, the fit. This philosophy suited and fitted perfectly, a country such as the United States, with a stripped-down Constitution, offering abstract rights, but no solutions for the survival of the "common" people. So, who was the Constitution for? For the people that drafted it: the owners of property.

As I repeatedly stressed in earlier pages, the American Constitution was a carefully designed hierarchical structure to imitate the Aristocracy—in the case of America—a republican building with fancy ornaments and symbols signifying that the property owners liked hierarchy and property ownership as the mark of those that should rule the new country. Obviously, I do not think the members of the Constitutional Convention were sitting down to draft a constitution, other than the racial bias—to disadvantage the workers of the nineteenth century or future generations of workers with their handy work. No, they were simply carrying forward those Enlightenment ideas of the time as to how to balance power against power—that was the problem of a monarchy, crown or dictator. They of course could not have known what the future was going to bring—the mass industrialization of America—that at one time stood as a marginal power on the east coast of North America—to a world power sitting astride the world.

4.2 The Fuller Supreme Court (1888–1910) & Substantive Due Process

The Fuller Supreme Court protected corporations across a spectrum of economic and commercial hurdles posed by the government such as tax, regulation, and labor issues.[7] This happened because the Fuller Court and its successor Courts functioned

[7] Siegan (2001). Siegan provides a historical background for the origins of modern property rights leading to the Fourteenth Amendment from a conservative perspective; White (1976), p. 86. "[T]he Fourteenth Amendment gradually came to be used by the Court to bar state regulation of industrial enterprises. Implicit in this. . .were two collateral themes: a disinclination on the part of the Court to protect civil rights of blacks as it became more inclined to safeguard the property rights of entrepreneur[s]." *Santa Clara County v. Southern Pac. R. Co.*, 118 U.S. 394 (1886), declared corporations are persons. Wiecek (1988), p. 99. "A narrow construction, such as was suggested by Miller in *Slaughterhouse,* would constrict the ability of the national government to protect blacks' rights, leaving the freedmen's future in the control of the Democratic, racist, ex-secessionist, ex-Confederate Redeemers who were then taking control of the southern state.") *See also, Slaughter-House Cases*, 83 U.S. 36 (1873). *Pollock v. Farmers' Loan and Trust Co.*, 158 U.S. 601 (1895) (Court held income tax to be unconstitutional). *Loewe v. Lawlor*, (*The Danbury Hatters' Case),* 208 U.S. 274 (1903) (Court decided that a labor boycott of D. E. Loewe & Company by the Hatters' Union was deemed a conspiracy in restraint of trade that violated the *Sherman Antitrust Act* and awarded threefold damages to the company.) Statutory efforts served as a threat but not much more

both as a legislative and judicial body.[8] The Fuller Court, took the Due Process Clause of the Fourteenth Amendment, and used it to support and protect corporate enterprise. The Supreme Court used the Reconstruction Amendments to conduct economic and industrial policy in America. That is, the Court "redirected" the newly minted 14th Amendment, from helping the former slaves to building corporate America. The Waite Court considered corporations to be "persons." Property worship came to an apex in world history. And taxation was a dirty word. So, what could exist was nothing but a "skinny" state. The Fuller Court finished off income taxes. "Since the government coffers were empty, the corporation was left free of government supervision and only the most perfunctory oversight could be supported given the general philosophy of "limited" government. The federal and state efforts to control the corporation were inadequate."[9]

The Court essentially read into the Constitution Herbert Spencer's *Social Statics*, a survival of the fittest philosophy.[10] Further, the philosophy of natural rights embodied in the *Bill of Rights* were in full use in the justification of the suppression of workers. That is, the use of Natural rights to embody a survival of the fittest ideology in the industrial and corporate jungle.[11] The Due Process Clause became in essence a natural right for the protection of property in the American class system. "A fragmented state, federalism and separation of powers, allowed the Fuller Court to combat so-called "class legislation" using the Due Process Clause. And to further

with the passing of the *Sherman Antitrust Act* and *Clayton Act*. Some early success at regulatory control, *Munn v. Illinois*, (*The Granger Cases*), 94 U.S. 113 (1877), *Budd v. New York*, 143 U.S. 517 (1892), *Standard Oil Co. of New Jersey v. United States*, 221 U.S. 502 (1910), *Swift and Co. v. United States*, 196 U.S. 375 (1905), and *United States v. American Tobacco Co.*, 221 U.S. 106 (1911) (state regulatory and federal monopoly cases showed the government meant business by actively using police power and the *Sherman Antitrust Act*). But eventually, as the Due Process Clause gained economic substance, it became harder and harder to control corporations.

[8]De Santis (2000), p. 12. Chapter 1, "The Rise of Industrial America"—the role of the holding company in evading antitrust); *See also*, Wiecek (1988), pp. 134–135. "Congress in the Clayton Act of 1913 had vaguely attempted to exempt organized labor from antitrust prosecutions by providing that labor was "not a commodity or article of commerce," and had flatly prohibited labor injunctions unless necessary "to prevent irreparable injury to property." The Court nullified these provisions in a series of cases that upheld use of the labor injunction to stop secondary boycotts (*Duplex Printing Press v. Deering*, 1921) and to halt picketing in a printing boycott (*American Steel Foundries v. Tri-City Central Trades Council*, 1921). For good measure, the Court also voided a state statute that prohibited injunctions against peaceful picketing (*Traux v. Corrigan*, 1921)."

[9]Skouras (2011), p. 41; *see further*, Shapiro (1986), *see generally*, Williams (1988) for a general view of the forms of American economic activity before and after the Civil War and the consolidation of the corporate model of enterprise by the last decade of the nineteenth century; *see specifically*, Williams' subsection, "The Age of Corporation Capitalism: 1882-," pp. 343–469.

[10]Spencer (1851) (a social-Darwinian philosopher).

[11]The two previous Courts to the Fuller Court (the Chase Court (1864–1873) and Waite Court (1874–1888), all post-Civil War Courts, set the groundwork, or better put, cleared the ground of debris unfavorable to property interests, and by the time of the Fuller Court (1888–1910), the Supreme Court was reaching the apex of destabilizing democracy through its decisions negating legislation and regulations unfavorable to property or capitalist interests. *See further*, Hendel (1951).

consolidate property power it embedded the Due Process Clause in a philosophy of natural rights even though natural rights were not supposed to be the preferred method of legal analysis."[12]

Is the Fourteenth Amendment a new source of constitutional renewal?[13] Some have regarded the Civil War Amendments to be a major update to the Constitution.[14] The Supreme Court essentially infused the Due Process Clause[15] of the Fourteenth Amendment, with the necessary power, to bludgeon all legislation it found abhorrent and interfered with property rights. With the concentration of new industrial power, the Supreme Court posed as an obstacle to legislative will.[16] Corwin goes on to summarize the activity of the Court between 1887 and 1937. The liberty of contract and laissez-faire ideology took the wind out of any legislative effort to control the economy. According to Corwin, Justices Holmes and Brandeis were not heard as far as the Court was chopping away at social legislation. "The Court had converted judicial review, declared Justice Brandeis, into the power of "a super legislature," while Justice Holmes complained that he could discover "hardly any limit but the

[12] Skouras (2011), p. 42.

[13] The Fourteenth Amendment forbids the states of depriving any person of life, liberty, or property without due process of law. A similar provision is found in the Fifth Amendment with restrictions that apply to the federal government. The Due Process Clause traces its origin to the *Magna Carta*. For additional research on the Fourteenth Amendment, *See*, Curtis (1990) and Nelson (1988).

[14] Kammen (1987). *See also*, Levinson (2006), (a broader critique on the undemocratic nature of the Constitution). Wiecek (1988), p. 116. Wiecek says: "Bradley's dissent in *Slaughterhouse* was more far-reaching. In a brief passage, he conjured up the doctrine of substantive due process out of the natural rights tradition. . .the transformation of the concept of property from tangible objects (e.g., land, wagons, horses) to intangible rights and expectations, such as the abstract right to sell one's labor or the expectation of profit. [P]rocedural due process enabled courts to oversee the rules by which trials were conducted. Substantive due process, on the other hand, protected property rights from legislative impairment."); *See generally*: Foner (1988); *Civil Rights Cases*, 109 U.S. 3 (1883) (Civil rights for blacks were ignored and economic rights for the emerging corporation were privileged); *See also, Plessy v. Ferguson*, 163 U.S. 537 (1896) (The Fourteenth Amendment does not prohibit private citizens from discriminating against blacks, with regard to hotel, theater, or railroad accommodations. The Court promulgated the doctrine of "separate but equal" in the segregation of black America).

[15] Siegan (2001), pp. 219–226. Siegan claims that the Supreme Court Due Process interpretation of the 5th Amendment to the Constitution, during the roughly 80 years between the adoption of the Bill of Rights and the passing of the 14th Amendment, set the precedent as to how the Court should also interpret the Due Process Clause of the 14th Amendment. Obviously, the matter has generated controversy with conservatives and progressives moving to their respective corners in the use of language and the linguistic arts to settle the determination of the phrase "due process." If the analysis presented here is correct, that is, that the Supreme Court usurped the power of judicial review, then the fact that Siegan points to prior Court precedent in its interpretation of the phrase is of no significance here, since the Supreme Court has no authority or legitimacy to interpret or fix the clauses of the Constitution as it sees fit or at its pleasure.

[16] Ely (1995), pp. 63–64. *See also*, Tiedeman (2001), Cooley (1998), Ely (1991), Halper (1990), Swisher (1930), McCurdy (1975), Furer (1986), and Kens (1997).

sky" to the power claimed by the Court to disallow State acts "which may happen to strike a majority" of its members "as for any reason undesirable."[17]

The case of *Lochner v. New York*[18] (1905) became a landmark case in economic due process review. It took a few decades of preparatory work by the Supreme Court to reach this point. *Lochner*[19] became the new landmark in overturning legislation hostile to property interests.[20]And the Justices became the high priests of property protection. By the use of a "thin" Constitution to drive down the hoards looking to breach the walls of property protection. The Supreme Court became the last guardian between property interests and *We the People*.

Why did the Court focus on economics/property issues during the Gilded Age? Because property protection is a foundational principle in defense of the American Constitution. What does that mean? As the Industrial Revolution sped up the pace of change, it became necessary that these changes do not upset the apple cart. So, changes taking place in society needed to comport with the constitutional protection of property. The massive wave of humanity, on the move from farms to factories, along with massive amounts of immigrants mostly unskilled, had to be incorporated into urban centers without interfering with private property. And any legislation or regulation had to meet a standard of "reasonableness." What is reason? What is reasonable? How do we know what is reasonable? Could my reason differ from

---

[17]Corwin (1978), p. 223.

[18]198 U.S. 45 (1905); this landmark case has thrown up voluminous debates as to its status between revisionists and anti-revisionist scholars trying to properly characterize its reach and domain. For these debates, *see* also, Bernstein DE "Lochner Era Revisionism, Revisited: Lochner and the Origins of Fundamental Rights Constitutionalism," George Mason University School of Law, Law and Economics Working Papers, can be downloaded at the Social Science Research Network Electronic Paper Collection: http://ssrn.com/abstract_id=395620.

[19]*Lochner v. New York* became a landmark case because it came at the intersection of the changeover between the Agricultural Age and the shifting over to the Industrial Age where worker rights were few and capitalist powers were increasing or solidifying. The case involved bakery workers. New York passed legislation that forbade any employee in a bakery to work more than 60 hours per week. Lochner was convicted of allowing his employees to work more than 10 hours per week. The issue arose as to whether the 14th Amendment was violated by the New York legislature. The Supreme Court took the case and responded in the affirmative. The right for individuals to make their own contracts was violated by this legislation. The Court did not buy New York's argument that the legislation was necessary because bakery work conditions posed a threat to the health and safety of the workers; *see further*, the construction of the liberty of contract by the Supreme Court to cut the legs off States passing legislation to help workers. Beth (1971), p. 64. "The construction by Justice Rufus W. Peckham and his colleagues of the doctrine of liberty of contract to stop the states from regulating wages and other working conditions was a logical deduction from the existing common law."

[20]Wolfe (1986), pp. 4–5. "New York State prohibited employment in bakeries for more than sixty hours a week or ten hours a day. The Court acknowledged the established state power to regulate matters relating to safety, health, morals, and general welfare, but it argued that this power had to be limited, for otherwise "the legislatures would have unbounded power." The question was whether this exercise of state power interfered unreasonably in the "liberty of contract"—the freedom of employers to buy, and employees to sell, labor on mutually agreeable terms. The Court thought that the statute impermissibly interfered with such freedom and struck it down."

yours? Can there be such a thing as a reasonable standard? Could there ever be an "objective" standard of reasonableness or reason? Many philosophers cut their teeth on such amorphous concepts.[21] What does the phrase "liberty of contract" mean? What does the term "liberty" mean? Why is the Supreme Court in the best place to serve as that "limiting" power? Who appointed the Court to serve as a surveyor and delimiting power of legislative will?

The *principle* may be stated this way:

> Property is all there is. Whether you see the "reasonableness" of this statement is your affair. My "reason" and your "reason" are epiphenomena. The core is all. Reasons are later justifications.

What is clear is that language and linguistics mark important territory in the law. Just as land or territory held on a battlefield, linguistic demarcation points to conquered mental territory in the justification of legal action. After the Civil War, the Supreme Court began a march toward slowly transforming the Fourteenth Amendment as a protector of property. In the *Slaughterhouse Case* (1873),[22] the Due Process clause was read as a procedural clause, but Justices Field and Bradley in dissent pushed for a broader interpretation of the clause.[23] It started moving further with the *Munn v. Illinois*[24] decision with Field in dissent pushing for a broader reading of the clause.

---

[21] I will have more to say on this concept of "reasonableness" in the other sections of this work. However, it should be noted ahead of time that a concept such as "reason," used by philosophers for centuries is a rather slippery concept and packs lots of fuzziness into it. Philosophers have cut their teeth on such amorphous concepts for millennia. So, there should be no great expectation that this concept will be unpacked satisfactorily here.

[22] Wolfe (1986), p. 148. "The post-Civil War Supreme Court resisted invitations to employ substantive due process for a generation. In the *Slaughterhouse Cases* (1873), for example, the Court construed Fourteenth Amendment due process for the first time and held that it was limited to procedural matters. But this holding met with vigorous dissents from justices such as Field and Bradley who urged the Court to see in due process a broad protection of fundamental rights, substantive as well as procedural." *see further*, Beth (1971), p. 67. "The uncertain slide of the Supreme Court into laissez-faire had begun with the Court's decision in the Slaughterhouse cases in 1873."

[23] Beth (1971), p. 67. "Here (the *Slaughterhouse* case) the Court had staved off by a 5-4 vote. [T]hat the due process clause of the newly adopted Fourteenth Amendment should be turned to the protection of private business from the depredations of government. [F]our dissenters were not so sure that the federal system should not be changed, but they seemed to be more concerned with the protection of business property than with individual human liberties. It is significant that in the *first case seriously to introduce the idea that the due process of law could be applied to the substance of laws rather than merely to legal procedure[s].*" (my emphasis).

[24] Wolfe (1986), p. 148. "The Court's apparent early rejection of substantive due process, however, contained the seeds of a future reversal. In *Munn v. Illinois* (1877), for example, the Court faced the question of whether Illinois could regulate grain elevator rates. Relying on a common-law doctrine of a business "affected with a public interest" could be regulated, the Court upheld the Illinois statute. Field dissenting, arguing that... "If this be sound law, if there be no protection, either in the principles upon which our republican government is founded, or in the prohibitions of the Constitution against such invasion of private rights, all property and all business in the State are held at the mercy of a majority of the legislature.""

By the time of *Mugler v. Kansas*[25] it started to become clear that the Court was carving out this clause for special treatment in protecting property from legislative and regulatory interference. The linguistic form need not conform to the substantive form. The regulatory body could use pretty language to restrict the use or sale of liquor in Kansas, but the practical outcome should not be restrictive of property rights or else the Supreme Court will pierce the veil of linguistic niceties and strike down the legislation.

Finally, by 1890, in *Chicago, Milwaukee, and St. Paul Railroad v. Minnesota*,[26] the Supreme Court began to utilize the doctrine of Substantive Due Process.[27] "Rather the "procedures" involved here were related to the substance of the law: the railroads in effect were demanding a participation in the process of setting the rates, that is, a share in the (delegated) legislative process."[28] And by 1897, the concept was baked into Supreme Court philosophy, in the case of *Allgeyer v. Louisiana*.[29] "*Allgeyer* was quickly followed by *Smyth v. Ames*[30] (1898), which held that railroad rates set by states were subject to judicial review in order to ascertain whether railroads were being deprived of property arbitrarily. For the next forty years, then, the Court was knee deep in the business of setting railroad rates: it became a kind of Super-Railroad-Rate-Commission."[31]

We see the Supreme Court bifurcating legislative action: legislation aimed at protecting health and safety of workers as acceptable to the Court. Legislation aimed at restricting property rights as unacceptable to the Court. The former is fine, the latter is an interference of property rights. With the case of *Lochner*[32] (1905), the Court was unable to find that working in a bakery was an inherently dangerous work. With an earlier case, *Holden v. Hardy*[33] (1898), the bifurcation was legitimate. The Court began a long march after *Lochner* in the invalidation of contracts that

---

[25] 123 U.S. 623 (1887).

[26] 134 U.S. 418 (1890).

[27] Wolfe (1986), p. 149.

[28] Wolfe (1986), pp. 149–150.

[29] Wolfe (1986), p. 150. "Finally, in 1897, the Court completed this development of substantive due process with the first clear cut decision based on it, *Allgeyer v. Louisiana* (1897). [B]ut the holding of the case was based on the due process clause: "The liberty mentioned in that [the Fourteenth] amendment means, not only the right of the citizen to be free from the mere physical restraint of his person...In the privilege of pursuing an ordinary calling or trade and of acquiring, holding, and selling property must be embraced the right to make all proper contracts in relation theret[o]"".

[30] *Smyth v. Ames* (1898).

[31] Wolfe (1986), p. 151.

[32] *Lochner v. New York*, 198 U.S. 45 (1905); Lochner bifurcated the concept of the State regulating for health reasons and interfering with private property (hours a worker may work).

[33] *Holden v. Hardy*, 169 U.S. 366 (1898), Court upholding the law limiting the working hours of miners as a matter of health due to the dangers posed in mining work.

interfered with property rights.[34] It moved to wage regulation, hours setting, railroad rate setting, price regulations, and many other matters it deemed an interference with freely negotiated contracts.

> The Court was more steadfast in its rejection of legislative regulation of wages. In *Adkins v. Children's Hospital*[35] (1923), it struck down a congressional establishment of a minimum wage law for women in the District of Columbia. In order to protect health and morals, the wage was to be set at the level necessary to provide for the necessities of the women. The Court recognized that there might indeed be a moral obligation for the community to support its needy, but it rejected the imposition of that duty on the employer. Liberty of contract—both the employers' and the employees'—was impermissibly infringed, especially by a minimum wage law that was based on something other than the true worth of the work.[36]

Labor contracts, *Adair v. United States*[37] (1908) and *Coppage v. Kansas*[38] (1915), were curtailed by the Supreme Court. The Court sort of appointed itself as the overseer of a society undergoing rapid change from agriculture to industry.[39] Justice Holmes was cognizant of the fact that the Court was acting like a super-legislator during this period and found himself, along with Justice Brandeis, in dissent in many cases.[40] In short Justices Holmes and Brandeis did not fit in well with a *laissez-faire and social Darwinian* Supreme Court in early Twentieth century America.

What is clear is that a Supreme Court, with the power of judicial review is in a position, to re-order society according to its own plans, not by the will of *We the People*.[41] Where property protection becomes the standard of the good society, all that interferes with private property protection is bad. Legislation aimed at ameliorating the pain and suffering of the unskilled and propertyless worker was not in the capacity or within the scope of the legislator authority because the legislator tipped the scales of justice in favor of the propertyless over the propertied—those that want to help the propertyless, at the expense of the propertied, are deemed as illegally

---

[34] Ely (2007), p. 88. "Because judges are influenced by social forces and intellectual currents in general society, the principles of laissez-faire constitutionalism gained currency among Supreme Court justices in the 1880s."

[35] *Adkins v. Children's Hospital*, 261 U.S 525 (1923).

[36] Wolfe (1986), p. 152.

[37] *Adair v. United States*, 208 U.S. 161 (1908).

[38] *Coppage v. Kansas*, 236 U.S. 1 (1915) (the employers allowed to implement "yellow-dog" contracts that forbade employees from joining a union.

[39] Wolfe (1986), p. 153 "The Court applied this rule to strike down price regulation in various areas. Besides food, fuel, clothing (at least where competition exists and theater ticket resale (*Tyson and Bros.*), these included employment agency fees and private cabs. The Court also guaranteed against state attempting to proscribe them, either completely or for private citizens, the legality of entering certain "honest callings." *Adams v. Tanner* (1917) struck down a state provision of employment agencies that collected fees from employees. *New State Ice Co. v. Liebmann* (1932) overturned an Oklahoma law prohibiting private sale and distribution of ice without a permit."

[40] *See*, Urofsky (2009) on the life of Justice Brandeis.

[41] The Supreme Court re-ordering society is a rather strong statement. It might be clearer or better put to say that the vision of the legislature or We the People can be frustrated, blocked, or re-imagined by the Court according to its lights.

interfering with the sacred rights of property ownership. "Support for laissez-faire philosophy simply reflected hostility by businesses to increase government regulation that accompanied the industrial revolution—regulation that was designed to protect workers, women, consumers, and competitors."[42]

The mechanical and Newtonian principles embodied in the Constitution regarding the priority and centrality of property protection were applied regardless of conditions on the ground. The Newtonian mechanics, embodied in the American Constitution, were rigid enough to allow the Supreme Court to serve as the ultimate decider as to how property is to be distributed in the United States—to withstand the need for legislative and regulation change and reform on the ground level. Combine this rigid Newtonian mechanics with Social Darwinism philosophy, and it entails an asymmetrical challenge for living animals to survive the experience in the urban jungle of industrialism. It was nature's way of weeding out the weak, and the judges using the Constitution as a scalpel to finish off the propertyless commoners. The Justices were simply carrying out their duty to protect society from any unnatural assistance (by Regulators/Legislators) and the redistribution of property from one group to another or from one class to another.

Nothing was off the table for the Supreme Court, not even sick chickens! "In *A.L. A. Schecter Poultry Corp. v. United States* (1935), often referred to as the "sick chicken case," the Court declared a federal law unconstitutional based on an insufficient direct effect on interstate commerce. *The National Industrial Recovery Act of 1933*, a key piece of New Deal legislation, authorized the president to approve "codes of fair competition" developed by boards of various industries."[43] Before Roosevelt threatened to pack the Court, most of Roosevelt's New Deal legislation was struck down as in one way or another interfering with commerce or property. That is, again the Court was behaving in a mechanical and Newtonian way as it did during the Gilded Age. Even though conditions changed on the ground, with the collapse of the market in 1929 and the ensuing Great Depression, the Court was acting to protect property over legislative efforts to meet the needs of the commoners. The Supreme Court aligned itself with the business interests over *We the People* or the unwashed masses.[44] Chemerinsky nicely summarized the Supreme Court opinions that brought down Franklin Delano Roosevelt legislation in the effort to fight to stabilize American society during the Great Depression.[45] Chemerinsky

---

[42] Chemerinsky (2018), pp. 109–110.

[43] Chemerinsky (2018), p. 114.

[44] Corwin (1964), p. 109. Corwin characterizes this period of Business not lifting a finger to help stabilize a social and economic order undergoing deep transformation. The Supreme Court had no interest in rocking the Business boat. Corwin says: "What is more, no single important measure of the past forty years meant to correct business practices in the interests of a wider public can be pointed to which has the support of Business. The Interstate Commerce Act did not, The Sherman Act did not, the Federal Trade Commission did not, the Clayton Act did not, the Federal Reserve Act did not. On the contrary, Business presented in every one of these instances an almost solid front of opposition."

[45] Chemerinsky (2018), pp. 114–117.

does a good job listing the Great Depression cases that gave the Roosevelt administration a run for its money, as the Court destabilized his whole economic program.[46]

From 1798 until the Civil War, the Supreme Court helped consolidate the power of the Federal government, by interpreting the Constitution in such a way as to grant the federal government maximum power to control and regulate interstate commerce. However, after the Civil War and until the New Deal, the Court was hostile towards regulatory bodies interfering with property and business interests. The example of the Bigness of corporations and the Court's interpretation of Antitrust laws, to minimize the interference and growth of corporations, was front and center of its policies or doctrines. After 1937, the Supreme Court granted Congress the permission to regulate property and the economy after being threatened by President Roosevelt to pack the Court. "From 1937 until 1995, not one federal law was declared unconstitutional on the grounds of exceeding the scope of Congress's powers."[47]

Other efforts to curtail Federal legislation from interfering with property rights involved the Tenth Amendment. According to Chemerinsky: "But in *Hammer v. Dagenhart*, [t]he Supreme Court said that the Tenth Amendment meant much more than this. The Court held that Congress violated the Tenth Amendment if it attempted to control production of goods, even though it was exercising its constitutional power to regulate commerce among the states. The Court concluded that the Tenth Amendment reserves control of production to the states for their exclusive control."[48] Since 'production' and 'commerce' were not the same thing, the States were free to manage their own production without Federal legislation. In short, the Court would bend over backwards to thwart federal legislative laws aimed to weaken property rights. The Supreme Court gave the Substantive Due Process a pause after President Franklin D. Roosevelt threatened to pack it, as one after another of his New Deal programs fell dead.

4.3 Corporate Expansion and Monopoly

The Corporation served as a perfect vehicle to accumulate capital and diversify risk. As corporate power grew unchecked, it started to swallow up public power. Once the Corporation reached the early stages of aggrandizement,[49] it could set its own terms

[46] Chemerinsky (2018), p. 115.

[47] Chemerinsky (2018), p. 117.

[48] Chemerinsky (2018), pp. 111–112.

[49] Pole (1979), pp. 76, 77. "The popular name of the type of capitalist economy that sprang up rapidly in nineteenth century America was a 'free labor' economy, perhaps because it was labor rather than capital that needed to be convinced of its freedom. In the third quarter of the century, Standard Oil's legal advisors began to devise the trust as a form of corporate government for multiple branches of business, within a few years, the increasingly monopolistic aspects of the

and agenda as to its best interests—the public or *We the People* be damned.[50] Monopoly[51] power turned the corporation into a ferocious and vicious animal that could devour whatever got in its way. Of course, this was not an overnight process. It took many decades to work itself out, with the State occasionally threatening to tame the beast—from time to time attempting to put it into a regulatory cage using its primitive tools of antitrust law. However, the corporation, along with other large property interests, long enjoyed constitutional protections by way of the Supreme Court—to clear whatever was thrown in their way, starting with defanging the early antitrust laws such as the *Sherman Act.*[52]

---

corporate form of business became a matter of major public concern, but the more heavily concentrated and monopolistic the system became, the more firmly did its political and business spokesmen commit themselves and the nation to the conviction that the system incorporated all that was the best of free private enterprise and of what came to be called economic—eventually 'rugged'—individualism." (p. 76) J.R. Pole, a distinguished British historian with a focus on American history, says that the above tale told by progressives has been countered later in the twentieth century by two studies that demolish this sad story favored by progressives. He goes on to say: "In the aftermath of the New Deal these views were demolished, primarily by two important studies of Massachusetts and Pennsylvania, one by Oscar and Mary Handlin, the other by Louis Hartz. They showed that early American state governments were as mercantilists and as interventionists—in intension if not always in power—as the royal government they had over-thrown. These monographs represent an important step in the liberation of historical interpretation from a particular nexus of political dogma." (p. 77) This footnote may not be the proper place to challenge Pole's thesis. Nevertheless, a brief response needs to be generated. The American political system does not govern America, the legal system, by way of the Judicial branch of government, by way of the Supreme Court as the final arbiter of how property law, contracts, commercial law, antitrust, etc. function on the ground level. J.R. Pole might have confused how the British parliamentary system (free of judicial review oversight functions) from the American system of government. His focus on early America is the wrong standard to judge post-Civil War America. Although he has many interesting things to say about the relationship between Britain and America in the eighteenth century and early nineteenth century, there came a point of divergence. One big point is the post-Civil War America. J.R. Pole seems to conflate early America with the rising Industrial power America where the courts started intervening on a different quantitative and qualitative scale with legislatures. In the domains of property, contract, commerce, tort, etc. the Supreme Court interfered with the legislative will and ruled for corporate America over a We the People America.

[50] Bates (1976); Hays (1957), p. 37. "The stark reality of social conflict deeply stunned Americans who had cherished the view that class divisions did not exist in their country". Beatty (2008), p. 200. Beatty says: "In "The Owners of the United States," a writer in the *Forum*, extrapolating from the 1880 census, figured that 25,000 people owned half the wealth and 250,000, 75 to 80 percent of it. "Who owns the United States?" he asked. "The USA is practically owned by less than 250,000 persons." Using the 1890 census, a contributor to *Political Science Quarterly* calculating "The Concentration of Wealth" found that "4,047 families possess as much as 11,593,887 families." "This result," he wrote, "seems almost incredible""); see further, Mitz and Cohen (1971) and Holbrook (1954).

[51] Adams and Brock (1986); Baran and Sweezy (1968); Fine (1964).

[52] McCloskey (1994), p. 84. "It involved the Sherman Act, which had been passed by Congress in 1890 to "protect trade and commerce against unlawful restraints and monopolies." In 1895 the Court held that the law did not, and indeed could not, forbid monopolies in manufacturing, because manufacturing is not a part of interstate commerce and affects interstate commerce only

How has the Supreme Court helped property interests and the monopoly interests over the People during the Gilded Age[53] and Progressive Age? By using its power of judicial review, during the early Industrialization stage[54] of America, the Court could do as it liked regarding Congressional regulations by either defanging them or delimiting them because the formal state in America was weak and immature—America was simply left with a "nightwatchmen" state to oversee the massive shifts of capital and workers at the hands of large-scale enterprises. Empowered by a *laissez-faire* ideology and a rendition of individualism, making collective action extremely difficult to achieve. In short, working Americans had, long been convinced by a political philosophy that favored individualism over collective action, while at the same time corporations were consolidating and aggrandizing their power.

According to Gillman, in 1895 alone, the Supreme Court was very busy cutting down the legislature: "In 1895 alone the Court struck down the income tax, approved the use of injunction against labor strikes and boycotts, and interfered with the administration of antitrust laws. Soon thereafter it began to nullify legislation designed to improve the dismal condition of workers."[55] What is clear from the historical record is that monopoly control, via Antitrust policy, is uneven and haphazard at best. Only when the effects of monopoly power begin to pinch is there a popular ruckus. Some offering is made to break-up the business gods that be, by way of antitrust threats, and after a period of quietude, the business operates as usual until the antitrust cage is reopened and the cycle begins anew. The reason for this periodicity is simply that the threats of antitrust are forgotten, the business enterprise is emboldened again, and the cycle continues. The underlying condition as to why stronger measures are not taken against monopolists is because they have the American Constitution as their protector and the Supreme Court standing at the ready to read the Constitution in their favor. The maxim: *property protection over equality*. Sanders summarizes the number of ways the Court interfered with economic policy at the end of the nineteenth and early twentieth centuries. That is, tax policy, antitrust policy, labor policy and other economic efforts were derailed by the Court. "From 1897 to 1903, frenzied trust building, undertaken more often by great

---

"indirectly." To allow the national government to regulate this subject would be to permit encroachment on the reserved powers of the states. (*United States v. E.C. Knight Co.*)" *see further*, Sanders (1986), pp. 157–158.

[53] If we can say that the state function of America during the Gilded Age and Progressive era was fragmented (deliberately so by the nature of the Constitution), then we should be able to observe how such a vacuum of political power can be claimed as a matter of default by emerging corporate power. As the nature of rural America changed due to industrialism, it continued to operate under "limited government" principles even though industrialism required direct government intervention in the private sector if it was to control the power of the corporation. That is, the corporate state will refer to the default power as a result of constitutional fragmentation and the Founder's creation of a weak Federal government.

[54] Cochran and Miller (1961) (*See, e.g.*, Chapter Nine, "The Rise of Finance Capitalism". See also, Lears (2010) and Kolko (1984).

[55] Gillman (1993), p. 2.

financial houses than by the manufacturers themselves, gave lasting form to American industrial structure. The merger movement peaked in 1901, with an elephantine example: the formation, as a New Jersey holding company, of the world's first billion-dollar corporation, United States Steel (USS)."[56]

Theodore Roosevelt attempted to put some muscle behind the *Sherman Act*, but he made a distinction between "good" monopoly and "bad" monopoly. In other words, Roosevelt did not consider all monopolies as a bad thing. Sanders says: "Roosevelt's policy was highly selective, based on a distinction between "good" and "bad" trusts that maximized his discretionary power. He was in no way opposed to corporate concentration *per se* but was determined that the national government—or at least *his office*—possess power that matched (and, in a showdown, exceeded) that of the corporate giants. He only supported new legislation that expanded executive discretion, and condemned the Sherman Act itself because "its full enforcement would destroy the business of the country."[57]

The internal plumbing of the American Constitution is all about the protection of property. So, any effort by the government to interfere, confiscate, or regulate property has a herculean task in front of it. The Founders believed that without strong protections of property all that is left is anarchy and savagery—a fallback to the state of nature and a Hobbesian world of "each against all".

4.4 Mechanical Constitutionalism Versus Organic Constitutionalism

As the Nineteenth century reached its midpoint, the legal foundations were shifting as commercialism and capitalism were becoming a force to be reckoned with. That is, the Agricultural Age was passing slowly from the scene, and the agricultural society's legal system was undergoing transformation and preparatory work to accommodate commerce, that will eventually supplant agricultural life and alter the conditions of life in the fullness of time, by way of gutting legal protections and regulation that were attached to the agricultural way of life (even though the passing from the Agricultural Age to the Industrial Age will take another 40 or 50 years). The markings were on the wall as commerce was beginning its rise and would eventually substantially transform the nature of society and its ways of being within-time. Replacing a way of life, by allowing the common law to be transformed, as

[56] Sanders (1986), pp. 158–159. According to Sanders additional mega mergers for their time were: "United States Steel was but one of the great industrial combinations put together between 1897 and 1903. The list of new trusts also included Eastern Kodak, Amalgamated Copper, Borden's, Quaker Oats, United Shoe Machinery, International Harvester, United Fruit, and two smaller trusts, Jones and Laughlin and Republic Steel. Over a thousand companies in mergers in 1899 alone. A few years later, over on industrial fields were e hundred dominated by a single firm."

[57] Sanders (1986), p. 161.

preparatory or clearing house, for trade and commerce to become the handmaidens of modern industry.

Just as the Civil War was to restructure the American political system, the legal system was being updated to accommodate the needs of commerce and the rise of capitalist society. The legal system, especially those aspects involved with contract, commerce, corporate formation, and industry, according to Horwitz, were undergoing transformation. Horwitz says: "Anticommercial legal doctrines had been destroyed or undermined and the legal system had almost completely shed its eighteenth-century commitment to regulating the substantive fairness of economic exchange. [L]aw, once conceived of as protective, regulative, paternalistic and above all, a paramount expression of the moral sense of the community, had come to be thought of as facilitative of individual desires and as simply reflective of the existing organization of economic and political power.[58]

That is, the instrumentalist theory of law was tied to a utilitarian moral philosophy flexible enough to accommodate the needs of the emerging non-agriculturalist society that was on the horizon but not yet birthed. Jeremy Bentham, John Austin, and John Stuart Mill were prevailing in the Nineteenth century—that is, their pragmatic, efficiency, and utility school of thought was suitable for the emerging business interests—whether be it in law or economics.[59] It also appears that the future was going to be dominated by a flexible ethics called utilitarianism, and a market economics based on new contract[60] and monetary exchange—all under principles of market efficiency economics. Those old moral codes and common practices of the agriculturalist society could only be a hindrance to the emerging society on the cusp of birth—the birthing of the industrial age—a new dawn that will

---

[58] Horwitz (1977), p. 253.

[59] Jeremy Bentham (1748–1832), *A Fragment on Government* (his utilitarianism and jurisprudence: *https://plato.stanford.edu/entries/bentham/;* John Austin (1790–1859), *https://plato.stanford.edu/entries/austin-john/* and John Stuart Mill, https://plato.stanford.edu/entries/mill-moral-political/.

[60] Horwitz (1977), pp. 253–266. "Chapter 8: The Rise of Legal Formalism"—Horwitz attempts to make the case for the transformation of contract law, as understood and practiced during eighteenth century America versus the first half of the nineteenth century. That is, the "fair price" doctrine had to be done away with in favor of utility exchange between parties. "During the first half of the century, legal writers and judges were largely successful in shifting fair price conceptions from the law of contract and in shifting the focus of contract law to the determination of whether there had been a "meeting of the minds." As a result, one of the central problems of the "new" contract law was the development at the same time barring any substantive inquiry into the equivalency of an exchange, which now had come to be regarded as "subjective" and "political."" (Horwitz, pp. 261–262) On similar lines as contract law, Horwitz also illustrates the transformation taking place in property law by way of takings and eminent domain. By removing this power from the legislatures willing to compensate the victims of such actions with "just" compensation which could be very damaging to the business interests, it was better to let the judiciary and courts in making this determination rather than the legislatures. That is, judges were more likely to be more restrained than legislatures in compensating the victims of the takings or eminent domain actions—that is, to transfer the power to the judiciary and judges to limit and reduce any redistribution or confiscatory actions that legislatures were prepared to make the victims whole (Horwitz, pp. 259–261).

eclipse a way of life, the life of agriculture and farm society that was a way of life since the dawn of civilization.

The *principle* may be stated this way:

> Utility, practicality, and what works ideology leaves out moral agency that respectively can regulate the conditions of change, upheaval, and new forms of earning a living under fair principles—that is, the function of utility and the function of justice become discontinuous.

According to Horwitz, foundational and preparatory work was underway to clear away the debris accumulated over the ages of common law accretions and replaced with utilitarian ethics (or instrumentalism) and economics of business enterprise—as a way of allowing business and enterprises to supplant the farming society. And new accommodations were needed in supporting the trades and businesses as they began to open up an alternative space to farming. "As in the analogous case of the mill acts, there regularly appeared to be considerable "slippage" between actual compensation and the fair market value of appropriated land, especially since "consequential" or "speculative" damages were often left uncompensated, until around 1840 the rising entrepreneurial groups, though regularly suspicious of this confiscatory potential within their midst, had used the eminent domain power ruthlessly to their own advantage."[61] Horwitz appears to some degree to reverse the Marxist principle that the economic conditions set in motion the superstructure that forms the legal system. That it just might be the case that the law prepares the way or clears the underbrush before capitalist production can be set in full motion. The motions of the capitalist needs to be undergirded and supported by the legal infrastructure. What Horwitz is saying is that the Agricultural Age legal structure needed to give way to the Industrial Age legal infrastructure.

What is happening is the transformation of the law of 'takings' from providing compensation for the takings of property to a more restrictive and uncompensated takings of property. As state taxation was increased to pay for these takings, it required the termination or restriction of these means, also, for the costs of economic development. The fear that the increased taxation was redistributive because it went to compensate the owners whose property was taken by eminent domain. So, what was to be done to assist the rising business class interests, in taking and using property for development, if the business class did not want the State to increase taxes to pay for these takings? The Supreme Court could step in and allow the taking of property by eminent domain, and rule whether it required compensation or not, by developing its own tests and mechanisms of what constituted a taking of property. This could clear out agricultural or landed property for preparation for industrial use and consolidation—that is, by clearing out the land for commercial interests more worthy than what their previous use during the Agricultural Age. Otherwise, the legislature might overcompensate outdated property/lands that needed to be improved to accommodate the new industrial development—why let the petty farmers, tradesmen and others out-of-date workers and businesses interfere with

[61] Horwitz (1977), p. 260.

Big Business and Big Industry? "Creating for the first time a sharp distinction between public and private takings—no doubt drawing spiritual guidance from the earlier and analogous public-private corporation doctrine of the *Dartmouth College* case—the court refused to accept what before had been a standard and virtually unchallenged utilitarian justification of these acts."[62]

A preparatory clearing was taking place throughout the Nineteenth century of debris from an agricultural society. As the old ways of life receded from the farming horizon a new dawn was breaking for the corporations. As indicated previously, the key function of the Supreme Court during this period was to maintain the priority and privileged status of property and its protection.[63] This period saw the breakdown (the Civil War) of the American constitutional system because it could not adapt itself to meet the pressing conditions of its time. Similarly, today, in our own time, the Constitution lacks the mechanisms to adapt to our generations' needs. This is because of the cumbersome and layered structure to protect property over any other social need. The core protection of property at the center of the Constitution spills over to general social dimensions. A Constitution that cannot adapt to changing times or altered environmental condition will either be discarded or re-structured.[64]There is a third option, utilized by President Woodrow Wilson, after leaving the academic world and his careers as a political scientist, for the real world of drag out fights of beasts and animals, in the political arena, where these species of animals are prepared to skin each other alive, the use of "new" interpretations, to make the Constitution yield the results needed rather than going through the trouble of amending it or restructuring. That is, we will leave the "original" Constitution standing, but as life goes on, we will operate under an interpretive "living" Constitution that is more flexible in deflecting the arrows and challenges of any given era.

> The Fuller Court used the Due Process Clause to maintain "limited government" but not limited corporate power. [W]hat is clear is that the perpetuation of the idea of "limited government" serves and served the corporate interests perfectly. The Justices believed that the private market and individual freedom would come together to rectify the excesses of industrialization. Consequently, the Court adopted laissez-faire approach that left America at the mercy of the emergent corporate state without any checks or controls as to its size, function, aims, and residues of its existence.[65]

---

[62] Horwitz (1977), p. 260 (reference to a NY court case involved in 'takings' law).

[63] Ely, Jr. (1992), *see further,* Ely, Jr. (2005); Ely, Jr. (1991), p. 213; McDonald (1958); Barnett (2003), p. 111; Siegan (2001); McCurdy (1975), p. 970; McCurdy (1978), p. 631; Murphy (1963), pp. 64–79; Jones (1966), pp. 602–627; Jones (1967), pp. 752–771; Epstein (1985, 1995); Berger (1989, 1997).

[64] Purcell (1973), p. 75. "As early as 1881, Justice Holmes, then a young lawyer in Boston, had published his famous study of the common law, which he placed in an evolutionary Darwinian framework. Holmes argued that practical expedients, necessitated by the needs and conflicts of human society, were more central to the development of law than were any logical propositions."

[65] Skouras (2011), p. 7.

Ultimately, the Supreme Court fused property and business interests with public interests. *We the People* were a second act for the Court if we mattered at all. The Supreme Court versus the government, defending business from governmental intervention and regulation. McCloskey says: "In this second great period of constitutional history, then, running roughly from the end of the Civil War to 1937, the major interest of the Supreme Court as a molder of governmental policy became the relationship between government and business; and the major value of the Court was the protection of the business community against government."[66]

4.5 Property and Judicial Review

As more and more countries around the world examined the American model of separation of powers, it started to have great appeal for them too. Especially after their defeat in the Second World War or during the decolonization periods or after the collapse of the Soviet Union, and these countries had a conversion experience on the road to Damascus. That is, given the supreme power exercised by the United States, it would bode well for them to extract some features of the American system—division of powers to break up authoritarian tendencies and the power of judicial review to protect property, usually going under such sweet-sounding names as "human rights" or "civil rights" or a "Bill of Rights" if they wanted to impress the new overlord masters in the United States.

That is, we should not accept European countries or any countries word that they have recently adopted the practice of judicial review under the goodness of their heart and must dig deeper for roots that lead to aristocracy. As we have shown so far and will continue to point out for the remainder of the book, how the United States hides the principles of Aristocratic rule. These republican principles would be of special appeal to the Europeans with a heritage heavy and weighted down by aristocratic rule for millennia. That is the hiding of property protection under democratic labels and a "thin" Constitution. Using democratic labels but laced with poison pills in case the "unwashed" masses want to desecrate the halls and walls that keep them out of the sanctuary. The bottom line—the core of property rights—must be protected at all times.

So, it would be convenient for European countries and other countries around the world that have adopted the American system of judicial review to throw in a Bill of Rights into their Constitutions. In case they have any troublemakers, they can pretend that they are all about "human" rights, "civil" rights and other goodies, but hide the fact that the protection of "property" rights is the center and core of their constitutions. This is basically the Lockean philosophy that ties liberalism,

[66]McCloskey (1994), p. 69. "Historians like Charles Beard and J. Allan Smith and Brooks Adams were telling us, as early as the first decade of the twentieth century, that the Supreme Court was remarkably friendly to the pleas of "vested wealth."

individualism and the labor theory of value into a golden noose for the workers and the unpropertied. The Europeans must be salivating in the protection of all these goodies. So, the property right is bundled up with rights to liberty and free speech, freedom of religion etc. Not telling the average joe and jane that they have a right to freedom, liberty, religion on empty bellies. Therefore, any modern analysis or comparative must first begin with the unbundling the property right from the other rights—from the non-property rights. Because the property right is unlike the other rights that might have good justification of special protections under a Bill of Rights.

The analyst must go directly for the throat and remove the property right from the Bill of Rights if he expects to understand the modern function of the Property Aristocracy within capitalist systems. Because property right is the core or the core right that is being protected—all the others being subsidiary or better put secondary or tertiary—the property right being the core—the sun that bend light from distant stars or the gravitational field or black hole that sucks all in. We should expect to find other countries that have adopted the American practice of judicial review to be also protecting property as the core of their societies. Of course, other rights are mentioned in the American Bill of Rights, as they are mentioned under many other countries' Bill of Rights—which is simply trying to maintain a new society of the Aristocracy of Property under the color of democratic labels.

We might suspect that other European countries, which converted into democracies and converted in mass of adopting the American system of democracy and judicial review, might also be using the judicial review technique to indirectly maintain aristocratic systems under the color of democracy. This would not only be true for the Commonwealth countries based on the Anglo traditions such as Canada, Australia, New Zealand, South Africa, Hong Kong, and others, but also for those continental European states emerging out of the shattering experience of the Second World War—such as France, Germany, Italy, and others.[67] The British did not adopt the American system of judicial review[68] as cover or color of democratic rule because the English never overthrew their monarchy and if anything, monarchy suggests is aristocracy Writ large as we will see later. The point being that other countries adopting the American system may be also trying to protect property rights under color of democracy and judicial review. It could simply be a trick of labels by hiding property rights under human rights. So, it becomes imperative that any undertaking of analysis or comparative that the underbrush is cleared out or else the analysis or comparative will fall stillborn.[69]

Why should we suspect or question the motives of the European countries, adopting the practice of judicial review? One good reason might be that the Europeans always lived through hierarchical systems of government. The second

---

[67] Post World War II, the Germans have adopted judicial review and a strong one. According to German Basic Law, German courts are empowered with judicial review power. However, only the Federal Constitutional Court is empowered to overturn legislation.

[68] Van der Schyff (2010).

[69] Brewer-Carias (1989) comparative study of judicial review systems.

good reason might be they destroyed themselves with two World Wars and are the primary drivers of their populations and their colonies driving them to the major killing fields that was World War I and World War II, just to mention the twentieth century. Should we look into previous generations, the Europeans have consistently attacked one another over land, religion, ethnicity, and many other factors. Given the topology and geography of the European landscape, conflict was unavoidable. Even the British with different geography and topology were not immune from the constant struggle for land and territory either on their own island or the continent. So, given the above history of the Europeans, we can only hope by their formation of a European Union that this might decrease their fights with one another and on the global scene. But, we should be very careful and always with a watchful eye toward them, despite their European Union formation and the dressing of their constitutions with nice Bills of Rights.[70] And, as indicated earlier, as to the deadly nature of the human animal, the Europeans proved to be a deadly people, but should other peoples of the world gain a similar status of money, weaponry, and technology, that they would be the exception to the rule. The non-Europeans would be just as deadly as the Europeans.

The *principle* may be stated this way:

> The combination of technical power in the hands of the human animal is an extremely dangerous thing, regardless of being European or non-European. Such a combination of a layered brain (amphibian, reptilian, and mammalian) can only lead to the species destruction.

References

Adams W, Brock JB (1986) The bigness complex: industry, labor, and government in the American economy. Pantheon Books, New York

Baran PA, Sweezy PM (1968) Monopoly Capital: An Essay on the American Social Order Modern Reader Paperbacks, New York, NY

Barnett RE (2003) Constitutional legitimacy. Columbia Law Rev 103:111

Bates JL (1976) The United States 1898-1928: progressivism and a society in transition. McGraw-Hill Books, New York

Beatty J (2008) The triumph of money in America 1865-1900. Vintage, New York

Berger R (1989) The fourteenth amendment and the bill of rights. University of Oklahoma, Norman

Berger R (1997) Government by judiciary: the transformation of the fourteenth amendment, 2nd edn. Liberty Fund, Carmel

Beth LP (1971) The development of the American constitution 1877-1917. Harper Torchbooks, New York

Brewer-Carias AR (1989) Judicial review in comparative law. Cambridge University, Cambridge

Chemerinsky E (2018) A progressive reading of the constitution for the twenty-first century. Picador, New York

Cochran TC, Miller W (1961) The age of enterprise: a social history of industrial America. The Macmillan Publishing, New York

Cooley TM (1998) Treatise on the constitutional limitations which rest upon the legislative power of the states. Law Exchange, Clark

[70]Dorsen et al. (2003) comparative constitutionalism studies.

Corwin ES (1964) In: Mason AT, Garvey G (eds) American constitutional history. Harper Torchbooks, New York
Corwin ES (1978) The constitution and what it means today, 14th edn. Princeton University, Princeton
Curtis MK (1990) No state shall abridge: the fourteenth amendment and the bill of rights, 2nd edn. Duke University, Durham
De Santis VP (2000) The shaping of modern America 1877-1920, 3rd edn. Harlan Davidson Inc., Wheeling
Dorsen N, Rosenfeld M et al (2003) Comparative constitutionalism. Thomson-West, Rochester
Ely JW (1995) The chief justiceship of Melville W. Fuller 1888-1910. University of South Carolina, Columbia
Ely JW Jr (1991) Economic due process revisited. Vanderbilt 44:213
Ely JW Jr (1992) The guardian of every other right: a constitutional history of property rights, 3rd edn. Oxford University, Oxford
Ely JW Jr (2005) Property rights and democracy in American constitutional order. In: Hall KL, McGuire KT (eds) The judicial branch. Oxford University, Oxford
Ely JW (2007) The Guardian of Every Other Right: A Constitutional History of Property Rights, 3rd edn. Oxford University Oxford UK
Epstein RA (1985) Takings: private property and the law of eminent domain. Harvard University, Cambridge
Epstein RA (1995) Bargaining with the state. Princeton University, Princeton
Fine S (1964) Laissez-Faire and the General Welfare: A Study of Conflict in American Thought, 1865-1901. The University of Michigan, Press Ann Arbor, MI
Foner E (1988) Reconstruction: America's unfinished revolution 1863-1877. Harper and Row, New York
Furer H (1986) The Fuller court 1888-1910. Associated Faculty Press
Gillman H (1993) The constitution besieged: the rise and demise of Lochner era police powers jurisprudence. Duke University Press, Durham
Halper LA (1990) "Christopher G. Tiedman, 'Laissez-Faire Constitutionalism' and the Demise of Small-Scale Property in the Gilded Age," 51 Ohio State Law Journal 1249.
Hays SP (1957) The response to industrialism 1885-1914, 2nd edn. University of Chicago, Chicago
Hendel S (1951) Charles Evans Hughes and the supreme court. King's Crown Press, Columbia University, New York
Holbrook SH (1954) The Age of the Moguls Doubleday and Comp, New York, NY
Horwitz MJ (1977) The transformation of American law 1780-1860. Harvard University, Cambridge
Jones A (1966) Thomas M. Cooley and the interstate commerce commission: continuity and change in the doctrine of equal rights. Polit Sci Q 8:602
Jones A (1967) 'Laissez-Faire constitutionalism': a reconsideration. J Am Hist 752
Kammen M (1987) A machine that would go of itself: the constitution in American culture. Vintage, New York
Kens P (1997) Justice Stephen Field: shaping American liberty from the gold rush to the gilded age. University of Kansas, Lawrence
Kolko G (1984) Main Currents in American History Pantheon Books, New York, NY
Lears J (2010) Rebirth of Modern America, 1877-1920 Harper Perennial, New York, NY
Levinson S (2006) Our Undemocratic Constitution: Where the Constitution Goes Wrong (And How We Can Fix It) Oxford University 2006. Oxford UK
McCloskey RG (1994) In: Levinson S (ed) The American supreme court, 4th edn. University of Chicago, Chicago
McCormick RL (1997) Public life in industrial America 1877-1917. In: Foner E (ed) The new American history. Temple University, Philadelphia
McCurdy CW (1975) Justice Field and the jurisprudence of government-business relations: some parameters of laissez-faire constitutionalism 1863-1897. J Am Hist 61:970

McCurdy CW (1978) American law and the marketing structure of the large corporation 1875-1890. J Econ Hist 38:631
McDonald F (1958) We the people: the economic origins of the constitution. University of Chicago, Chicago
Mitz M, Cohen JS (1971) America, Inc.: Who Owns and Operates the United States Dell Books, New York, NY
Murphy P (1963) Time to reclaim: the current challenge of American constitutional history. Am Hist Rev 69:64
Nelson WE (1988) The fourteenth amendment: from political principle to judicial doctrine. Harvard University, Cambridge
Nichols RF (1963) The American leviathan. Harper Torchbooks, New York
Nozick R (2013) Anarchy, state and utopia. Basic Books, New York
Pole JR (1979) Paths to the American past. Oxford University, Oxford
Purcell EA Jr (1973) The crisis of democratic theory: scientific naturalism & the problem of value. University of Kentucky, Lexington
Riis J (1997) How the other half lives: studies among the tenements of New York. Penguin Classics, New York
Sanders E (1986) Industrial concentration, sectional competition, and antitrust politics in America 1880-1980. In: Studies in American political development, vol 1, pp 157–158
Shapiro M (1986) The supreme court's "return" to economic regulation. In: Studies in American political development, vol 1. Yale University, New Haven
Siegan BH (2001) Property Rights: From the Magna Carta to the Fourteenth Amendment Transaction Books. Piscataway, NJ
Sinclair U (1985) The jungle. Penguin Classics, London
Skouras G (2011) On the formation of the American corporate state: the Fuller supreme court 1888-1910. J Jurisprud 9:37
Steffens L (1957) The shame of the cities. Hill and Wang, New York
Swisher CB (1930) Stephen J. Field: craftsman of the law. University of Chicago, Chicago
Tiedeman CG (2001) A treatise on the limitations of police power in the United States considered from both a civil and criminal standpoint. Law Exchange, Clark
Urofsky MI (2009) Louis D. Brandeis: a life. Pantheon, New York
Van der Schyff G (2010) Judicial review of legislation: a comparative study of the United Kingdom, the Netherlands and South Africa. Springer, New York
White GE (1976) American Judicial Tradition: Profiles of Leading. American Judges Oxford University Press. Oxford UK
Wiecek M (1988) Liberty under law: the supreme court in American life. Johns Hopkins University, Baltimore
Williams WA (1988) The contours of American history. W.W. Norton & Comp., New York
Wolfe C (1986) The rise of modern judicial review: from constitutional interpretation to judge-made law. Basic Books, New York

Chapter 5
The Idea of Democracy and Congressional Government: The Reality and the Fiction

5.1 Tocqueville, *Democracy in America*

How are we to understand the idea of democracy? Is this old Greek idea of a community (polis) of members coming together to vote on governing themselves sustainable beyond the small village or town level?[1] Maybe a small village or town can apply this idea in the real world or make this utopian idea a practical one. Could a Jeffersonian style democracy be possible in America? Morone summarizes Jefferson position nicely, on modeling the United States, on the New England town model.[2] Assuming for a second, that democracy is possible on a small scale, can it also be achieved at the State level? That is, how are larger entities like Cities or States to apply the same principles for themselves? Let us look at the ground rules or foundations of democracy. Why is it important that every member of a community be given a right to vote? Who determines which issues need to be voted on and which do not? Is there a goal to this voting enterprise? If so, what is it? If we say the goal is 'justice' or 'equality,' what does that mean? If the idea of 'justice' or 'equality' is just as much an ideal concept as the idea of 'democracy,' then what? From the pragmatics of voting to the need for justice, are we not moving from the practical to the metaphysical?[3]

> All the English colonies, therefore, at the time of their inception, shared a great kindred spirit. From the start, they all seemed destined to promote the development of liberty, not the

[1] Fishkin (1991), p. 1.

[2] Morone (1990), pp. 5–6 "Americans would return to citizen participation in a wide variety of ways. The Left pursues it in, perhaps, its purest form, through neighborhood democracy, worker participation, and community organizing."

[3] The idea of democracy and the idea of justice—practical or metaphysical?

G. Skouras, *Constitutionalism and Democracy*,
https://doi.org/10.1007/978-3-031-66906-4_5

> aristocratic liberty of their mother country, but *middle class*, democratic liberty, a complete example of which had still not been encountered in the history of the world.[4]

Aristocratic liberty versus middle-class/democratic liberty?[5] What does it mean? And is Tocqueville suggesting that the American New England model[6] is like the

---

[4]Tocqueville (2003), p. 40. It should be noted here that Tocqueville is espousing a liberal nineteenth century view of the class system in America rather than a communitarian understanding of class. The American class system as understood by the Aristocratic people like Tocqueville versus the actual class system of the commoners are not in sync. Appleby (1984), pp. 8–9. Joyce Appleby points our attention to the contested notion that American intellectual history was either shaped by "Lockean liberals" or "Enlightenment" men. She says: "Instead we have been taught through the work of Bernard Bailyn and Gordon Wood that the ideas that animated colonial leaders were ancient ones, going back to classical texts of politics. [C]lassical theory emphasized that civil society was fragile, that men lusted after power, that stability required a carefully constructed constitution. It also taught that there were two orders of men—the talented few and the ordinary many—and because there were inevitable social divisions, a properly balanced constitution would balance the powers of these two groups. But constitutional stability rested ultimately in this classical paradigm upon the exercise of civic virtue—upon the capacity of some men to rise above private interests and devote themselves to the public good." Morone (1990), p. 17 reminds us that: the original historical school understood the Constitution and the men that drafted it to be classical eighteenth century liberals, with a philosophy of the pursuit of liberty means the pursuit of property and incorporated such a classical liberal philosophy into the Constitution. At some point later in time, mostly in the twentieth century, another historical school, called communitarianism, challenged the monopoly of the liberal philosophy being so embedded in the Constitution. This communitarian school emphasized the "shared" values of the Founders not just as being property acquisition exponents but also valued "community" and other non-property related values as well. Morone says: "This world view, argued Bernard Bailyn, informed the colonists as the English began to meddle in New World politics; the imperial menace to republican ideals helps explain why the settlers moved so swiftly to revolution. The next step was Gordon Wood's powerful exposition of how classical images of communal republic shaped the first American decade until they were swamped by factional conflicts and displaced by the Constitution. [I]n its most sweeping form, articulated by J.G.A. Pocock, the republican view would displace the liberal interpretation of America. For Pocock and the scholars who follow him, the republican paradigm is an analytic key to American history and culture. From the other side, social scientists who see a liberal nation have been long and loud in their critique."

[5]Wilentz (2005), p. xvii. Wilentz says: "Important elements of democracy existed in the infant American republic of the 1780s, but the republic was not democratic. Nor, in the minds of those who governed it, was it supposed to be. A republic—*res publica*, or a "public thing"—was meant to secure the common good through the ministrations of the most worthy, enlightened men. A democracy—derived from *demos krateo*, "rule of the people"—dangerously handed power to the impassioned, unenlightened masses. Democracy, the eminent Federalist political leader George Cabot wrote as late as 1804, was "the government of the worst." Yet by the 1830s, as Alexis de Tocqueville learned, most Americans proclaimed that their country was a democracy as well as a republic."

[6]Baker (1991), pp. 21–27. Baker gives us a general view of the status of Bostonians and a general sense of overall class in America. That is, it was assumed that the American aristocracy or a subset of the Bostonian and New England patricians were the perfect model to rule America, sturdy Puritans and tracing their origins to the original settlers—forming the American aristocracy. So, if an aristocracy existed in America, it was an Aristocracy of merit by way of the Bostonian Brahmin in the North, and in the South the slaveholding planter class—large slaveholding plantation Aristocrats—that could provide the leisure time for culture, education, and learning. These were the types of Americans the Founding Fathers imagined or hoped would rule America as a matter of

medieval town? If all the townships are independent entities, how can they all come together to form a whole society or nation? Or is town structure the be all and end all or is the *sine qua non* of democracy fully embodied? Tocqueville suggests that all this is based on the types of constitutions. He notes that France's constitution is unalterable. The British constitution is changeable by Parliament at will, as ordinary law. But in America the constitution is neither unalterable nor can Congress simply pass a law to alter it. The fact that America has a written constitution has given way to speculation as to why Americans have allowed judges the power of judicial review.[7]

Tocqueville says:

> I realize that this refusal to allow judges the right to declare laws unconstitutional gives indirect power to the legislature to alter the constitution, since it no longer encounters any legal obstacle in its way. Yet, it is still better to grant the power to alter the constitution of the nation to men who, however imperfectly, represent the will of the people than to others who represent only themselves.
>
> It would be even more unreasonable to grant English judges the right to resist the will of the legislature since Parliament, which makes the laws, also shapes the constitution and consequently cannot, under any circumstance, call a law unconstitutional when it stems from the three authorities: King, Lords, and Commons.[8]

Tocqueville goes on to suggest that neither the French model of constitutional interpretation nor the British model applies to the United States.

> In the United States, the constitution rules both legislators and ordinary citizens. It is, therefore, the primary law and cannot be modified by a law. Hence, it is right that the courts obey the constitution rather than all the laws. This touches the very essence of judicial authority; it is, in a way, the natural duty of any judge to choose from legal provisions those which bind him most strictly.
>
> In France, equally, the constitution is primary among the laws and judges have an equal duty to take it as a basis for their decisions. But, by exercising this duty, they could not fail to

---

course—those that possessed the necessary breeding, culture, education, history, and talent needed for rulership. Baker (1991), p. 23. According to Baker: "[B]rahmins, like the English from whom they were descended, respected the authority of the past and shared the conviction that white, Protestant, conservative Boston, its eighteenth-century heart still beating steadily, represented social and political perfection. They sincerely believed Jacksonian democracy contemplated the ruin of New England, and they agreed in principle with the social critic and Harvard professor Charles Eliot Norton that meaningful political reform would be accomplished not by extending more power to "the people," but through strong leadership by the "intelligent and prosperous classes"—democracy by the noblesse oblige." (p. 23) In other words, We the People or the "unwashed" masses had no business with political rulership.

[7]It is of interest to note that the British and French do not allow for judicial review, but the British Commonwealth countries allow for judicial review. It also the case that the German and Japanese governments have judicial review which were based to some degree on the American Constitution after their defeat in the Second World War. Also, after the Indian colonial break from the British, they have adopted the power of judicial review. However, it should be noted when doing comparisons of their constitutions, that the culture, history and deep disposition of each country must be examined in depth before one can see how their legal systems function in practice.

[8]Tocqueville (2003), p. 119.

> trample on a duty more sacred than their own: namely that of society in whose name they are acting. In this case, ordinary reason has to yield to reasons of state.[9]

To sum up, according to Tocqueville, the British, French, and United States have three different constitutional models. Each of these models requires a different interpretative strategy. The American model grants the most powers to the judiciary.[10] Tocqueville confessed his fears about the American model this way: "I have looked at the legislative and executive power of the Union. It remains to consider the power of the judiciary. Here I must be frank to the readers about my fears. Judicial institutions exercise a great influence upon the destiny of the Anglo-Americans and hold a very important place in the political institutions properly so called."[11]

The role of the Supreme Court,[12] with the power of judicial review, is not simply a judicial body but also a political body. It assumes that other political bodies will counter-balance it. However, under democratic conditions, with the spread of the vote along large distances and many voters, the Court has an advantage in its concentration of power in the hands of relatively few Justices, five justices are sufficient to carry the day versus the millions of voters dispersed to the winds. Hence, *We the People* could never compete with the Supreme Court, in giving it direction or guidance, given the fragmentation and dispersal of voters over large territories. This implies that Americans consent to be governed by a majority of five justices out of nine on the Court. Does the true meaning of democracy in America mean government by five Supreme Court justices?

It might be best to say that democracy is a murky concept once we step outside the institutional structure that government by the majority can be clear cut. That is, outside of metaphysics, democracy via majority rule is the only pragmatic concept—but only if the foundations or groundwork are established as to who qualifies as a voter and who determines these rules as to the accounting and systemic process for a "fair" vote and a "fair" process that will represent generally the "will" or the "preference" of the general public.[13] Once we step outside this procedural domain, and entertain the substantive concept of democracy, we are lost souls in search of a

---

[9] Tocqueville (2003), pp. 119–120.

[10] Tocqueville (2003), p. 175.

[11] Tocqueville (2003), p. 162.

[12] Tocqueville (2003), pp. 175–176 "To this reason of primary importance we must add a still greater. Among the European nations, courts see before them only private individuals; but one might say that the Supreme Court of the United States summons sovereign powers to its bar. When the court usher, at the head of the steps of the court, pronounces these few words: "The state of New York versus the state of Ohio," one does not feel part of an ordinary court of justice."

[13] History has taught us that who counts as a voter and the rules for setting up the machinery of voting is vital to setting up a workable and practical democracy. Any failure with this process renders democracy as a metaphysical project. So, any attempt to bring these ground conditions or ground rules to life are critical for fair elections. History, also, warns us that this process will be contested and fought over every inch of the way. If a society cannot overcome these battles and difficulties, it will never be able to set up a practical or workable democracy and must content itself to some sort of authoritarian regime.

body.[14] Therefore, a "thin" democracy—of giving voters a choice—is the basic procedural way of taking the broad public into account.

A majority of the public—regardless of their educational status or capability of understanding the issues or have any interest of the issues of the day—regardless of their race, ethnicity, religion, etc.—are given a voice as to what happens to them. That is, as citizens living under a body of law, they have a voice and a vote on all public matters. Whether they are manipulated by advertisers or propaganda is a risk that must be taken if any form of democracy is to be established. It has always been assumed that the educated voter is less at risk of manipulation by special interests. Whether this proposition is true or not we leave for another day or others to investigate. A major criticism of democracy, modern or previous generations, is that the commoners or We the People are not in a position to decide on major issues of the day, without a persuasive orator, demagogue, or populist twisting this mass mind of the public and taking advantage of this vulnerable population to serve his or her interests. Very true, indeed. But it can also serve as a discipling process. If the public makes a poor choice, then it ought to be prepared to pay the consequence no matter how harsh the outcome is. As long as we are prepared to allow the general public to vote, we cannot protect them from their vices, selections, or dreams. Should they make a poor selection, with the candidate of their choice, they must be prepared to pay the consequences and amend their choice in the next electoral cycle. Now, that is procedural democracy. Now, you want to ask about the substance of democracy?—go ask a metaphysician. It is hard enough to figure out the accoutrements needed for a fair vote as is and you also want to talk substance? Our civilization places certain limits and constraints as to what is doable in our civilizational time and given the current disposition of our species.

That is, "majority" rule is the only route to practical democracy. This of course begs the question, what happens to the "losers" of an election? Does democracy need at least two political parties to give the voters the option to vote for an alternative party? What happens if there is a plurality of parties, and no single party can reach majority rule? All these questions are a part of setting up the political system. The ground rules will determine the disposition of the losers and by what rules a failure or a system failure in the selection of a viable alternative, in a competitive race, needs to systemically be re-evaluated, and systemic failure on the procedural front, is democratic failure and would require new thought as to the workability of procedural democracy. It may look easy to count the votes, but the internal plumbing to set up the system is serious work.

In our stage of civilizational development, we should avoid questions like what "is" democracy and focus on working the ground rules for fair elections. Otherwise, we will be stuck in the muck of metaphysics. Pragmatic questions are these: who sets the ground rules for majority-based democracy to work? We the People? We the

[14] At our current civilizational development, our best hope is to establish a workable democracy. If we attempt to link democratic processes with substantive issues of "equality," "justice," "fairness," and the like, we are lost souls.

Aristocratic People? We the Workers? We the teachers? Etc. What if democracy is not defined by individual voters but by classes? Which class sets the ground rules? The upper class? The middle class? The poor? A "thin" democracy of picking candidates for office cannot perform miracles.

What does democracy have to do with class rule?[15] In a democracy, is it the majority of people that matter or do all the people matter? If there is such a thing as a numerical majority, there must also be a numerical minority. What happens to those that are excluded from the majority or form minorities in a democracy? If the aim of society is to create a middle class that rules in a democracy, then what happens to the lower class or upper class in that democracy? Does Tocqueville have something to say to us about that? If so, what? Clearly if minorities are not to pose continuous problems for the majority[16] in a democracy, they must somehow be dealt with. How are they to be dealt with?

The American system has attempted to divide and conquer by dispersing citizens along state lines, natural geographic line drawing, and testing, among other efforts, to jump over in order to minimize the damage of the "wrong" voters being allowed to cast a ballot. The losers in a democracy, the minority party, could at least be assured of their dignity and freedom, as long as there exists a *Bill of Rights*, which could shield individuals from dangerous majorities regardless of who wins a particular election. Of course, the idea of a *Bill of Rights* is an anti-majoritarian tool to protect people from the ill effects of democratic rule. It is a poison pill to ensure that a majority of the commoners do not do evil things to the losers of the election. The writers of the American Constitution were able to justify such a poison pill, as the *Bill of Rights*, by appealing to a higher authority, either to Locke or God. That is, they are God-given "rights" and cannot be stripped away with every new election and vote. They cannot be taken away by way of the democratic vote or majoritarian rule—forming the counter-majoritarian problem. According to the Framers, these

---

[15] According to Plato, democracy is mob rule. Wilentz goes on to say: "Since Plato, doctrines of hierarchical authority had dominated political thought, whether classical (favoring the rule of the wise), Christian (favoring the rule of the holy), or some mixture of the two. According to these doctrines, most humanity was unsuited for public duties more elevated than the drudgery of farm animals. History seemed to support hierarchical theory. The fate of popular government in the ancient Greek city-state and the Roman republic had been tragic. Periodic peasant uprisings and urban disorders, from the late fourteenth century on, persuaded the articulate classes of Britain and Europe that the "people" were dangerously unstable and incapable of rational thought. "The beast," "the rabble," "th' idiot multitude" reappeared with contemptuous regularity in the learned treatises, poems, and plays of the early modern West." Wilentz (2005), p. 5. It also appears that the only "equality" Tocqueville was able to find in America was in the prison system that he was studying. Damrosch says: "A leading theme of *Democracy in America* would be that despotic regimes can give people equality but deny them freedom, and Sing Sing was a perfect illustration. In their report Tocqueville and Beaumont wrote trenchantly, "All the inmates are treated alike; there is much more equality in prison than in society. [E]ven while society in the United States gives the example of the most extensive liberty, the prisons of that country present a spectacle of the most complete despotism."" Damrosch (2010), p. 39.

[16] *Federalist # 10*, Madison's solution that the majorities can pose the "tyranny of the majority" while minority rule can pose the counter-majoritarian problem.

natural rights were based on British common right of reason—the natural reason that all human beings are endowed with and the ability of the human to tap into "reason" to ascertain god's will and purpose in this world.[17]

So, if we have a bifurcation between democracy and natural rights, which is superior and which is inferior? If there is a dispute between democracy (majoritarian rule) and natural rights which side must yield? Well, is it not obvious? In a society grounded on religious belief, God must be the superior ruler to man-made rule and law. That is, natural law must be superior and determinative over democratic rule. Obviously, the society that the people of the Eighteenth century lived in—and especially the Framers of the American Constitution—were imbued with the presence of God in everyday affairs. Of course, the Eighteenth-century Englishman and American lived in a pre-Darwinian society where people were human "beings" and very distinct and superior to the other "animals" in god's kingdom. But what happens to this schema, that the Framers brought to bear in their Constitution-making and civilization, in a post-Darwinian world—where human beings are animals just like all the other animals around us?

5.2 Wilson, *Congressional Government* (1885)

Woodrow Wilson, in *Congressional Government*, found that the Constitution that the Founders stitched together needed re-stitching.

> Wilson's thesis was a striking one: the Constitution is inadequate as a basis for modern government. It established a government in which the legislative and executive powers were separate and thus gave the nation a government unable to meet the needs of our day. "The government of a country so vast as the U.S. must be strong, prompt, wieldy, and efficient," he wrote, but the division of function and authority in the Constitution (especially separation of powers) frustrated this necessary goal, and also obscured responsibility.[18]

Wilson believed that the Federal-State duality form of government needed mending, and that a centralized government was needed to manage a continent. That is, the old form of "checks and balances" was unable to respond to an expanding nation in late Nineteenth century America. According to Wolfe, Wilson pulled back from some of the ideas in *Congressional Government* with the publication of his book early in the Twentieth century, *Constitutional Government in the United States*.[19] Although

[17] *U.S. Bill of Rights*, the philosophy of rights largely deriving from the *Magna Carta*, British Constitutional history, and John Locke's political philosophy.

[18] Wolfe (1986), p. 206. *See*, Wilson (2002a, b).

[19] Woodrow Wilson, *Constitutional Government in the United States*. The origin of this book is a series of lectures Wilson delivered at Columbia University in 1907. Wilson may have suffered from a grand or optimistic perspective of how We the People could achieve a more efficient government, especially as a youth or an armchair political scientist. But in later years, with becoming a politician, he may have gone from an "optimist" to a "realist" as the hard politics of his day smacked him in the face. For a reporter's perspective of how politicians can be ground down. For a down to earth view,

Wilson still believed in the rigidities in the American system of government, according to Wolfe, he found that the art of "interpretation" left room for reading the Constitution more broadly and having sufficient flexibility to meet the changing times.[20] "The Constitution, according to Wilson, was "constructed upon the Whig theory of political dynamics, which was a sort of unconscious copy of the Newtonian Theory of the universe." Whig government, like the Newtonian Universe, was composed of bodies governed by the "nice poise and balance of forces which give the whole system [i]ts symmetry and perfect adjustments.""[21]

Wilson rejected a Newtonian theory of government for a Darwinian theory of government. Wilson, concluded, perhaps under the influence of the Darwinian natural philosophy of his times, a much more flexible reading of the Constitution was needed, as a "living" document rather than as a "frozen and dead" document as the Originalists would later claim in the twentieth century.[22] Wolfe believes that Wilson's interpretation of the Constitution is not very consistent.[23] It appears that

---

see Greider (1993), p. 17. Greider gives a ground floor look of reality on the basement floor: "Politicians, rather like priests or police officers, are regularly exposed to the least attractive qualities of human nature—gaudy dimensions of greed and confusion and mindless fear. It requires strong character for a politician to resist cynicism and retain an idealistic sense of the democratic possibilities. The speeches invoking "the people" as the sacred source of political power have taken on a mocking ring for many."

[20] Wolfe (1986), p. 208. Wolfe says: "The reason was Wilson's new understanding of constitutional interpretation. "Fortunately, the definitions and prescriptions of our constitutional law, though conceived in the Newtonian spirit and upon the Newtonian principle, are sufficiently broad and elastic to allow for the play of life and circumstance. Though they were Whig theorists, the men who framed the federal Constitution were also practical statesmen with an experienced eye for affairs and a quick practical sagacity in respect of the actual structure of government, and they have given us a thoroughly workable model.""

[21] Wolfe (1986), p. 208.

[22] For example, Justice Antonin Scalia called the text of the Constitution as "dead, dead, dead" and so fixed for all times as the Framers left it; *see further*, other variations or play on the originalism of such doctrines that fix once and for all the "meaning" of the document at its last draft or official approval by the powers that be. Of course, they take aim at Justices or scholars that believe that the Constitution is a "living" document and are willing to be more flexible as to its alteration or meaning over the course of historical time as the conditions on the ground change and a certain amount of linguistic drift alters or shades the meaning of words in the course of historical time. And the further the time and space from the original document, the greater the likelihood for constitutional upgrade, modification, and pragmatics of understanding it and where the original understanding in the course of time has become amorphous and fuzzy. So rather than laying down ironclad laws of interpretation and faithfulness to the original document, a certain leeway of breathing space becomes necessary to breathe new life into an old document that was created in a different space-time and for a different culture and society. Of course, pragmatics done in a willy-nilly way can be just as incurable as fixing a document as dead, as fossilized, there for all to see for all of time. Language and communication are not fixed systems that operate in some metaphysical universe but must yield to the exegesis of the times with pragmatic understanding. *See further*, Habermas (1981a, b, 1992, 1998).

[23] Wolfe (1986), p. 205 "What was Wilson's new view of the Constitution? A favorite phrase, repeated in several places, was that the Constitution is a "vehicle of life," and not a "mere lawyer's document." For instance, "no lawyer can read into a document anything subsequent to its execution,

Wilson gave up on his plan to replace the federalist structure with a more parliamentary type of structure—Congressional Government—given the difficulties that would entail and by re-interpreting the Constitution in a more open way, he could get what he wanted as President. "[W]ilson prepared the reader to accord less importance to original intent. He went on ultimately to relegate the intention of the framers to a secondary role. The Constitution contains no theories, he said; it is a practical document."[24] Wolfe says that Wilson found Jefferson's views more compatible to his than the views of Hamilton and Marshall. That is, that the text of the Constitution was open to creative interpretation rather than a solid "meaning." Wolfe goes on to say: "The case for the latter view presupposes, to a considerable extent, that there is no real "true meaning" of the Constitution (excepting only the most basic and obvious provisions), or that the "true meaning" was deficient for the needs of the nation. That is a view, however, that Hamilton and Marshall certainly did not share."[25]

The *principle* may be stated this way:

> Wilsonian doctrine of a flexible constitutional interpretation is one of pragmatism. Darwinian organicism, over Newtonian mechanics, is better at preparing the Nation to respond rapidly to emerging problems. Flexibility in constitutional interpretation allows it to bend with the wind. Opponents of such flexibility stress the fact that a constitution is no ordinary law and must withstand the storms of time or the passing troubles.

According to Wolfe, Wilson focused on the "technocratic" nature of government and a pragmatic way of reading the Constitution to solve the problems of early Twentieth century America. Wolfe goes on to contrast this technocratic sense of government with the "revisionist" historians' more radical view of American government and critical review of the Constitution, that also popped up in the early Twentieth century. "Woodrow Wilson's attack on the Constitution—directly in *Congressional Government*, more subtly in *Constitutional Government in the United States*—arose in what he called "the first reason for free, outspoken, unrestrained constitutional criticism." This initial criticism was based on what can almost be called a "technocratic" view of the American government. Wilson wanted government to be "strong, prompt, wieldy, and efficient," but he devoted little attention to what government was supposed to accomplish with these characteristics."[26]

The *principle* may be stated this way:

---

but we have read into the Constitution of the United States the whole expansion and transformation of our national life that has followed its adoption." Thus, the Supreme Court, Wilson wrote, had adapted the Constitution in ways that would have amazed its framers of the simple days of 1787," for "the powers drawn from it by implication have grown and multiplied beyond all expectations."

[24] Wolfe (1986), p. 210. "One problem is that Wilson's view of the original intention of the framers of the Constitution was not very accurate. His characterization of the original theory of the Constitution as "Whig theory" or "Newtonian theory," which prevailed over the very different theory of Hamilton," misrepresented the founding period." (pp. 209–210)

[25] Wolfe (1986), p. 210.

[26] Wolfe (1986), p. 216.

Revisionist historians and others noticed at the turn of the 20th century that the American Constitution was a class-based document and not meant to be favorable or inclusive of all classes, esp. the lower class.

By the time Wilson came to office most of his theoretical understanding of the Constitution was tempered by the practical realities on the ground. Wilson, the political scientist, became Wilson the politician. Besides the loss of the possibility of establishing Congressional government in the United States, just the opposite happened. He preferred the presidential prerogative to Congressional discussion and debate model. That is, as a political science professor, he saw the soundness of establishing Congressional government, but as President of the United States, he saw the wisdom of wielding raw power through the prerogative. Is it any wonder that King's in the past treasured most of all their prerogative powers?

However, unlike Theodore Roosevelt, he did not see pure raw power being wielded as a sledgehammer as the most pragmatic tool in his toolbox. Roosevelt would club someone over the head if he believed the other's policies were wrong for America. Wilson would do it too but with a Southern style gentility. His professorial background rendered Wilson as too theoretical-conceptual, armchair theoretician, in some ways, maybe a bit naive idealist, such as pursuing world peace through a system like a League of Nations that he proposed, which the more hardheaded rejected as a bridge too far. It is not the case that Wilson was weak, and Theodore Roosevelt strong, but the fact the Great World War derailed both his pragmatism and idealism. Having been drawn into the Great War, all bets were off—there is no need for Congressional Government or Constitutional Government during war times, what is needed is the Presidential Prerogative. The Kings loved it and so do modern Presidents. He ended up with his idealism dashed on the horrors of the Great War and broken in body and mind—died the death of countless leaders that start with high hopes but end up with dead dreams.

Further, on the domestic front, even under the tutelage of Louis Brandies, Wilson was not very effective in turning back the power of monopoly. Louis Brandeis, designated the 'People's lawyer',[27] with his experience and fights with large businesses and corporations, were insufficient to turn the tide of monopoly washing over the nascent American democracy. It might be argued that Roosevelt was more effective in fighting monopoly power than Wilson, if only to show the monopolists who is boss. Unlike Wilson, Theodore Roosevelt had fought the monopolists and was prepared to fight them again and again. However, Roosevelt was no man of the people or for the people. He was a Machiavellian power-interests man. He had no use for democracy. Democracy for Theodore Roosevelt was to formalize or legitimize his victories on the battlefield called elections. He wanted to show his strength, by tallying up victories, against the upsurge and power hungry and greed of the new monopolists. For Roosevelt, it was to show and prove raw power was necessary to

[27] Louis Brandies (1856–1941) took many high-profile cases in favor of the common people, We the People, in his legal career and fought corporate and monopoly interests. He was elevated to the Supreme Court by Woodrow Wilson in 1916.

get things done and the hell with Congress and its debating society of rulership. He was about Aristocracy and the privilege Aristocracy grooming the 'strong' for leadership and rulership. Here is how Matt Stoller gets to the gist of Roosevelt: that he was an elitest and power hungry—more inclined to aristocratic virtues than to mob rule. Stoller says: "He venerated war and violence; manhood meant proving oneself in combat. "A Quaker may be quite as undesirable a citizen as a duelist," he wrote. Roosevelt "loathed one of the founders of the country, Thomas Jefferson, because he saw in Jefferson's statement that his "passion for peace" were words of an effete weakling pacifist.""[28]

Remember that this man was President of the United States for most of the first decade of the Twentieth century. Roosevelt wanted to fight the monopolists to show who was stronger, the monopolists or the President of the United States. It was a combat to prove himself, with democracy and the People as simply a backdrop to the action. Wilson too thought about taking on the monopolists, but not as a match of raw power of the political and the commercial, but as having the monopolists play fair in the capitalist arena. However, Wilson along with many other academics, scholars, and political commentators, in the early Twentieth century, were prepared to take drastic action to revise and reform the American Constitution, as it had come to be interpreted in their day. Wilson was prepared to go so far and no further. But Wolfe tells us that other early Twentieth century revisionist historians and political scientists were even more radical than Wilson, regarding the form and substance of the American Constitution. That is, they viewed the Constitution not as a tool or a means to more efficient government but as a document supporting established interests. "Revisionist historians led the way by arguing that the Constitution was a deliberately undemocratic document, intended primarily to protect the class interests of the framers."[29]

According to Wolfe, these revisionist historians[30] were ready to pounce and eviscerate the American Constitution.

> The framers were intent on preserving from popular majorities, and *liberty*, "as the framers of the Constitution understood the term, had to do primarily with property and property rights." The framers fully realized that only by checking democracy could they retain their economic ascendancy, and they accomplished this especially through the dominance of the Supreme Court, which institutionalized the rule of the conservative legal profession. The result of this—especially since the development of industrialism—had been the oligarchic power of the capitalists over the people.[31]

[28] Stoller (2019), p. 2.

[29] Wolfe (1986), p. 216.

[30] Wolfe (1986), p. 216. "Foremost among these political scientists and historians were J. Allen Smith, Charles Beard, and Vernon Parrington. Smith's, *The Spirit of American Government*, published in 1907, was a no-holds-barred attack on the Constitution that argued that the latter was a reactionary document intended to prevent popular control of government and giving only as much power to the people as was necessary in order to have it ratified successfully."

[31] Wolfe (1986), p. 216.

Historians and political scientists, early in the Twentieth century, found serious problems with the American Constitution. Beard, Parrington, and Smith suspected that the Constitution was an undemocratic document in the business of protecting class interests.[32] "Beard particularly developed the economic side of this argument in his very influential *An Economic Interpretation of the Constitution of the United States*. According to Beard, the economic class interests of the founders were the foundation of the Constitution."[33]

The Constitution was basically viewed as a reactionary document by Beard, Parrington, and Smith. Wolfe says that the Constitution represents "great property interests". He puts it this way: "They settled on republicanism as a compromise between monarchy and democracy and, "influenced by practical considerations of economic determinism more than by the theories of Montesquieu," elaborated a system of checks and balances to protect property."[34] True enough, but in fairness to the Founders, they could not have seen the role of political parties will play to make their system work. It was assumed that great statesmen will ascend to the top offices in the land rather the self-seeking and aggrandizing politicians looking to score points in a debate. Also, true enough, property ownership is the *sine qua non* of the American qualification and participation in the American dream. Lack of property is a sure sign mark for disqualification for higher office. Eventually, the emergence of the political party system turned the Founders dreams upside down. But even so in a capitalist America, money talks.

Holmes was an early adopter of a Darwinian view. Nevertheless, even though he preferred an "organic" rather than a "mechanical" philosophy of jurisprudence, he was not of the Social Darwinian camp. He also was not a part of the "laissez-faire" school of thought and often found himself as a dissenter from the majority of the other Justices on the bench.[35] What appears to be happening here is that a "living" constitution is susceptible to a certain amount of change without killing the patient. That is, if changes need to be made to a given constitution under an organic theory, then why have a constitution at all because as the changes mount up, and eventually, you end up with a different constitution—another more practical way of seeing the matter is of a boat that needs repairs at sea, and each piece of lumber is replaced to prevent it from sinking—so as each piece of lumber is replaced, does any part of the original boat still exist even though all the original planks were replaced when it returns to port?

[32] Beard (1986); Parrington (1927); Smith (1965); Hofstadter (1979).

[33] Wolfe (1986), p. 217.

[34] Wolfe (1986), p. 217.

[35] Wolfe (1986), p. 229. See further. Holmes along with Brandeis were opposed to the Supreme Court correcting for the deficiencies in legislative action, as long as the legislation was adopted under the aegis, We the People, once the People spoke, it was the end of the matter. The Court had no further business poking its nose or second guessing the will of the People. So, if the People or We the People wanted the legislation, then who was the Court to stand in our way.

Powers such as the presidential "prerogative"[36] that go beyond the law may make sense to use during an emergency, in dealing with a house on fire for example. But it should be understood that whether the house on fire is saved or burned to the ground, it no longer exists as before the operation. Presidents, like Jefferson, Lincoln, and Franklin Roosevelt, which have acted through presidential "prerogative" may have had some justification, by acting extra-constitutionally, during extremely difficult situations by taking out the firehose to stop the house from burning down. But at the same time utilizing unspecified, vague, and special powers from above, such as 'god given powers,' or 'extra-constitutional' powers may save the house from burning down but also pose a serious threat to *We the People*, once the emergency passes, and these special prerogative powers are not returned to the shelf or shelved. Therefore, it bears asking, before drafting a constitution, just how much change could it withstand before it too is burnt to the ground and no longer relevant? Is it better to save half a house by using extra-constitutional provisions or let the whole house burn to the ground and start all over again?[37]

So, in dealing with major institutions, in a democratic polity, there is always the danger that some passion will innervate those in power to grab ever more power for themselves than may be justified only under authoritarian institutions, and a polity and society slips slowly into authoritarianism, ever so slowly, until what might have been called or labeled democratic institutions, fade away ever so slowly. The power of judicial review, just like the power of presidential prerogatives, is the way of losing one's democracy—an ever so slowly motion and slight-of-hand, until over the historical span of the United States, it was not noticed that an unelected body (the Supreme Court) has a big role in ruling the country—power slipping ever so slowly from democratic processes—from election of congressional representatives—to appointed judges' ruling America, all under the idea that the judiciary is simply the "least dangerous" branch of government.

[36] Prerogative power derives from kingly power—that the king cannot do wrong and is free to take the initiative to protect his people or have his will obeyed by the people.

[37] Levinson (2006), pp. 102–112. Abraham Lincoln, (suspension of writ of habeas corpus), Jefferson, (Louisiana Purchase), Franklin Roosevelt (regulatory property restrictions and administrative state actions)—arguing for a leader's use of discretion in taking decisive action without authority, if need be, during times of emergency and danger through the use of prerogative—"prerogative" versus constitutional law.

5.3 Electoral College, Radical Historical Contingency, and the Illusion of Democracy

The Electoral College[38] is an affront to democracy.[39] This practice should have been abolished after the Civil War. It is a holdover practice from a slavocracy era. Yet, since it is embedded in the Constitution and the American political system, there is no "will" to eliminate the practice without massive change to society. Unless one believes in a "living" Constitution that adapts with the times, then one usually falls under the "originalist" camp of dealing with a "dead" Constitution that is unchangeable, unless one is prepared to undertake super-majoritarian efforts to amend it. Procedural democracy is drowned out under the protections of an "originalist" meaning or interpretation of the Constitution—that neglects the fact that a Civil War was fought to amend it through the Civil War Amendments—amounting to a Second Constitution, if not a Second Constitution, at the very least, a dramatically altered document sanctified by the blood of over 600,000 dead, in order to cross over from slavery to freedom via Civil War.

Chemerinsky believes that the Preamble to the Constitution serves as a beacon for democratic principles and as a way of progressively reading it.[40] He believes that the Preamble holds legal force. Most scholars view the Preamble as "aspirational" rather than a substantive part of the Constitution. Regardless of your position on this issue, the bottom line is that the Founders deeply embedded the Electoral College in the Constitution. As I see it, there is no need for Chemerinsky or others to use the Preamble to justify a "living" Constitution. In my opinion, the *Civil War Amendments* are sufficient to restructure the Constitution to increase the representative capacity of the system. The Civil War should be taken as a rupture in the fabric of the

---

[38] The Electoral College is a product of a different age—the Age of Slave owners, or slaveocracy—it was the norm or at least accepted as an essential institution in America for the people of the eighteenth century. Slavery, in general, has been a way of life since time immemorial. It cannot be the case, unless people still subscribe to the position that slavery is good, and owning slaves still receives civilizational approval—although 100% abolition has not been achieved today and even though some would take up the practice again around the world if allowed or given the opportunity—civilizational judgment has been reached that owning slaves is wrong—then the electoral college must fall and should have fallen with the Civil War and the freeing of the slaves. It was no longer necessary to classify slaves as 3/5th of a person. Why the electoral college still exists has to do with property, no longer owning other human beings, but property ownership that could be endangered if the electoral college fell and allowed for democratic rule—majoritarian democracy.

[39] Levinson (2006), pp. 81–97. (the problems of the Electoral College laid out) ("This means that "predictable states" are simply written off, so far as campaigning is concerned. And the battleground is shrinking. A *New York Times* editorial noted that, in 1960, "24 states, with 327 electoral votes, were battleground states." By 2004, "only 13 states, with 159 electoral votes, were."" (p. 88); *see further*, Dahl (2003), p. 30. "If the Framers had been aware of the central importance of political parties to the democratic republic, would they have designed their constitution differently? They might have. At the very least they would not have created the absurdity of an electoral college."

[40] Chemerinsky (2018), pp. 82–83.

United States—from its slavocracy days to a renewal or rebirth—with real resolve to increase the freedom and dignity of all Americans. Those that died on the fields of Gettysburg, Chickamauga, Spotsylvania Court House, and many other battlefields for something higher than State's rights. Unfortunately, American history has made the defense of State's rights the signature or *sine qua non* of Freedom in America. And the stain of cleaning up slavocracy almost becomes an after-thought. That is, the Constitution should be interpreted differently after the Civil War than it was before it. State rights are meaningless if *We the People* are not free and subjected to super-majoritarian criteria to get anything done.

Of course, it was a catastrophe and a tragedy that confronted those living or dying on the battle fields. There can be no winners in a civil war. If a civil war happens, it happens because two sides cannot compromise. If compromise is essential for humans living together, once the compromise component disappears—that is when the guns, swords, and canons make their appearance. History does not move by hindsight. History moves on the contingency of the moment, the urgency of the moment, by accident, and by unpredictable human agents in the flow of time. Those contingency moments, which unfold by unknowable elements or facts, like a subatomic particle might pop up under quantum conditions. The subatomic particle does not ask nor give any reason nor asks for causal mechanisms to determine its behavior. It simply is. Its facticity is the "nowness" or the "instantaneous" spark of its existence and then disappears into nothingness.[41] Nature is what it is and asks nothing of the human animal to confirm the agent's understanding as to why it is what it is. As to the causal explanations and as to why a subatomic particle pops up here rather than there, it might be the case that there is no there there. That is, what the human animal considers time and space might not be one and the same in all possible world conditions. It is "in" the nowness of space and time and again disappears into nothingness which is empty space or a vacuum. History too cannot predict the popping up of events, under the uncertainty or contingency conditions, by the introduction of human agency into the equation. The human animal is simply a contingency in space and time. Nothing more.

For the Founders believed the movement of history is by great "men" that were expected to rule America from up on high, with *We the People* giving them our validation. That is, someone like Oliver Wendell Holmes, Jr., would have been the type of person capable of taking leadership roles in America. Those men of substance that could take up the burden of leadership such as George Washington. Those that came from *We the People* class could only be thankful that such giants would step forward and lead us or rule us. Chemerinsky points to Alexander Hamilton's remarks in Federalist # 68 as to the need for a select group of people to pick the president rather than the commoners or We the People because the

[41] The idea of "nothingness" here is being used in a philosophic sense. Under modern scientific explanations there is no "nothingness." If one takes vacuum space and removes all known matter from it, it does not become empty space. With all known particles or entities removed, it might be assumed that there is nothing there. But in fact, there still exists something in a vacuum or the empty nothingness.

commoners lack the required knowledge to make such an important selection.[42] As I pointed out many times before, the Framers' distrusted democracy. What does this say? It says democracy is not the prime interest of the Framers' drafting of the Constitution. It says the prime interest is private property protection. And, so, they designed a constitution with those values in mind. Property protection first, everything else secondary or tertiary. Further, under an Electoral College the small states gain more power than under majority rule.[43]

The original design of the United States was flawed at the foundational level because it was based on the theory that democracy was not workable in a country with a collection of independent state systems with a disproportionate number of people—the North having larger populations than the South. So, it was necessary to include a three-fifths clause in the Constitution to bulk up the Southern States' population by the inclusion of slaves, but obviously the slaves could not vote. So, federalism[44] essentially means a non-democratic system at its core and the need for the establishment of the Electoral College to balance things out between the populous states and those sparsely populated states. And, so, grant them greater representational power than they would otherwise have.

The *principle* may be stated this way:

> If democracy is not a feasible or workable system for the Founders, what is to be done to unite the thirteen colonies? Make the unequal equal. Treat each colony on the principle of equality regardless of how unequal each is to the others. If independence is not to be compromised for the small states, all states must be treated alike. This will obviously destroy any pretense to democracy.

Somehow the Southern states were able to assert extensive power over the more populous Northern states in the drawing and composition of the Constitution. Consequently, what resulted was a lopsided entity tilted in the Southern direction with no regard for popular rule, democracy, or *We the People*. Afterall, Southerners had some of the most talented and aristocratic minds on their side, being a slave society gave them the leisure to study history closely. Jefferson and Madison could hold more than their own against any Northern intellect.

It appears that countless generations of intellectuals looking at judicial and legal matters made it clear that the American form of government is not democratic. This is true and accurate accounting based on the foundational document of the United States, the Constitution. However, over the course of many generations of scholars and intellectuals, looking over the matter, concluded that the United States is a republic, and that it is close enough to being a democracy. In other words, many scholars note that, based on the Constitution, America is not a democracy. Nevertheless, we can go on and treat it as if it were a democracy because it is neither a monarchy, nor an aristocracy, nor a dictatorship. So, by default a republican form of government gives it the closest approximation to democracy and makes it possible to

[42] Chemerinsky (2018), p. 84.

[43] Chemerinsky (2018), p. 84.

[44] Dicey (1982), pp. xci–cviii.

grow this republicanism, over time, into a democracy of sorts. This is false. The United States is no closer to being a democracy than any other system. However, the "appearance" is given that the republican form of government is closer to a democracy than a monarchy or aristocracy. It is not. The republican form of government is the "embodiment and entanglement" of monarchy and aristocracy. So, the theory that republicanism can be transformed into a democracy is no closer to the truth than that monarchy or aristocracy is capable of being transformed into a democracy.

The *principle* may be stated this way:

> Give the "appearance" of being a democracy without any such intention or will from the Founders. Be as inclusive as possible in letting citizens believe that they are fit for rulership without ever intending that such an absurdity would come to pass. The use of the word "Republic" fit the Founders perfectly. In other words, present the "form" as a democracy but hold the "substance" as an aristocracy.

What appears to be the case is the conflation of republicanism and democracy to protect property from the majority or majoritarian rule. Slavery was going to be a problem in writing a constitution for a people, since the slave lacked the full rights of a people. Basically, slaves were a form of property. How was the South going to protect its property from majoritarian or democratic rule? Conflate republicanism with democracy by layering in requirements to fend off the "mob", or "unwashed" masses, or *We the People* from interfering with other peoples' slaves/property.

Also, notice how the power of judicial review could be used to undermine public interests and protect private interests—property protections. The Supreme Court tasks itself the priority of the protection of property. Slaves counted as "people" but not "100% of a person," just three-fifths of a person—how else was a slaveholder to get equal representation with the free states if he did not have his slave property protected by way of equal protection in the Constitution. A formula made for disastrous consequences, not only for the hundreds of thousands that died on the battlefield, but forever more marking the United States as either a slaveocracy before the Civil War or a near slaveocracy after the Civil War.

It seems that the issue of 'equality,' whether it involve slaves and freemen, or equal voting power, or equal social standing—the concept of 'equality' and, as was with the concept of 'liberty,' were more "aspirational" references than reality in the Constitution.[45] That is, they sound good on paper or in theory, but must have very

[45] Wilentz (2005), pp. 27–28. "As of 1790, fewer than half of the original thirteen states provided an approximation to white manhood suffrage by replacing freehold qualifications with minimal taxpaying requirements. [T]o the extent they did shift, at least in theory, it was often toward sharpening the distinction between persons and property, linking the upper houses of the new legislatures to the representation of propertied interests—on the presupposition, stated most starkly in Massachusetts, that "men possessed of property are entitled to a greater share in political authority than those who are destitute of it." Revolutionary state-builders hedged in the democratic-element by establishing bicameral legislatures (except Pennsylvania and Georgia); by approving property requirements, sometimes quite severe, for officeholding; by retaining powerful appointive state and local offices not elected by the people; and by continuing malapportionment of the legislatures to favor the wealthier and more settled districts."

little potential of realization in fact under conditions of unlimited acquisitiveness by the human animal.

The Supreme Court has done its part in preserving the Constitution as best determined by its own interpretation—by the right to have the sole and final interpretive power over the document. That is, the Supreme Court serves as a compounding power in resisting changes to it that are not approved or sanctioned by the Justices. The Court believes that its reading and interpretation of the Constitution are the Court's domain and province. Outsiders may submit opinions, data, or any other kind of evidence to persuade the Court to change direction, but it must have the last word on any matter dealing with the Constitution. So, it must disabuse all entrants of any belief that any other interpretation is better or superior to their interpretation of the document. By precluding other co-equal branches of government such as the Legislature, the Executive or State and Local governments from providing an alternative reading of it.

Obviously, slogans such as "liberty" or "freedom" or "equality" could not have any import in America other than window dressing. The Supreme Court could also bring additional fire power to the scene as being the final arbiter of what the Constitution means and being able to utilize the *Bill of Rights* as a *poison pill* to cut up any incursion or attack on the backbone of American law—*Natural Law or God's Law*. The Court could simply roll out natural law defenses, as contained in the *Bill of Rights*, to kill off any rights or laws enacted by majority rule that threatened to carry off another person's slaves or property under the dressing of majoritarian rule. It was simply all window dressing because the Founders were not stupid people and well understood that an 'experimental' system called democracy could be bad for their property, businesses, lands, profits, or any other possession of value to them. As indicated earlier in this book, other nations of the world have seen the wisdom of the Founders of America in including a Bill of Rights in their constitutions. If they expect to remain a civilized nation, then a Bill of Rights as a poison pill to kill off any usurpers, radicals, or populists threating to do damage to property interests.

Therefore, the values that the Framers of the American Constitution held cannot be the same values that America continues to have after undergoing a Civil War, the transformation from the Agricultural Age to the Industrial Age, major global wars and economic depressions—surely there must be an upper limit of American constitutionalism of the newly freed Colonists, hugging the eastern coast of North America during the Eighteenth century, and the constitutionalism of an America of the Twenty-first century.

What does it mean to be a core value? Why is 'equality,' for example, important? Is the concept or idea of equality a legal matter? An economic matter? A philosophical matter? A social matter? A mathematical matter? An equation of sorts? What if the idea of equality is "vague," should it be contained and maintained in the Constitution? Is equality a matter of justice? If so, why? What does it mean to say two things (persons) (animals), etc., are equal? If "equality" is a metaphysical concept, then what? Should metaphysical concepts still be maintained in the Constitution as aspirational matters, as is the *Preamble to the Constitution*, or be able to do work within the document, carrying water for the *We the People*? Whether such "vagueness" is important, as to praying to unseen gods or the need of human animals for mythmaking, will be left for another day. But if the Constitution is a practical document, not a metaphysic, then any reading or close interpretation must be able to distinguish the aspirational phrases contained therein and those pragmatic phrases or portions of the document that will carry water for *We the People*. Just like the *Preamble* is recognized as sweet sounding but lacking thunder, so too those phrases or portions that are vague may sound good but have little power to affect change in society or protect society. Since there are no specifications or limits to vague language, it can only serve as mythmaking or as aspirational but delivers nothing of substance in the end.

The *principle* may be stated this way:

> A certain degree of vagueness, a certain degree of cloudiness, and a certain degree of indeterminacy is built into linguistic systems. The ideas contained in language are carried with raw words that point in directions not always hitting their targets exactly but approximately. Linguistic slippage is a condition of communication.

The Electoral College is clearly an anti-democratic institution. But it is there for a reason. It counterbalances 'majoritarian' rule with 'constitutional' rule. The mechanism that was put into the Constitution, on the account of slaves and small sized states, lasted longer than any other poison pills in the constitution in killing off democracy and continuing the practice of protecting property from the "common" people. Can a pillar or a core part, embedded in the Constitution be removed or discarded no matter how surgically, by the Amendment process? No, it cannot. Why not? Because the Constitution as a whole, is not a democratic document. One can comb through the document and remove many other things offensive to democratic principles, in which case the document will remain a potholed document. The Constitution was never designed to be a democratic document to begin with. So, even if the Electoral College is removed, what next? So, modifications eliminating core doctrines of the Constitution dissolves the Constitution. "The problem of the Electoral College is compounded by state laws that provide that electoral votes are awarded on a winner-take-all basis. In all states except Nebraska and Maine, the candidate who wins the popular vote in a state—even by the narrowest margin—gets all of the electoral votes from the state. This, too, greatly increases the chances of the Electoral College choosing a president who lost the popular vote."[46]

The Electoral College is only one feature of the American Constitution that makes it undemocratic, lest we forget that Senators were also selected by their States' legislature. Making the Senate also an undemocratic institution, now add the power grab by the Supreme Court usurping the power of judicial review, and the Presidency grabbing power during emergency situation, by way of "prerogative," we end up with each co-equal branch of government power grabbing for themselves what they can and leaving the people to suffer what they must—that is, *We the People* having a very undemocratic and unrepresentative society on our hands—viewing this compounding effect, we see that *We the People* have mostly been left out of the

[46] Chemerinsky (2018), p. 88.

Constitution. Of course, over time and many struggles a few doors opened-up. But at its core, then as today, the American Constitution presents many structural problems by way of *We the People* gaining an entry to full American citizenship and the "original" intent philosophy simply supporting this undemocratic document by requesting that democratic means be used to amend it without taking notice that that is precisely why the Constitution was built in the first place to protect itself from the "unwashed" masses—that is protect itself from democracy itself. And this problem of democracy will continue to plague the Twenty-first century as it did previous centuries.

In sum, the Constitution (parts thereof), the Senate, the Powers of Judicial Review, Presidential Prerogative powers, the *Bill of Rights* (parts thereof), and the Electoral College have been superseded by history. That is, all these mechanisms and poison pills are designed to rob *We the People* from expanding the democratic franchise to all adult people of the United States. They are a historical anachronism that has hung on our necks despite wars, revolutions, depressions, famines, etc. without revision or elimination with the passing years. Why? Because they serve tradition, the establishment, and the elite interests of society. The *Brahmins* like it that way and will fight to the end to keep it that way.

References

Appleby J (1984) Capitalism and a new social order: the republican vision of the 1790s. New York University, New York

Baker L (1991) The justice from beacon hill: the life and times of Oliver Wendell Holmes. Harper Collins Publisher, New York

Beard C (1986) An economic interpretation of the constitution of the United States. The Free Press, Los Angeles

Chemerinsky E (2018) We the people: a progressive reading of the constitution for the twenty-first century. Picador, New York

Dahl A (2003) How democratic is the American constitution? Yale University, New Haven

Damrosch L (2010) Tocqueville's discovery of America. Farrar, Straus and Giroux, New York

Dicey AV (1982) Introduction to the study of the law of the constitution. Liberty Fund, Carmel

Fishkin JS (1991) Democracy and deliberation: new directions for democratic reform. Yale University, New Haven

Greider W (1993) Who will tell the people: the betrayal of American democracy. Simon & Schuster: A Touchstone Book, Chicago

Habermas J (1981a) Theory of communicative action: reason and the rationalization of society. Vol I (trans: McCarthy T). Beacon, Boston

Habermas J (1981b) Theory of communicative action: lifeworld and systems. Vol II (trans: McCarthy T). Beacon, Boston

Habermas J (1992) Between facts and norms: contributions to a discourse theory of law and democracy. MIT, Cambridge

Habermas J (1998) On the pragmatics of communication. MIT, Cambridge

Hofstadter R (1979) The progressive historians: Turner, Beard, Parrington. University of Chicago, Chicago

Levinson S (2006) Our undemocratic constitution: where the constitution goes wrong. Oxford University, Oxford

Morone JA (1990) The democratic wish: popular participation and the limits of American government. Basic Books, New York

Parrington V (1927) Main currents in American thought. University of Oklahoma, Norman

Smith A (1965) The spirit of American government. The Belknap Press of Harvard University, Cambridge

Stoller M (2019) Goliath: the 100-year war between monopoly power and democracy. Simon & Schuster, Chicago

Tocqueville A (2003) Democracy in America. Penguin Books, New York

Wilentz S (2005) The rise of American democracy: Jefferson to Lincoln. Norton, New York

Wilson W (2002a) Congressional government. Routledge, New York

Wilson W (2002b) Constitutional government in the United States. Routledge, New York

Wolfe C (1986) The rise of modern judicial review: from constitutional interpretation to judge-made law. Basic Books, Inc., New York

Chapter 6
The Jurisprudence of Democracy v. Judicial Review: History, Intention, and Finality

6.1 Legal Realism

The law could be the product of debate or command. It could be the outcome of negotiations or simply the outcome of raw power. However, whether the law is 'legitimate' or 'just' is an ethical matter. If "ideal" democracy is not possible, then clearly the law will be made by a portion of the community that has the power to do so. Since all in the community will not participate in the law-making process, it is clear it will be delegated to those in power. Whether those in power or command have authority to produce and enforce the law is a matter of whether they achieved their power through brute force or some other way less brutal method. So, how comes it to be that those that make the law are 'legitimated' or accepted by the public? In our time three forms of regimes claim power to make laws. One type is the authoritarian type—that makes laws by command. A second type is through some form of representation of *We the People* and may involve negotiations and argumentation in making the law. And the last is some sort of admixture between authoritarianism and democracy.

What is clear and emphasized, thus far here, is the proposition that: *No responsible State should allow law-making by the Judiciary.* There is no legitimation process to allow judges to serve as lawmakers. "[M]odern American judicial history has been largely through the lens of legal realism, which argues, among other things, that judges are, and have always been, legislators or "politicians in robes." If this is true, then the only difference among judges is the particular political preference they seek to advance."[1] As said earlier, many nations have adopted the American model of judicial review after the Second World War and the decolonization period of the twentieth century. So, it should be of interest to us to ask the question what particular features of the American model of judicial review appealed to them? I fear that the comparativist will also come short of a good answer. Adopting models from

[1] Wolfe (1986), p. 13.

G. Skouras, *Constitutionalism and Democracy*,
https://doi.org/10.1007/978-3-031-66906-4_6

successful and strong countries is nothing new in the history of mankind. It is said that imitation is the strongest flattery. All we can say here, is that any comparative study that does not go down to the roots of the matter must be mostly a matter of speculation.

Legal realism is that law as determined by conditions on the ground rather than in the high tower of the theory world. Law as actually practiced by judges rather than found in textbooks. That is, the power conditions that prevail in practice, rather than in formal or theoretical codes, decide cases and not abstract principles. In the case of the Supreme Court, during this transformational period from Agricultural society to Industrial society, it played the role of legislator and judge.[2] Even though under formal systems, the Supreme Court is not to make law and policy, realism holds that its practice indicates otherwise.

What is legal realism?[3] The philosophy of legal realism is the stripping of legal fictions from the formal system of "objective" law and an "objective" judiciary interpreting law in some "neutral" way.

---

[2]Legal Realism is a legal philosophy that challenges the view that law is an autonomous and independent practice free from the personal views of judges. It challenges the view that judges can be "objective" and free from personal, political, social, economic, and cultural beliefs and can objectively judge laws and rules free from these human influences. *E.g.*, Realisms was not a unified philosophy and involved many variations. Here are some of the Legal Realists: Oliver Wendell Holmes, Roscoe Pound, Jerome Frank, Karl Llewellyn, Robert Hale, Felix Cohen, Louis Brandeis, Benjamin Cardozo, Felix Frankfurter, William O. Douglas, etc. *Lochner v. New York* (1905) set the stage for early twentieth century legal realism. It continued to build to a boil with the rise of Franklin Delano Roosevelt and the rise of the modern regulatory and administrative state: cases post-Gilded Age and Progressive era Court rulings: Ackerman attempts to argue the revisionist case that the legal realism of early twentieth century America, and *Lochner* in particular, was a product of their age and that we should not evaluate these cases with the lens of post-new Deal America. He argues in *We the People: Foundations* that: "If, then, something was fundamentally wrong with *Lochner*, it has to do with the particular way middle republican courts conceptualized the nature of fundamental rights. It is here, however, where anachronism distorts modern vision in condemning the middle republic's emphasis on private property and freedom of contract. Given the popular repudiation of laissez-faire during the New Deal, it is no longer right for modern courts to interpret constitutional liberty in free market terms. But before the 1930's, things looked very different. Even during the early republic, the courts had marked out contract as a domain of freedom peculiarly appropriate for national protection.". Ackerman (1991), p. 100 see further, Kens (1998);

Home Building & Loan Association v. Blaisdell, 280 U.S. 398 (1934)
Nebbia v. New York, 291 U.S. 502 (1934)
West Coast Company v. Parrish, 300 U.S. 379 (1937)
National Labor Relations Board v. Jones & Laughlin Steel Corp., 301 U.S. 1 (1937)
United States v. F. W. Darby Lumber Company, 312 U.S. 100 (1941)
Wickard v. Filburn, 317 U.S. 111 (1942).

[3]Horwitz (1992), pp. 169–192; Horwitz sees the realist doctrine as continuous over a period of time starting with the *Lochner* decision and the Progressives but notes a distinction between the type of realism of the Lochner era and Pre-World War I and the realism developed in the 1920's and 1930's in academic circles. The turn of the century realism reflected the power relation of law for the establishment versus law for the *We the People.* In other words, he has a more nuanced view. Nevertheless, I would argue that the sharp break in historical time between the Agricultural Age and the onset of the Industrial Age brought forth the realization that sugar coded doctrines of legal

The *principle* may be stated this way:

> Legal Realism exposed the legal system to be like other power systems when stripped down to its essence—relying on power rather than argumentation or a supposedly metaphysically "neutral" stand.

Horwitz makes clear that the Realism, pre-World War I and post-war, was the realization that the Enlightenment project of the Eighteenth century was dead upon arriving on the doorstep of the Twentieth century.[4] Left perhaps dead in the fox holes and horrors that was First World War.[5] Horwitz divides realism before the First World War and realism after the First World War. That is, Americans, like the Europeans, realized the Enlightenment is dead. He puts it thus: "Pre-war Progressive intellectuals represented what might be called a Victorian world view, one that, while often deeply skeptical of revealed religion, was nevertheless self-confident about the ability of reason to arrive at civilized and humanitarian values. The Realist generation, by contrast, had lost much of the pre-war faith in reason, both as a reliable source of moral understanding and as a powerful internal guide to law."[6]

Also, Wolf defined Legal Realism this way: "Legal realism necessarily strikes at the heart of the early American notion of judicial power as "judgment" rather than "will." Whether each traditional description of judicial power is sincere or naïve, or conscious window dressing to conceal its undemocratic character, they are distorted perceptions of the reality, according to modern realists."[7]

The *principle* may be stated this way:

> The distinction between "will" or "judgment" as far as the judiciary is concerned may be laid to rest. The judiciary is an organization, just like any other organization. How an organization behaves depends on its purpose, rules of operation or procedure, and the social space it occupies within a nation-state. When the Crown, for example, is able to operate above the law, then this entity is the sole absolute determinate of that nation-state. When the Judiciary has the final say as to policy over millions of Americans, it has become the kingmaker.

---

neutrality, fairness and balance went out the window as new power systems came in to replace the old agricultural system. The new labor power required a different legal system to accommodate the proletariat. And those in power or the establishment, stuck in the Agricultural Age, were unable to change the system and so power politics and "might makes right" doctrines flourished at the close of the nineteenth and early twentieth century America. The power jurisprudence simply followed the new worker (proletariat)-capitalist relation. The might of the new industrial age determined the range and scope of rights available to the new workers, the proletariat.

[4]Horwitz (1992), pp. 169–170. "Legal Realism was neither a coherent intellectual movement nor a consistent or systematic jurisprudence. [I]ndeed, defining Legal Realism with precision is not at all easy. [T]here is much more continuity than discontinuity between Realism and the underlying critical inspiration of Charles Beard's *An Economic Interpretation of the Constitution* (1913) or of Hohfeld's "Fundamental Legal Conceptions" (1913) or, indeed, of Pound's great pre-war writings." *see further*, White (1976); *see further*, from a limited government perspective and critics of the Progressive movement: Marini and Masugi (2005).

[5]Horwitz (1992), p. 170.

[6]Horwitz (1992), p. 170.

[7]Wolfe (1986), p. 13.

I want to further address a point I earlier promised the reader, dealing with the concept of "reason" and "reasonableness." After the devastation that was World War I, and all the other horrors that mark the Twentieth century, it might be a good idea to further explore this concept of "reason" both in a broader philosophical sense and in a more restricted jurisprudential sense.[8] I want to take up the matter here and briefly state and argue the matter. Immanuel Kant, entitled his *magnum opus*: *The Critique of Pure Reason*. Kant and the Enlightenment generation that he belonged to must have thought very highly of this concept, to name his work, *The Critique of Pure Reason*, and in the case of the Age or period he flourished in as *"The Age of Reason."* This Age must have discovered something special about this concept of reason to devote themselves to it—either to showcase it or critique it. So, what is so special about "reason"? It appears, for them, to be a key metric in the differentiation between "sense" and "rationality." That is, the human being and the animal all have "sense" data that influences their behavior. But human beings, unlike other animals, also possess "reason." Well above the remainder of the animal kingdom. This special tool or capability enables the human animal to transcend the sense-based world, and by examination of itself and nature, render a true picture of reality. Placing the human being in a far superior position to other animals—whereas, other animals rely on the senses and instinct, the human being has the additional benefit of the reasoning faculty.

Now, let me cut to the jurisprudence and legal philosophy as to how this concept influenced and influences law. Since human beings have this special "reasoning" ability, morality, ethics, and law demand that human beings exhibit a higher level of responsibility for their conduct and actions. With the devastation that was the First World War, it put the stake or dagger into the heart of what was known as the *Enlightenment Age*. It rendered suspect the notion that human beings are more special in their daily activity than all other animals. That is, the human being is like all other animals, and not "gifted" with this special power or entity called "reason." With this discrediting of reason, the human animal fell from the enchanted grace that it was placed upon by the *Enlightenment*—and fell to the ground where all the other animals live.

It appears that Hobbes was one of the earliest political philosophers to clearly assess the dangerous nature of the human animal. It would require two World Wars and the horrors that was the Twentieth century to drive that point to a wider range of scholars and intellectuals. Even those living today may not fully appreciate just how a dangerous animal the human being is because excuses for its actions and behaviors can always be found. I wrote briefly on one of the causes of such behavior in an earlier paper.[9] In that paper I lay out the matter in terms of evolution and biologism: the layers of the human brain make for a very unstable structure because it is an admixture of brain layering—not simply contain mammalian brain—but is a

[8] In the United States, the Founding Fathers and drafters of the American Constitution were men of the "Age of Reason" as were many others in North America as well as Europe.

[9] I previously commented and analyzed this issue in: Skouras (2020).

layering of brain from the earliest evolutionary days, of nature layering reptilian brain on top of amphibian brain, and on top of these two layers sits the latest in evolutionary development, the mammalian brain. This mixture or layering of brain structure makes for a very unstable and dangerous animal. But even Hobbes may have underestimated the exact extent of danger such an animal poses not only to other creatures of the earth but to its own kind. So, although Hobbes may have assessed it as a dangerous animal, I think, now that we live after the horrors of the Twentieth century, we may properly assess it as an "exceedingly" dangerous animal.

However, regardless of the evolutionary scale or the biologisms of the human animal, the law uses the "reasonable" standard of analysis—a standard that went out in flames and poisonous gas that was the First World War. So why after more than a hundred years after that war would legal institutions be using the "reasonable" standard model? That is, the law still required and requires "reasonable" conduct or behavior from the agent. There is of course currently being used the "reasonable person standard" to evaluate the conduct of those facing legal liability. The law never caught up with the fall of reason. In the case of American jurisprudence, the "reason" standard is alive and well in the legal system. This "legal fiction" has taken hold with both conservatives and progressives in the legal profession. It is assumed that lawyers, judges, and other interested parties accept "reason" as the gold standard of modern jurisprudence. I hope that along with the other practices singled out here for analysis such as the "power of judicial review," "the presidential prerogative," and "senatorial anachronism," I will have at least thrown some light of modern practices that should have been laid to rest or abolished well before entering the Twenty-first century. The power of "reason" being just another outdated system that continues to plague the legal and political system. With the continued belief that the human animal is better than the other animals because it has "reason" on its side.

The American legal system needs to clear out such outdated and anachronistic systems that have a pre-modernist origin if progress is to be made in updating the system by way of adaptation—just like any animal needs to adapt to its environment if it expects to survive. Systems that do not adjust fail. This happened in the American system that was forced to transform itself not by planning but by the brute force of history changing one domain to another—an Agricultural system to an Industrial system. Horwitz says that this transformation was well anticipated by the legal system.[10] However, it is not clear just how successful the legal system was in

[10]Horwitz appears to say that the legal system adjusted first, by the nineteenth century transformations in law and was already prepared to accommodate the Industrial Age. That is, the law was already outgrowing the Agricultural Age well before the Civil War. Clearly, the indicators of the late eighteenth and early nineteenth century transformations in economic and social systems were gaining steam and were coming to America. However, that is different from fully knowing the impact the Industrial Age will have on the farmers and future proletariat when it fully arrived, and the further transformations needed by the legal system to account for the new reality on the ground and the devastation the new worker-life transformation and impact will have on those transported and transformed workers from the farms to the cities—from farmers and agricultural workers to the new proletariat.

preparation for the Corporate age. Clearly, the signs of the Agricultural age was passing but whether the law could do much to accommodate the change may have been a matter of contingency. It seems to me that law follows the economic dynamics of the age, not set the dynamics. The motion of the economic whirlpool swept the law into its vortex—as the motion of body and the power of the steam engine generated a new world—the world of agriculture of thousands of years of human existence was coming to an end. Let me stipulate here that just because the agricultural age was passing from the scene that this is a universal statement of the nineteenth century. Simply because some parts of the world had undergone this transformation, it should not imply that all parts of the globe also undertook to modernize. This created and is still alive today the modern colonialist project. That is, those nations that modernized survived, those that failed to modernize, under the laws of and development of our civilizational horizon—were swallowed up and digested by the strongest powers. As I mentioned earlier, the laws of the jungle are final.

Another power dynamic was the belief in earlier times that the legal system that operated under "will" was different from one operating under "judgment." I seriously doubt it. Wolfe appears to say that our modern understanding of judicial review was not necessarily the same as in previous eras of American history. He thinks that the modern form of judicial review, based on legal realism, is more aggressive in nature than the early version of judicial review. That there was a clear distinction between legislative 'will' and judicial 'judgment'. I do not believe the two can be separated out and easily compartmentalized. I do not believe the distinction can be carried out in practice. Lawyers are not psychologists that know what is 'one's will' and what is 'one's judgment.' If there was such a distinction in early American cases, most likely it was the judges that set the terms or demarcation between will and judgment. But be that as it may, it might have been the case that, during early America, overturning legislation via judicial review was in its infancy, but as the judiciary became more and more confident, in the use of this power, it assumed more and more legislative control by throwing its weight around as to what the Constitution said on any given matter or issue. That is, judicial review during the early era was in its infancy and not fully developed by the Court to take down legislation on a massive scale, and, also, the economics of an agrarian society was very different from modern industrial society. And the opportunity to do massive damage to an agricultural society was minimal. Only during the American Civil War era, and during the transitioning stage from agricultural society to an industrial society, did it become clear the massive damage the Supreme Court was capable of inflicting on *We the People*. The first evidence of combining legislative power with judicial power, in one body, came with the *Dread* Scott[11] case. Who in early America could believe that the power the Court had amassed in being able to send

[11] *Dread Scott v. Sanford,* 60 U.S. 393 (1857); this case may not have been the "proximate" cause of the Civil War but set-in motion or set the table for further hostilities. I will later in the chapter consider the jurisprudential issues of "proximate" causation and general causation.

more than 600,000 soldiers and civilians to their death in the Civil War? It became very clear, by the close of the Nineteenth century, that the Court was using its massive power to quash the workers and protect the capitalists and property owners.

Are law and politics a *continuum* or *discrete* entities? "Law carried an unusual burden in this conception. It was hoped that it could provide a non-political cushion or buffer between state and society. Unless law could be rendered non-political, how could it avoid simply becoming an instrument of democratic politics?"[12] Can politics be removed from the law? Or better put, can the law be made and applied under conditions of 'equality' or 'neutrality'? Attempts to constitutionalize "equality," according to Horwitz, was a difficult process. He examines how Michigan's Chief Justice Thomas Cooley, in his *Treatise on Taxation*, attempted to do it. "There were substantial difficulties confronting anyone who wished to constitutionalize taxation. Treating equality as a fundamental principle of justice, Cooley sought to make this norm applicable regardless of whether a state had specifically incorporated it into its constitution."[13]

According to Horwitz, since the American Revolution, with all the 'democratic' talk, and I suspect with the fear entailed later in the Eighteenth century by the French Revolution, that the Founders found out, by the close of the Eighteenth century, that democracy could be a very dangerous thing especially to those with property. That is, would it not make sense to attempt to fence in *We the People*? If law can be made "neutral," would that not advance the peace? "The separation between law and politics has been an early aspiration of American legal thinkers. Operating uncomfortably within a democratic political culture that has been obsessed with the threat of "tyranny of the majority," American jurists since the Revolution have striven to embody "a government of laws and not of men" in a conception of an autonomous system of law untainted by politics."[14]

The *principle* may be stated this way:

> Can law be "neutral"? Can fish fly? The notion of neutrality is a hard problem for history, the social sciences and philosophy. The concept of neutrality is irrelevant as far as the world of nature is concerned. Neutrality is discontinuous with the natural world and a metaphysical subject as far as history, law, and the social sciences is concerned.

---

[12] Horwitz (1992), pp. 9–10.

[13] Horwitz (1992), p. 22.

[14] Horwitz (1992), p. 9 Horwitz does a good job of the use of "implied" argumentation by constitutional scholars that might lack access to more direct language: "Cooley's argumentative strategy is a prominent example of what Edward Corwin has called the "doctrine of implied limitation." Since separation of powers is a basic doctrine of American constitutional law, the argument went, the legislative branch was confined to acts of legislation. Taxation is within the definition of the legislative power only when it is used to raise revenue. It follows that an unequal tax, being clearly for redistributive purposes, is not within the legislative power. Unequal taxation was thus defined to be in fundamental conflict with the theory underlying separation of powers and was unconstitutional even without a specific provision requiring equal and uniform taxation." (p. 22)

What is happening here? Democracy requires treating every vote equally. No one's vote counts for more than one and no one's vote counts for less than one. Equality of vote implies equality of taxation. Taxing some more than others is treating equal voters unequally or differently. There is no issue of fairness in the neutral and scientific enterprise. Equality means one person one vote (we will disregard the Electoral College for a minute). One tax applied equally to every voter/citizen. So, what is Cooley doing? He is attempting to protect private property from unequal taxation. He is going back to the Founding Fathers principle that property is sacred and underlies the American constitutional system. In other words, it is protected from taxation because property is a natural right and must be excluded from the democratic vote.

Basically, Cooley is reminding us that the goal of the American political system is not democracy, but the protection of private property. And since private property is God given and under God's special protection or nature's protection, any interference with property must be a violation of God's will. Wherever we look in America we find the protection of property as God's will commanding us to protect it, especially from the "commoners." The influence of the Protestant ethic appears again and again in American history. The *Enlightenment* might have banished the deity to the outer reaches of the universe. But America grew up under the tutelage of a stern Protestant ethic, and even some Enlightened Founding Fathers, drafting the Constitution, could not remove property or God from being emblazoned within it—basically, the Founding Fathers were helpless in any attempt of removing God and natural law from the legal system, even if they wanted to. Afterall, America was not France, and the American Constitution was drafted before the French Revolution. But even if it had been drafted after the French Revolution, with all its beheadings and terror, there was no way that a stern Protestant nation was going to banish God from the land, especially if such a god was serving as the protector of property rights. It was too embedded in society, politics, law, and culture to be discarded based on some French Enlightenment principles. In short, the sacredness of property was under divine protection in America!

Further, according to Horwitz, early in the Nineteenth century a debate broke out about the codification of the law. Is the law "politics" or a "science" of sorts? "The underlying argument between Jacksonian proponents of codification and the orthodox defenders of the common law system turned on whether judges "make" law or "declare" law. The question of whether law is "political"—and, hence, to be appropriately determined by democratic legislators enacting code—or, instead, is "scientific," and thus capable of being expounded by judges, was at the heart of the codification controversy."[15]

America being conceived as a place where "individualism" is supposed to rule rather than "collectives," it becomes important that the individual is not overrun by the collective, like *We the People*, operating as a mob of "unwashed" propertyless people. So, how is a philosophy of individualism to maintain itself in a sea of

---

[15] Horwitz (1992), p. 9.

democracy that will later in the Nineteenth century become a tidal wave of democracy? It had to be a trick of labels—good advertising copy to claim "individual" freedom in a sea of a collection of States—Confederation or subsumed under a Federal government, Federalism—to convince citizens of their individuality and freedom. In other words, it must have had to be a '*linguistic turn*' rather than a political or philosophic turn to convince every citizen that they are "individuals." So, then it follows: if each citizen is an individual, but they come to vote as collectives, for instance as a class of "commoners," in each election, how can this individualism be preserved through an enterprise such as voting? That is, "*fear of tyranny of the majority*," has been the bane and hallmark of American democracy. Why? Because as said many times over here, America is not a true democracy but rather an Aristocratic Republic.

Well, this is a linguistic problem, not a real legal, political, social, or economic problem—the answer is simple. It is staring out right at our faces. America cannot be a democratic country. It has defined democracy in a truncated manner. So that some things that are equal are good and other things that are equal are bad. The concept of democracy has been called upon to do double duty. This confusion has made the "counter-majoritarian" problem a real concern for a democratic system. Of course, if America was set up as a democracy, it would indeed be a problem, but given that America was set up as an Aristocratic Republic, then majorities are not the "real" problem unless they breach the walls of Republicanism.

The *principle* may be stated this way:

> Is not democracy based on voting that creates winners and losers? Where do the losers go to cool off their heels? Could majority rule be transformed into a tyranny of some sort? Aristocratic Republics can take care of the "majoritarian" problem by "checks and balance," "electoral college," "the power of judicial review" and with the use of many other major poison pills to ensure that those commoners do not rule in any meaningful way even if they constitute a majority.

6.2 Originalism Doctrine: The "Dead" Constitution

Does the Constitution authorize the legislative branch to establish a national bank? Can the United States create a Federal Reserve system under the Constitution? Arguments can be made in either direction. If no direct language becomes handy, the constitutionalist theorist can move to "implied" language as backup. If "implied" language cannot be stitched together, perhaps historical context or other literary theories can be brought to bear to get the job done. When dealing with document interpretation, the examination of the "four corners" of the document may not yield the desired results. Of course, there are modernist and postmodernist literary theories that can be tried out. But where is the end point? Is there an end point to documentary reading and interpretation? Obviously, when dealing with documents without clear "meaning" or incomplete exposition, a debate is inevitable with various factions, with groups going to their corners to find their favorite strategic theorist or doctrine that they can appeal to get the results required. Looking for patterns of "intent" and "meaning" within a document or from outside the document can become a battle of the social, economic, cultural, and most important military victories. To the victors go the spoils, as the old saying goes. There must be some truth that those with the guns interpret things their way or else. As is the case with military combat, the victors write history their way—so is the case of legal interpretation—the victors, that can put down the challengers, will enjoy their preferred reading of the Constitution. There is nothing magical about combat by document. Can the original constitutional "intent" mean the same exact thing to the generation living in the Twenty-first century as it meant to the generation of the late Eighteenth century?[16]

What is the philosophy of originalism?[17] Is it possible to maintain the integrity, stability, meaning, and intentionality of documents over long stretches of historical time? Justice Antonin Scalia believes it can be done. His originalism: "Justice Scalia, in countless speeches, proclaimed that the Constitution is "not a living document" and is "dead, dead, dead."""[18]

> Why? Conservatives repeatedly emphasize that they want a method of interpretation that avoids forcing justices and judges to make value choices. In one of the initial and most influential arguments in favor of originalism, Judge Robert Bork (who was later nominated for the Supreme Court and rejected by the Senate) said that "a Court that makes rather than implements value choices cannot be squared with the presuppositions of a democratic society.[19]

How does "values" system shift decision-making in the Twenty-first century back to the Framers' Constitution? Justice Antonin Scalia, Randy Bennett, and Justice Amy Coney Barrett believe in originalism or a "dead" constitution philosophy.[20] That the Constitution is frozen at the time of its writing. And remains so thereafter until it is properly amended by its own terms. Originalism doctrine sounds a lot like an eternal god philosophy where this eternal god cannot change—it is the same today as it was yesterday as it was a billion years ago, by containing its own infinity and being its own infinity, it could be no other than an eternal unchanging being (document, doctrine, philosophy, constitution). This is also a natural rights doctrine that secures individual liberty but not collective liberty. So, majoritarian[21] rule is an illegitimate guide in protecting these God-given individual rights. The individual secures these rights upon birth and not given to them by mortal men and women. "In attacking this state of affairs, Barnett starts with its premise: that we should not be concerned about

[16] Original intent debate—originalism seems to have emerged simply to counter progressive readings of the Constitution. That is, a conservative counter-offensive of those that they view as tinkering, misreading, misunderstanding, or otherwise have low opinion of the original document and are simply out to portray it wrongly or are otherwise unfaithful to it. Some originalists, like Justice Scalia, would prefer that the phrase "original intent" be dropped or switched for the phrase "original meaning." The difference being that the latter phrase is more verifiable than the former.

[17] *See,* philosophy of originalism: Bork (1978); *See further*, Rakove (1996).

[18] Chemerinsky (2018), p. 28.

[19] Chemerinsky (2018), pp. 29–30.

[20] Barnett (2003), p. 103; Barrett (2017), p. 61; Kay (1988), p. 226; Barnett (2014).

[21] Barrett (2017), pp. 62–63.

the counter-majoritarian nature of judicial review. Instead, Barnett claims, we should be concerned about the majoritarian nature of legislation. Democratic majorities pose a consistent threat in minority rights."[22]

Richard Kay as a supporter of originalism says: "This essay will critically examine the reasons given by modern scholars for rejecting the conventional norm of judicial review—adherence to the original intentions of the Constitution's enactors. While variously phrased, their reasons may be subsumed under the general objections: 1) Adherence to the original intentions is impossible; 2) It is self-contradictory; and 3) It is wrong."[23] It appears that the "intentionalism" doctrine is derived from a plurality of angles even by the "originalists" themselves. One type of originalist might focus on what the Framers "intended" to convey using their language. Other originalists may forgo the "intent" aspect and simply focus on the "meaning" of the language used by the Framers, taking the standard to be the average competent reader living in late Eighteenth century America.

Modern progressive writers, like Chemerinsky, argue that judicial review is antimajoritarian.[24] "Constitutional judicial review, by an unelected Supreme Court, is intentionally antimajoritarian and it is logically impossible to make such review consistent with a definition of democracy as simple as majority rule."[25] But are those "originalists" also inclined to read the Constitution, and particularly the doctrine of judicial review, as an antimajoritarian practice? If they do, how do they propose to change the Constitution to make a pro-majoritarian document? Either they can reply that the Constitution is not anti-majoritarian or, they can go on and say that if it is antimajoritarian, that the Framers provided for its alteration within the stipulations of the document itself. So, if the document is to become majoritarian, it must overcome many provisions within itself that serve as poison pills to kill off any such attempt. Of course, the originalists can reply that any portion of the Constitution is subject to change, if the criterion for change contained within itself, is followed. Well, let us think about this for a moment: if the Constitution requires ¾ths of the Congress or ¾ths of the States in convention to so vote, isn't 3/4ths a super-majoritarian stipulation whereas majoritarian rule, conventionally means 50 plus 1? So, to become a majoritarian state, we must use super-majoritarian rules. What does this prove? It proves that the Founders were not democrats.

The debate between the progressive "living" constitution supporters and the conservative "dead" constitution supporters seem to be whistling in the wind. Many Americans from the early days were taught to worship the Constitution. However, the Constitution is neither for worship nor neglect. It is simply a document that hopes to serve as a road guide from point A to point B. If in the course of history, the route changes and the Constitution is not changed or amended, it leads one astray and one becomes lost wandering about finding new directions. If reform of the

[22] Barrett (2017), p. 63.

[23] Kay (1988), p. 228.

[24] Chemerinsky (1986), p. 47; Chemerinsky (1984), p. 1207; Farber (1989), p. 1084.

[25] Chemerinsky (1986), p. 49; *see further*, Hutt (2017), p. 2.

American constitutional system is in order, then there is a need for the transformation from the current Aristocratic Republic to a Democratic government. The first order of business being to dispose of any unnecessary entanglements between *We the People* and the legislature. So, this would require disposing of the Senate, as an outdated appendage to the system. The second basic requirement is to strip the Supreme Court of the power of Judicial Review, and lodge it with the legislative branch. And finally given that this will result in great power lodged with the legislative branch, it needs to be safeguarded by anchoring the Congress from below—workers' unions, workers' councils, and other civic institutions with broad representation in their communities to help anchor the Congress to *We the People*. This should provide better representation in the Congress, since it will be selected by—*We the People* generally and underpinned by 'We the Workers' and the local 'Civic' institutions in particular.

The *principle* may be stated this way:

> The current internal plumbing of the American Constitution is based on Aristocratic principles. To achieve reform this plumbing must be ripped out of the internal system and replaced with a modern plumbing system. The Senate and the Supreme Court power of Judicial Review are leftovers from a pre-Civil War world. They should have been ripped out during the Civil War. But any attempt to modernize, fix, or improve the internal plumbing of the Constitution should expect blowback.

To sum up, Congress, before being given Supreme power to serve, not only as legislator, but also as judge over its own legislation, must become more accountable to *We the People*, by first, the elimination of the Senate as an outdated aristocratic institution, and second, with the eliminating the Senate, it is to be replaced by Unions and Civil organizations, from below, to help inform and counteract a Congress that might become Imperial with its new power. This should increase Congress' anchoring to democratic majoritarianism and increase the points of reference from below rather than aristocratic holdovers, like the Senate, from above.

At the same time, the Congress must select a special committee to monitor the actions of the executive branch with particular focus on the Presidency. That is, during times of emergency or danger to the state, this Committee could serve as an accounting department, overseeing the use of executive power and making sure that the executive does not abuse those powers granted to it. Any emergency powers granted to put down a threat and return those powers once the threat is disposed of. The Committee could monitor to see to it that the Executive returns those emergency powers back into storage—seeing that the Executive does not pilfer emergency power and retains them along with its usual regular/daily power of executing laws. In other words, that the executive does not pilfer powers not reserved for its use outside the emergency, just like the Supreme Court pilfered the power of judicial review. What constitutes an emergency is easy to identify if history is any guide: War, Insurrection, Famine, Pandemics, etc. that are of such a magnitude to trigger emergency power authorization. This means the other two branches of government, the executive and judiciary, must be reduced in stature and power, as the Congress' power is increased during times of peace, but during times of war, the Congress becomes helpless and the Executive must step forward to wage and conduct the war under the oversight of the special Congressional Committee, to be sure those emergency powers granted for war purposes are put back into the safe at the end of hostilities. This recognizes a body the size of Congress is not designed to act quickly under emergency conditions. So, this standby Committee[26] must stand down once the emergency has ended, but not dismissed, in terms of planning ahead for future responses to emergency conditions. Otherwise, a slow deliberative body like the Congress, or a debating society, with its stalemates, lockdowns, inefficiency, etc. would sink the state under emergency conditions.

6.3 History & Interpretation

The Supreme Court brings nothing to the table in the decipherment of documents that other governmental bodies or scholars could not bring to the table. There is no reason that the Supreme Court is in a superior position to analyze and review the Constitution or statutes for consistency and compliance. As far as interpretation of law is concerned, the matter is not as simple as Blackstone lays out. "The best way to interpret the law is to explore the *intention* of the lawgiver at the time the law was made, says Blackstone, "by signs the most natural and probable." There are five basic signs: "the words, the context, the subject-matter, the effects and consequences, or the spirit and reason of the law."[27] However, in the Nineteenth century

[26]Decision by committee can be a good thing during times of peace and plenty of free time to ponder and consider matters slowly and cautiously after debate. However, decision-making and decision-taking by way of rule by committee, during emergency conditions, would be a nightmare of the worse kind. Therefore, the function of this sector of Congress that is selected must be on decision-making and action. Once the emergency is over, then this committee can stand down after the emergency but not be dissolved as to planning how to deal with the next or other types of emergency conditions.

[27]Wolfe, p. 18; *see also*, Blackstone (2016), *see further*, Broom (1896), p. 2. Broom writes in the traditional Blackstonian mode of legal interpretation. He says: "The *lex scripta* comprises the statute law of the land, the duty of interpreting which devolves upon the Judges, who are guided in such interpretation by various recognized rules or canons of construction, of which the primary, or, as it has been called, the "golden" rule, has been thus expressed—"to give to all the words of an Act of Parliament their plain and ordinary meaning, unless such a construction leads to absurdity or injustice[e]." [J]udges cannot "speculate upon the intentions of the legislature, which are neither expressed in terms nor conveyed by implication;" their "duty is to interpret the words of a statute according to their plain and grammatical meanin[g]."; Clinton (1989), pp. 1–2. "I argue that the American understanding of the judicial function during the eighteenth century was thoroughly Blackstonian, most pointedly embodied in that author's famous Tenth Rule of Statutory Construction. This principle holds that legislation may be overruled by common-law courts only when its application would necessarily result in absurdity, repugnancy, or impossibility of performance—in other words, when a statute is internally defective and self-contradictory, pp. 1–2.

there emerged another school of jurisprudence that said that law cannot be discovered in nature but was simple a social product of any given society.[28]

The *principle* may be stated this way:

> Interpretation, Intentionality, and Finality are Consciousness based actions. These actions cannot be fixed forever. Linguistic drift on the empirical-side and consciousness-drift on the other are not rationally or empirically compounded to produce a fixed state of affairs. With each state of affairs there is a shifting of consciousness and its directionality. Consciousness is not a permanent and ever-present entity standing at the ready to do x, y, or z.

Blackstone, in early America during the drafting of the Constitution, was taken as the gold standard in legal interpretation. However, the view of the law as a "neutral" enterprise encountered realist philosophy.

> A thin line, however, has always separated the apologists, who believed, like Blackstone, that a more abstract and systematic jurisprudence would reveal the deeper rationality of the common law, from the critics like Hohfeld, whose efforts at systematic jurisprudence were inspired by the belief that only a more abstract system of legal thought could expose the irrationality of common law modes of legal classification.[29]

Why bother with linguistic niceties about "intention," "meaning" and other semantic games if it can be proven or shown that the law can never be an "objective" or "value-free" entity? That the historical coloring of the law falls within the domain of human activities and conventions, and it is what it is, not because God-handed it down or found in the eternal writings of nature in the sky, but simply a "relativist" and "utilitarian" product of human activity. Regardless of what counts as law or what law is, it cannot transcend the boundaries of community, society, or civilization. Whether law is derived from myth, spirit, or a god can count as law within any given horizon.

Why is it important to capture the 'intention' of the law?[30] Is the capture of 'intent' closer to truthfulness or legitimacy? If the 'intent' is missing, does that mean that the law is being wrongfully misconstrued? What if using the category of 'intentionality' is the wrong category in the interpretation of laws? As far as we know intentionality is formed and spoken through language. The components of language are the words. Is it true that "words" may change but "ideas" do not change?[31] Are words the same kind of thing as ideas? We need to ask then what is

---

[28] Wolfe (1986), p. 158. "The late nineteenth century saw a continuation and an intensification of a long debate in jurisprudence over the nature of law. Blackstone represented the more classical position in the debate when he argued that judges (even common-law judges) did not make law, but rather discovered it, in the customs of the community, themselves represented a higher law, the natural law. In the nineteenth century, John Austin and Jeremy Bentham had represented the very different opinion that law cannot be "discovered" in nature because law is merely the command of the sovereign (there is no "natural law"), and from this perspective common-law judges were in fact *making* law."

[29] Horwitz (1992), p. 201.

[30] Kay (1988), p. 226.

[31] The relation between "words" and "ideas"—here is how structuralism deals with the problem: Hawkes (1977), p. 19. "Saussure inherited the traditional view already referred to, that the world

the relationship between words and ideas?[32] Words are carriers of ideas if you will, but ideas unlike words are not physical objects; ideas can be slippery if not properly captured by words (just as a law can be slippery if not properly reflective of the will of the people through the agent of their representation); words exist in space-time; ideas do not. Words originate in space-time and change over time—no word remains immutable over time.[33] But there is sharp distinction between words and ideas.[34] Is it true that words are the carriers of ideas? Of course, it may be questioned whether words capture "ideas" and bring them to consciousness.[35] What if the "word" is all that is or exists, and the "idea" is simply another word for the "word"? Of course, this is not a Platonic world of ideas existing in independent space-time outside the animal kingdom. What if 'ideas' are the same as 'words'? Why posit two entities when one will do?

As far as I know, we can never independently nor scientifically verify how ideas come into our consciousness (mind) other than through words.[36] Or under Freudian conditions, where our unconsciousness influences our conscious behavior, free of us knowing it. Whatever the unconsciousness does will eventually have to manifest

---

consists of independently existing objects, capable of precise objective observation and classification. In respect to linguistics this outlook yields a notion of language as an aggregate of separate units, called 'words', each of which somehow has a separate 'meaning' attached to it, the whole existing within a *diachronic* or historical dimension which makes it subject to observable and recordable laws of change."

[32] Hawkes (1977), p. 19. "Saussure's revolutionary contribution to the study of language lies in his rejection of that 'substantive' view of the subject in favor of the 'relational' one, a change of perspective closely in accord with the larger shift in perception mentioned above."

[33] Ogden and Richards (1989) (a modernist review of the use of words, ideas, and language).

[34] Plato (2016) (trans: Bloom A)—ideal v. real/platonic metaphysics versus Aristotelian physics; the platonic world of ideas, such a world where mathematics exists can be naturalized as long as the mind can grasp and synthesize or marry the two domains in consciousness via mind. However, the supposition of a mind outside a body is a place that generations of philosophers cut their teeth on, especially since the presentation of Descartes' philosophy of mind-body dualism. I will not go into any details here on this matter since it would take us too much off course as far as jurisprudence of judicial review is concerned. *See further*, Ogden and Richards (1989), pp. 1–23 (the relation between ideas and words can be problematic under modern linguistic understanding that uses systems and structures as foundations. Nevertheless, the bedrock of how "words" or "ideas" can be carriers of "meaning" is an ongoing concern.) *see in particular*, Chapter 1: "Thoughts, Words and Things,"; Ogden and Richards (1989), p. 7. "Further, much language, especially primitive language, is not primarily concerned with ideas at all, unless under 'ideas' are included emotions and attitude[s]." Ogden and Richards (1989), pp. 9–10. "Words, as everyone knows, 'mean' nothing by themselves, although the belief that they did. . .was once equally universal. It is only when a thinker makes use of them that they stand for anything, or, in a sense, have 'meaning.'"

[35] Hawkes (1977), pp. 19–20. "The *Cours* presents the argument that language should be studied, not only in terms of its individual parts, and not only diachronically, but also in terms of relationship *between* those parts, and *synchronically*: that is, in terms of its *current* adequacy. In short, he proposed that a language should be studied as a *Gestalteinheit*, a unified 'field', a self-sufficient system, as we actually experience it *now*."

[36] We will leave the problematics of this problem for another day. Here it is important to know that consciousness brings along with it, responsibility.

itself in behavior and behavior is action. That action eventually must translate itself into words that can made sense of by our minds. Whether the action originated from consciousness or the unconscious it will eventually be explained in words if at all. If it remains unconscious and does not affect behavior, then it is moot as far as attributing blame or causal connection to the subject or agent. Further, there may be such things as sounds, like musical sounds, which enter consciousness free from the word. But sounds at some point need to be translated into words if they are going to be appreciated by the mind. Otherwise, all we can say about sounds is whether they are pleasing, loud, harsh, etc. Similarly, visual or other sense data could enter consciousness free from words. But to organize the data requires a mind. And the mind is independent from data collection. Of course, whether the mind is the same as the brain opens additional scientific and philosophical problems that we are not going to deal with here. Many philosophers cut their teeth on this problem as well. But only make the point that the structure of any language system is never fixed for evermore.

The general point being that within the conscious mind, "intent" or "meaning" is not simply to be found by pointing to the artifacts left behind by another generation as those that espouse originalist doctrine would have us believe. What is intentional can be as mysterious as consciousness itself. That is, law and jurisprudence that relies on the idea of "intentionality" can be as complex as unraveling the origins of consciousness in animals.

The argumentation as to the "intent" of the law, has serious problems in that it requires "internal" correspondence to make that determination. If we apply the old philosophical principle that "all is change" or the modern scientific principle of motion, then we are really in a fix to set our NorthStar on these determinants. Of course, taking the dynamism and motion of the scientific world into the historical and social world, like animals such as us, is to cross the matter-consciousness barrier. That is to say, the dynamism of life cannot be captured or fixed forever in words. Words are the wrong entities for the job.

Bergson came close to explaining this process in his philosophy early in the Twentieth century.[37] Words can also be untrue because the motion of our bodies need not be equivalent to the changes in historical times or social times. The laws that govern nature are not one and the same that govern social-historical time.[38]

What was the "intent" of the Framers of the American Constitution regarding each phrase and clause of the document? Assuming we can start with a basic definition of the concept of 'intention,' what if the Framers did not "know," "fully know," or only "partially" knew what they "intended," as to how each phrase of the Constitution was to be interpreted? That is, what if the 'intent' of the Framers could not be ascertained from the document itself and one must turn to history and social context to bring color and help with their intentional meanings? What if the Framers

[37] Bergson's philosophy broke new ground early in the twentieth century, see: Bergson (1998).

[38] The German philosophers were very active in the development of the philosophy of history early in the nineteenth century, see: Herder (2004) and Hegel (1837).

lacked the full grasp of the "intent" that could be pulled out of their phrases in the fullness of time? "John Marshall, "the great Chief Justice," has been accused of seizing the bitter cup all too gladly and thus setting a pattern of usurpation for future judges to follow. As far as this indictment rests on the supposed "intent of the framers," it suffers from the weakness already remarked: that so few of the framers had any clear views one way or another about the subject."[39]

The State and legal system do not sit upon some utopian land, but on an instantaneous state of nature. Whether an animal has the luxury or the historical time to defend itself or nourish itself is the property of civilizational development—the animal can become food for another animal or have another animal as its meal. Regardless of the case, the State sits on top of nature not below it. In a utopian paradise, animals can dream up all the pleasantries and enjoyments they desire, but life under natural conditions is brutal. So that if the animal is to submit or give up power to a Sovereign, then the sovereign must be strong enough to allow the animal to live. Hobbes first noticed: "and which is worst of all, continual fear and danger of violent death, and the *life* of man, solitary, poor, *nasty, brutish, and short*."[40] He was able to distil the essential powers needed for survival both in the state of nature and within civilizational time. That is, fear of violent death demands that a strong leader can provide for the safety of the people. If the sovereign does not have sufficient power to do the job, then individual citizens must arrange for their own survival as they see fit. Regardless of whether the human animal is placed in a society or state of nature, a stateless animal roaming the jungle, the animal will first respond automatically and if given life beyond the "instantaneous moment" can plan and deliberate for-itself within historical time.

The *principle* may be stated this way:

> Fear of death is genetic in the code of all animals. Those with the strongest instincts in the "now" survive the "duration" window of tomorrow. Those that lack it are the meal of another animal or creature. The laws of the jungle are final.

So, 'sign interpretation' matters only under artificial conditions, within civilizational time. Those institutions that serve as the interpreters of the will of *We the People*, Congress, must be grounded on the experiences of the people on the ground level. The role of "interpretation" of the sign or signs matters not under automatic and instinctual response conditions. It is secondary. Does the human animal lose its instincts or give up its instincts in a civilized society? The Supreme Court cannot reserve the exclusive right to "interpret" the Constitution better than the masses of populations or *We the People* simply because the establishment says so or allows it to do so. Otherwise, the Supreme Court becomes the new Sovereign since it

---

[39] McCloskey (2004), p. 10.

[40] Hobbes (1994), p. 76; *see further*, Wilson (1995), pp. 1–5. For a modern challenger to Hobbes' view as to the dangerous nature of man, Wilson argues that the human animal also has a moral sense which therefore can serve as a countervailing force, and man not simply being a killer animal or man having to constantly fear a "violent death." Since the human animal has "moral sense," the fear of death feared by Hobbes is not eliminated but reduced and controlled to a certain extent.

possesses the power of final review—the final arbiter as to the meaning of the Constitution. Hobbes would have been amused to find out that the British-American colonies, along the East Coast of North America, would one day place the power of sovereignty in the hands of the Supreme Court. Of course, Hobbes did not care who exercised sovereign power, be it a monarch or a Supreme Court, as long as it had sufficient power to keep the peace. So, if the American people want the Supreme Court to be the final and ultimate power in the land, well that is their decision. Hobbes, however, would have been amused to find the judiciary as the ultimate power given his confrontations with the jurisprudence of Sir Edward Coke.

It cannot be good constitutionalism or jurisprudence to allow a single body to serve as "interpreter" of the People's will or *We the People*. That is, democracy cannot yield to a single body to serve as the final "interpreter" of its will. If Congress acquires such a power, once stripped from the Supreme Court, it must be under the condition that Congress operates under ground conditions. If Congress is stalemated or posturing or serving simply as a debating society, it must also be transformed to carry out the business of the People. If this is not occurring, it is because there are bottlenecks in the science of representation. Each Congressperson is there to look after the needs and concerns of his or her constituents, not to cut the knees off other congressional members, making Congressional representation a zero-sum game. No matter how imperfect this institution currently is, it is the best chance for some form of democracy to survive and at the same time fend off rival systems of power such as authoritarianism and dictatorships.

The *principle* may be stated this way:

> A citizen cannot become the victim of his or her government any more than a human animal can become the meal of a lion or tiger. Such an animal must signal as to what type of leadership and government will help it survive.

6.4 History & Consciousness-Intentionality

The historical point of consciousness of an event[41] is not the product of time itself but consciousness of the mind (brain) of the animal. An event could have occurred again and again over time immemorial but not have risen to consciousness,[42] until it can be separated from the background conditions. In other words, history is written

[41] Danto (1985), p. 2.

[42] Dallmayr (1984), p. 61. The pinning down as to what "consciousness" is has been an elusive task for both empiricists and rationalists. Dallmayr points to language for assistance in this matter. "Appealing to the teachings of the main founder of structural phonology, Trubetzkoy, the book identified the structural method with four basic principles of operations: "First, structural linguistics shifts from the study of *conscious* linguistic phenomena to the study of their *unconscious* infrastructure; second, it does not treat *terms* as independent entities, taking instead as its basis of analysis the *relations* between terms; third, it introduces the concept of *system*" or structure; and lastly, it aims at "discovering general laws" preferably through "logical deduction, which would give them an absolute character.""

against background conditions that shed light of an event to consciousness. That is to say that nature or the natural status of things is not history, history arises out of consciousness.[43] Otherwise, a natural event can occur endlessly without conscious attainment. "In Collingwood's understanding, history is a science of the mind or a *geisteswissenschaft* and as such it is to be contrasted with the science of nature."[44] "[A]ctions [t]o be explained rationally rather than causally. Whilst historians are committed to the view that "mind exists," natural scientists are similarly committed to the view that "matter exists.""'[45] "Further, philosophical propositions cannot be accommodated within a Humean epistemology since they are neither about relations of ideas nor about matters of fact."[46]

The *principle* may be stated this way:

> Nature does not care about history. Nature does not care about Time. The unrolling of Time is a product of the human animal's mind. Time is mind dependent. To use the metaphor 'of how Time flows'[47] depends on each animal's conception and experience of duration. How Events unroll in Time is a matter for science. Time is reversible in principle, but according to the 2nd Law of Thermodynamics, Time reversal is for all intents and purposes not possible. The arrow of time metaphor moves in one direction. The past, present, and future in principle, according to scientific laws, should be reversible. However, in practice and reality, Time is dependent on the scale of the observer. In matters of quantum physics, time is not real. It does not exist. But as to time on the Newtonian model, time is very real. Regardless of what the natural sciences tell us about Time, we as biological creatures, existing in a certain range of reality, time for us is measurable by clocks. And personal time for us is specific to each of us by way of duration. Physical clocks mark one Time, biological clocks mark another Time, and Mental Time expands or contracts, for us as biological creatures, according to Mind/Perception. So objective time cannot be measurable for human animals in the stream of consciousness because the perceiver ticks off time according to their personal condition. Events taking place in spacetime have meaning for that animal. Events outside this horizon are meaningless to flesh and blood animals.

Usually, it is taken that 'consciousness' is a pretty-mundane thing that all living creatures possess to one degree or another. And, of course, the human animal, in the opinion of human animals, has the highest degree of it. Whether this is true or not, we will leave for another day. What is important for our purposes here is the degree of consciousness necessary to establish a chain of causation for legal responsibility and the taking of legal action in the everyday world of action and reaction.

---

[43] Collingwood (1960); "Robin George Collingwood," Stanford Encyclopedia of Philosophy, Jan. 11, (2006) (revised May 13, 2015), pp. 1–33.

[44] "Robin George Collingwood," (2006) Stanford Encyclopedia of Philosophy, p. 7.

[45] Robin George Collingwood (2006), p. 7; See Hume (1978).

[46] Robin George Collingwood (2006), p. 8.

[47] Time flows is to be taken as a metaphor. Time does not roll over us. Time does not come to greet us upon birth. Time for us changes per our complex cellular activity. As complex animals we undergo continuous change. By contrast a simple or simples cannot be in time because their composition does not undergo change. The electron does not change. In its simple state, it will remain the same infinitely. We are complex animals that must continually undergo change and the cellular change of our complex being gives us the idea of time as a "flow" of sorts.

Consciousness is that transmission line that can bring together the world of the mind and the world of the flesh into concreteness. But as is the case with mind, consciousness cannot be fragmentary or broken or chopped up into smaller and smaller pieces for natural scientific examination and experimentation. Its validity does not depend upon empirical investigation but on mental coherence of putting the parts together and discovering that the whole is greater than the sum of the parts—so that the whole can come into being-for the mind.[48] Of course, this brings us back to a dualism of sorts espoused by Descartes. In his search for the connection between mind and body, he thought the *pineal gland* in the brain was the point of contact of these two entities. This is not the case. Students of philosophy, psychology, neuroscience and many other social or biological investigations and inquiries, since Descartes, have failed to connect the mind and body.

The *principle* may be stated this way:

> Consciousness is greater than the sum of the parts. Therefore, it exceeds scientific analysis and experimental investigation in seeking to get to the elemental world of nature. That is, reductive science is not the proper methodology in the exploration of consciousness.

Consciousness is currently the only viable candidate that can unite the two but getting a grasp or hold of consciousness has eluded all. So not being able to fully grasp how consciousness connects with the body can only leave us to posit spooky action-at-a-distance as the mechanism of connection between mind and matter. I do not think we need to go that far. We can simply posit the existence of consciousness without necessarily positing understanding of how it works in the body. That is, it is perfectly sane to proclaim that consciousness exists, and its origin need not be some other metaphysical universe foreign to flesh and blood animals, by simply saying that the electrical circuits in the brain and the generation of electrical activity (electrical current) therein simply generates sparks that generate consciousness-as-a-whole, even though it takes billions and billions of neurons generating the electrical activity. The patterns that emerge from that electrical activity generate "meaningful" structures for the understanding to process. This is not a reduction of consciousness to neuronal activity or electron activity. It simply suggests a possible explanation without pinning down the exact process of the transformation between electrical brain activity and the wholeness of consciousness—that is there is no need of breaking up the 'whole of consciousness' to elementary particles just because the process has eluded the scientific method and scientific explanation. Of course, this should not suggest or imply that if consciousness does not involve electrons or elementary particles, it means that we need to posit a spirit or ghost in the machine to make sense of it.

Whether electrical activity generates what we call "consciousness" is left as a pending matter for further future determination as we press on—that is, our civilization and time horizons see no way of reconciling the Descartes' mind-body problem—deem it as problematically structured or characterized *ab initio* as

[48] Hawkes (1977), pp. 15–17.

unsolvable—and press onward. Those that believe only matter exists will not find satisfaction here. Similarly, those that believe spirit, soul or mind exists will also find disappointment here. Like good pragmatists, we press on with the tools currently in our toolbox. We simply proclaim that once consciousness is generated (from whatever source), it becomes consciousness of ourselves and consciousness of the world around us. So, there is no need to posit a ghost in the machine, or souls, or spirits attached to consciousness.

The *principle* may be stated this way:

> Whether consciousness is a foundational entity is an open question. That consciousness is necessary to assign praise or blame to a person is a necessity. Events occurring outside of consciousness are beyond the horizon of the human animal and entail no moral responsibility or legal action.

However, even with a lack of full awareness of how consciousness emerges and operates, it nevertheless places the human animal in a position of responsibility for its actions. If a natural event happens outside the control of the human animal, it is not history nor a historical event. Its facticity is just that—a natural occurrence. The mind based and holistic re-play of the event in consciousness is different from the natural world causal events that shape the physical or atomic world. The concept "causal" may be a holdover from previous ages and may not fit the bill either in the social sciences or the natural sciences. That is, history cannot simply be a string of moments carrying the events to our consciousness, but the holistic organization of the events replayed in the mind. A mind that is incapable of consciousness cannot organize historical events either. The point being that the human animal makes history for itself. The process of simply recording events is not history unless processed by the understanding. The recording of events is a journal. Its transformation into history requires that these events be structured and restructured by the understanding to pull out meaning and explain the series of factual recordings. Beyond that there is simply raw space-time unrolling the film that inanimate and animate beings make as they try to make scratches on space-time. Henri Bergson may be one of the early Twentieth century philosophers of seeing the difference of time as a natural/mechanical/quantitative measure (the time of clocks) and as a life-force/organic/qualitative differentiator (time as duration independent of the tick-tick-tick of the clock) or as psychological time versus physical time. Time, not as a marker of consciousness (in the quantitative sense) but as an organic continuous flow (in a qualitative sense) of it.[49]

The *principle* may be stated this way:

> Human animals require consciousness to be aware of themselves and their environment. Absent this consciousness they are simply organic and inorganic matter undergoing continuous change or motion in space-time. The electron that exists today is the exact electron that existed a billion years ago and will be the exact electron existing a billion years from now. (A billion being a pointer for the human animal, not the electron.)

---

[49] Bergson (2001); for a critique of Bergson's holism/organicism and Hegelian philosophies, *see*, Bertrand Russell (1988), *Mysticism and Logic and Other Essays*.

Consciousness is not pure consciousness. Pure consciousness may be a product of angels or gods.[50] Human consciousness flows from the life-force and is directional. It is directed toward the finality of that animal. To be a human animal, as pointed out by Heidegger not long after Bergson is to be directed toward an animals' finality. Pure consciousness, without direction, is a metaphysical state for gods only.[51]

The *principle* may be stated this way:

> To be conscious is to be conscious of one's own finality. Pure consciousness is for the gods that have infinity on their side or exist as infinity. It is not for flesh and blood animals in finitude horizons. As far as moral and legal responsibility goes, the animal must first have consciousness before it can be assigned praise or blame.

Further, how a document is interpreted or deconstructed tells us about our conscious attainment of an event on the horizon of perception. The remnants, left behind by other eras or the marking left behind by a previous generation, such as the Framers of the Constitution, is to remind us of events not in our time. The intentionality of documents points to the actions in their times. If those documents are to have "meaning" for our generation, or across generations, they must be linked not by natural processes, such as that that links natural events or physical bodies, but a link that crosses consciousness from them to us. If eras change or undergo transformation or the previous civilization is washed away altogether, we are simply left with empty indicators and unlinked spaces signifying nothingness for us.

References

Ackerman B (1991) We the people: foundations. Harvard University, Cambridge

Barnett RE (2003) Constitutional legitimacy. Columbia Law Rev 103:103, New York

Barnett RE (2014) Restoring the lost constitution: the presumption of liberty. Princeton University, Princeton

Barrett AC (2017) Countering the majoritarian difficulty. Const Comment 33:61, University of Minnesota, Minneapolis

Bergson H (1998) Creative evolution. Dover, Garden City

Bergson H (2001) Time and free will: an essay on the immediate data of consciousness. Dover, Garden City

Blackstone W (2016) The commentaries on the laws of England. Oxford University, Oxford

Bork R (1978) The antitrust paradox: a policy at war with itself. The Free Press, New York

Broom H (1896) Commentaries on the common law, 9th edn. Sweet & Maxwell, Edinburg

Chemerinsky E (1984) The price of asking the wrong question: an essay on constitutional scholarship and judicial review. Tex Law Rev 62:1207, Austin

[50] For Hegel, pure consciousness might be the Absolute itself, God Itself in a Timeless universe and the pure identity of itself as itself forever more. The difference between the Platonic Timeless Other World and the Hegelian World of the Absolute Spirit is that Hegel brings to earth the spirit world as manifesting in nature, a pantheism of sorts while Plato keeps a pure world of the Forms in a metaphysical place that it timeless-in-itself; See, Hegel (1971).

[51] Heidegger (1962, 1972).

Chemerinsky E (1986) Wrong questions get wrong answers: an analysis of professor carter's approach to judicial review. Boston Univ Law Rev 66:47, Boston
Chemerinsky E (2018) We the people: a progressive reading of the constitution for the twenty-first century. Picador, New York
Clinton RL (1989) Marbury v. Madison and judicial review. Harvard University, Cambridge
Collingwood RG (1960) The idea of nature. Oxford University/A Galaxy Book, Los Angeles
Dallmayr F (1984) Language and reality. University of Notre Dame, Notre Dame
Danto AC (1985) Narration and knowledge. Columbia University, New York
Farber DA (1989) The originalism debate: a guide to the perplexed. Ohio State Law J 49:1084, Columbus
Hawkes T (1977) Structuralism and semiotics. University of California, Oakland
Hegel GWF (1837) Lectures on the philosophy of history. Dover Publications, Garden City
Hegel GWF (1971) Hegel's philosophy of mind (trans: Wallace W, Miller AV). Clarendon Press/ Oxford University, Oxford
Heidegger M (1962) Being and time (trans: MacQuarrie J). Harper and Row Publishers, New York
Heidegger M (1972) On time and being. Harper Torchbook, New York
Herder JG (2004) Another philosophy of history and selected political writings (trans: Evrigenis I, Pellerin D). Hackett Classics, Indianapolis
Hobbes T (1994) Leviathan. Hackett Publishing, Indianapolis
Horwitz MJ (1992) The transformation of American law 1870-1960: the crisis of legal orthodoxy. Oxford University Press, Oxford
Hume D (1978) Treatise on human nature. Oxford University Press, Oxford
Hutt DEB (2017) Against judicial supremacy in constitutional interpretation. J Const Theory Philos Law 31:2
Kay R (1988) Adherence to the original intentions in constitutional adjudication: three objections and responses. Northwest Univ Law Rev 82:226
Kens P (1998) Lochner v. New York: economic regulation on trial. University Press of Kansas, Lawrence
Marini J, Masugi K (eds) (2005) The progressive revolution in politics and political science: transforming the American regime. Rowman & Littlefield Publishers, Washington, DC
McCloskey RG (2004) In: Levinson S (ed) The American Supreme Court, 4th edn. University of Chicago, Chicago
Ogden CK, Richards IA (1989) The meaning of meaning. Harcourt Brace Jovanovich Publishers, San Diego
Plato (2016) The republic of Plato (trans: Bloom A). Basic Books, New York
Rakove JN (1996) Original meanings: politics and ideas in the making of the constitution. Alfred A. Knopf, New York
Robin George Collingwood (2006) The Stanford Encyclopedia of Philosophy https://plato.stanford.edu
Russell B (1988) Mysticism and logic and other essays. Rowman & Littlefield Publishers, Washington, DC
Skouras G (2020) Modernity, the commons and capitalism. Br J Am Leg Stud 9(2):368
White M (1976) Social thought in America: the revolt against formalism. Oxford University, Oxford
Wilson JQ (1995) The moral sense. The Free Press, Los Angeles
Wolfe C (1986) The rise of modern judicial review: from constitutional interpretation to judge-made law. Basic Books, New York

Chapter 7
Democratic Institutions Within Our Civilizational Time: History, Nature and Contingency

7.1 Nature vs. Historical Inquiry

Can democratic institutions be built in our historical time? If there is no agent, there is no historical time. The agent becomes the starting point of historical time. Whether an action has been brought about (caused) with thought or planned or by instinct or unconsciously, is of little importance in the mobilization of an event. However, the historical event can only be understood within the context of human action. If it falls outside consciousness of the agent, then it simply is a raw event without understanding its nature by the agent. An event that has intentionality or thought, can be recorded in historical time and understood by human beings. Events happening by nature or outside the actions or understanding of the agent, cannot be registered as history. Organic events have their own historical time which falls under the nature of their composition. Whether they are in the process of formation or disintegration is no business of agency. Organic nature encompasses time by whether they are composite or are what philosophers refer to as "simples" or physicists refer to as "elementary" particles.

We here will not dwell on the formations or decompositions of natural matter other than note that the human animal is a composite and therefore participates in this natural process. So, our concern deals with historical time generated by agents actions that are registered by the understanding and compose the record of our species actions. The event can terminate at another point, or it can cascade to other events with the original agent only having knowledge of the "proximate" cause or action. If the cause is nature itself without an agent, then it is not history nor fall within civilizational time. Mostly, the original agent will have immediate knowledge of the action set in motion, but further cascading is no longer traceable to the original agent and will cascade indeterministically and contingently from the original motion. Now, if this is the case, the amount of actions each agent undertakes per day will encompass the historical moment.

G. Skouras, *Constitutionalism and Democracy*,
https://doi.org/10.1007/978-3-031-66906-4_7

History for the human animal unfolds within the larger unit, the civilization. Trying to make sense of history outside the civilizational unit is like trying to catch air with your bare hands. Of course, within civilizations some believe that history is determined by economic forces, others by divine will and yet others from the biologisms of the species. For example, Marxists believe that the economic conditions on the ground are the drivers of history. Others may believe in a God that drives history and so on. That cannot be the case. History cannot be predetermined or ordered in a particular way. The directionality of history is contingent before the event unfolds. After the event unfolds its directionality can only be grasped by the mental faculty. History involves the contingency of human animals, with certain behavioral patterns, which shape it. Just as is the case with the Marxists or theists, biology too does not drive history because biology is a natural event.

Evolutionary biology goes to the structure and composition of an organism. Its evolutionary history is a natural event outside the control of the agent. This is not to say that the composition of the human animal is inconsequential to its traits and behaviors. The fact that our species is built on the layers of earlier organisms—for example, our brain structure sits on top of the amphibian and reptilian brain structures—that is the mammalian brain does not exist nor is it free from the ions of previous organisms developments. But this natural process tells us little of our historical development consisting of the doings of our species. It has no moral importance as far as human agent is assigned moral blame due to this substructure, since the same natural substructure is in all of the human animal's actions and not just applicable to some people. So, the biology of natural activity of nerves, muscles, bones, etc. is not a product of history but of nature. History is the mental re-enactment of events past. The determinants of history are radical contingent events, in the sense that the sum total of human actions cannot be predicted on a large scale. That is, history is not a process mirroring the unfolding of nature or the natural world. Nature in-and-of itself has no historical meaning, only scientific process or dynamism. However, history under the condition or domain of human agency gives the historical moments import.[1]

The laws of nature are written in a mathematical form. To discover them requires the mind engaging with the patterns and dynamics of the natural world until a computation can explain why a bridge does not fall if it has the correct geometry and construction.[2] Human actions are propelled by a multitude of drivers, as said above some consciously, others beyond the ken of the agent.

---

[1]Although Hegel has "history" fulfilling a goal, of Spirit, we need not accept Hegelian metaphysics, be they Christian or otherwise, to accept the phenomenology of history. That is, even though history has no goal, its understanding/explanation is best left to the mental process rather than a series of causally determined events. See, Walsh (1967); Hegel (1956, 2005).

[2]The nature of mathematics cannot be resolved here. It is said that god might in essence be a mathematician and works with the tools of arithmetic and geometry in the creation and building of his physical universe. Whether there is such a builder god, I know not of, but somehow this entity managed to place mathematics into the fabric of the universe, no doubt it will puzzle philosophers and mathematicians for some time to come. As to mathematics being mind-dependent or conceptual

Let us recap the historical moment from the natural moment. History as the mental reconstruction and "reenactment" of factual events. The event (natural phenomenon) in and of itself has no historical import. It acquires historical importance when human agency attempts to make sense and gather meaning from the chain of events set off by human agents. History is basically a mental enterprise stitching together a series of events. History is anchored in the facticity of the event as meaningful human action, but it is reconstructed and reenacted in the mental world of the human animal to gain meaning for that animal. History does not obey the laws of logic or mathematics; it unfolds and becomes meaningful by way of mind. Although logic/mathematics are conceptual entities, history depends on the unfolding event in space and time. Whereas mathematics exists in spacetime[3] of the natural world. Mathematics too is conceptual but must be distinguished in the way it mirrors or represents or maps the patterns of nature in number or geometric form;[4] whereas history is mind dependent in the interpretation and construction of a chain of events set forth by human agents. Professor Whitehead came to terms with these concepts as both being mind dependent.[5] The other, history being embedded in facticity/independent of nature. Between the facticity of the event and the process of Being lies history.[6] History describes events in time. Mathematics maps nature, since the patterns of nature lend themselves to symbolic and number descriptions.

The *principle* may be stated this way:

---

in nature or perhaps existing in some Platonic world of ideas, it is not likely unless being mind-dependent means that mathematical laws discovered by mind seem to also agree or match up with nature—that is, they map the patterns of nature.

[3](Minkowski Institute Press 2012). Minkowski unified Space and Time into a spacetime dimension. This is different from the Newtonian model where space and time are treated as independent properties. By rolling Time and Space into one, it leads to a different philosophical analysis of reality, very different from the treatment of the four dimensions of Newtonianism. See, Minkowski (2012).

[4]Cohen (1959), pp. 171–182, *see in particular*, the chapter on the distinction between mathematics as a formal system and mathematics as an applied system: Book II: Reason in the Natural Sciences, Chapter One. The Nature of Mathematics Section I. "The Distinction between Pure and Applied Mathematics."

[5]Logic and mathematics are mental entities that can conform to the natural world. To build a bridge requires the tools of mathematics unless you want that bridge to fall. History, unlike logic/mathematics, does not reflect the natural world nor describe the natural world-in-itself, but through mental activity reconstructs the world to make sense for the human animal events occurring in the natural world. The building of the bridge must conform to mathematics or else it falls. The history of the bridge need not conform to rules or laws of nature but as a reconstruction of human activity in nature. The natural world must obey the laws of mathematics. There are no such laws for history to obey. As said earlier, the natural world is of no importance to historical understanding unless human agency is involved. Otherwise, the role of time unfolds from one successive event to the next, from one moment to the next meaninglessly in and of itself. The British mathematician and philosopher, and long-time Harvard professor, Alfred North Whitehead, attempted in his major work, *Process and Reality*, to come to terms between the dialectic of Lockean empiricism and Hegelian idealism.

[6]Hegel (2005), pp. 341–360; see further, Vico (2001); Hegel (1988); Taylor (1975); Lauer (1987).

> The British empirical and utilitarian models came to America. But without challenge from Continental philosophy, they served simply as a can-do pragmatism. This resulted in rejecting or missing the rationalist philosophy—its phenomenology, and the role of mind in historiography. It basically yielded an incomplete historical methodology and philosophy that focuses on empiricism but neglects the phenomenological world.

American pragmatism lent itself well in attempting to attempt building democratic institutions on virgin grounds. But as indicated above, history is built on human contingency. That is, the human animal, as a contingent animal, can only build or create history on the basis of the foundations available to it. And as said earlier, the pattern of history is no pattern outside the mind. British history did not move in some predetermined manner from Monarchy to Parliament but through the prism of different forces acting on a body—centripetal forces to linear forces. The American colonies were advantaged in this process because they were not burdened with a historicity that embedded the monarchy in the system—moving away from one-man rule (Crown)—first to a republic and then to some attempts to democratize the original founding.

The British tradition relying on empiricism to inform its historicism can use a full exposition as to its defects. Observing history is not like a spectator sport, where the rules of the game and the name of the players are known before the game begins. There was nothing inevitable in British history that should eventually bring freedom to the commoners. Nothing suggested that the ancient and medieval way would be overcome in time. However, events in the natural world cannot be distinguished in a temporal-spatial way but are there as fundamental elements or as philosophers say, simples. What is left from nature is the sameness of the simples—nothing is left but electrons and quarks and the like. The sameness and uniformity of nature—an electron is an electron from here to eternity—as an exact copy of the phenomenon of the first electron that ever existed and will always contain those properties throughout the universe as an inorganic entity. The human animal or organic matter undergoes continuous change and could never be the exact duplicate it was a millionth of a second ago, with uniformity and motion being susceptible to scientific measurement.[7] History flows for us in the sense of memorial time.[8] As each civilization is washed away by time, something grasped by the mind remains, leaving traces of itself for the next civilization.

The *principle* may be put this way:

---

[7] See, Godfrey-Smith (2003); Bergson (1913); Whitehead (1985); Kuhn (2012); Collingwood (1945); Hempel (1942); Cartwright (1980). It should be noted that Hempel's model is not unchallenged. Hempel believes that Truth and Explanation are linked in the scientific process. According to Hempel's covering law model, Truth comes first which helps provide for the explanation.

[8] Whether space and time are real as in the case of Newtonian mechanics or ideal as in the case of Metaphysics or Mind-dependent systems we will not explore with any depth here, being outside the historical exploration for our topic. Nevertheless, understanding how history "flows" under either system is vital to understanding culture and civilization, and for us here, the legal bounds and determinants of legal action.

Electrons never change. Civilizations rise, peak, and collapse.

The British tradition of historical interpretation is more ground up, based on facticity and experience, in laying out the terrain and ground rules for building up a historical explanation than their Continental partners. That is, they see Continental interpretations of historical explanation as wanting, especially if it is based on speculative and metaphysical philosophy, by way of the German or other European countries, relying on a phenomenological method, as opposed to empirical-factual causal model. For the British, the unrolling of history, if you will, should be based on causal chains of being rather than the mental rearrangement of those connections in consciousness, or spirituality, or ghostly based entities. In other words, the British are a practical people expecting that historical events roll one after the other in some empirical-experiential trajectory. Certainly, in comparison to the German traditions of the eighteenth and nineteenth century, under review here, the British found German idealism not to their taste and looked at Germanic philosophy with a cold eye. The Germanic philosophical aspects of history as very speculative to appeal to the British character and mind.[9] That is, Germanic speculative history, of G.W.F. Hegel of the Nineteenth century, did not fare well in England, with the exception of a few British Hegelians[10] during the later-part of the Nineteenth and early part of the Twentieth century:

> But the study as conceived in this period was very much a matter of metaphysical speculation. Its aim was to attain an understanding of the course of history as a whole; to show that, despite the many apparent anomalies and inconsequence's presented, history could be regarded as forming a unity embodying an overall plan, a plan which, if once we grasped it, would both illuminate the detailed course of events and enable us to view the historical process as in a special sense, satisfactory to reason.[11]

Walsh goes on to make clear that speculative philosophy of history, simply based on reason alone, was not going to satisfy the English mindset for proof, facts, and experience.

> They professed to offer insight into history more profound and valuable than anything which working historians could produce, an insight which, in the case of Hegel, by far the greatest of these writers, found its basis not in any direct study of historical evidence (though Hegel was not as cavalier about facts as he is sometimes made out to be), but in considerations which were purely philosophical. Philosophy of history, as practiced by these writers, thus

[9] Walsh (1967), pp. 13–14.

[10] T. H. Green (1836–1882), F. H. Bradley (1846–1924), and Bernard Bosanquet (1848–1923). Also, involved in the idealistic camp were second generation J. H. Muirhead (1855–1940), J. M. E. McTaggart (1866–1925), H. H. Joachim (1868–1938), A. E. Taylor (1869–1945), and R. G. Collingwood (1889–1943). The last major figure in the tradition was G. R. G. Mure (1893–1979). The Hegelian idealism crossing the channel and starting to take hold as British idealism provoked the young Cambridge philosophers G. E. Moore and Bertrand Russell to begin and develop a new philosophical tradition, analytic philosophy. Although Bertrand Russell was a mathematical Platonist from time to time, he would reject the German version of idealism.

[11] Walsh (1967), p. 13.

came to signify a speculative treatment of the whole course of history, a treatment in which it was hoped to lay here in secret of history once and for all.[12]

The British and Germans have different views on the role and function of history. The British want to base history on facts[13] and the Germans want to base history on the mental power of reason. It seems that both sides are needed for the philosophy of history to move forward. History without facts is empty. History without mind is bare and purposeless.

In the case of the history of the common law, the British common law progressed through trial and error. Modification of law and legal procedure does not simply fall from the mind into the lap of history. Observation of what works and what does not work in dispensing justice is critical to any social development. However, the collection of facts and laws without the will-of-mind is a willy-nilly mountain of desolate facts looking for a home. On the German side of the equation, the Germans are correct, that the mind/reason is the template that human animals have for arranging and ordering the mental universe—according to those mental laws or actions that try to make sense of the physical universe. But the physical universe is not simply encountered by simply thinking it or the power of mind willing it. The mind can only work within a physical universe that anchors down the human animal itself. Hence, mind without facts or empirical investigation amounts to nothingness. Natural law or god's law may purport to have validity and legitimacy in cultures that accept God and a metaphysical universe as real. But this is not an absolute matter and cultures undergo transformation that can negative those accepted God-given laws with every revolution and upheaval. So ultimately those laws that remain in the books or archives can be examined and evaluated for their historical import as well as to their ground justness, validity, or legitimacy within the historical universe that they fall upon. The system of law, history, and the social sciences are not reducible to the microscopic level in order to explain the macroscopic level. Reductionism is no substitute for explanation. The legal system and other man-made systems are not analyzable the same way as natural processes.

The philosophy of Nature and the science of Nature are not one and the same things.[14] Scientific causal explanation is a project of observation and

---

[12] Walsh (1967), pp. 13–14.

[13] Walsh (1967), p. 14. Walsh says that the British mind was not very tolerant of the speculations of German philosophers: "By their own admission their object was to achieve a 'speculative' treatment of natural processes; and speculation, in this context, was not easily distinguished from guesswork. In its worst examples their work was marked by a fantastic apriorism which discredited it utterly in the eyes of the sober. Philosophy of nature was thus regarded with deep distrust by British thinkers, who transferred their dislike of it to philosophy of history, which they took to be nothing more than an attempt to do in the sphere of history what philosophers of nature were attempting in their own province. In each case both project and results were thought to be absurd."

[14] Maritain (1951), pp. 1–4. This Thomistic compromise between the natural sciences and metaphysics is not a good solution to the philosophy of nature. Clearly, the philosophy of nature should stand on its own rather than swished in between the natural sciences and metaphysics. That is, the philosophy of nature that is scaled for the human animal, not the theocratic divine being on the one hand and the microscopic or the light-distance travel scale on the other. There is a place for nature

experimentation to show the causal factors being investigated. That is, the connection between events in nature that can either be observed or brought under laboratory control. Historical explanation, on the other hand, cannot control history to examine the causal factors that produced a given event. The historian's laboratory is the tracing and collection of evidence left behind by other eras or civilizations and the creative, re-construction, and re-enactment of events, in the mind, to determine what happened and what plausible stories the events will yield. Does nature simply serve as the backdrop to historical events? No, it does not. Why? Because nature is ahistorical. What does that mean? Nature-Being is like the Kantian thing-in-itself.[15] It is the unknowable as far as (a finite animal such as our species) fitting into a temporal dimension of historical time. That is, it is just there that allows animals such as us to live and narrate our history. The history of the animal kingdom is meaningless to the universe.

The *principle* may be stated this way:

> This philosophy of nature and the scientific study of nature are not one and the same thing. History is explanation based. Science is "causal" or constant conjunction determinative. Since establishing the causation is a difficult process, science can fall back on correlation. Historical inquiry requires an agent and understanding.

There should be a clear separation between the nature of the natural sciences and the philosophy of nature. The former is empirical and fact-based, the latter is mind dependent. As far as the law and jurisprudence is concerned, it is mind-dependent because it is within cultural and political systems that fall on the human scale that animals such as us live on. So, law, morals, codes, regulations, etc., as existing within social systems, limit the range of our activity within the scope of the animal scale, and beyond this mid-range of existence, entities existing at the microscale or at the cosmological scale are beyond our day-to-day activity. Although we are mid-scale animals, the exceedingly small and the very large, are nature itself to us. Our systems would vanish without them to be sure. So, when it comes to a philosophy of nature, it should be understood as a mid-range philosophy for mid-range creatures. That the rules, codes, and laws are not immutable but a function of the social, cultural, political, and economic conditions within space and time and marking historical times for civilizations. The jurisprudence advocated here is basically a pragmatic one—to the extent it takes life as it finds it. The historical and jurisprudential meet at the crossroad of time and place. Our daily activity rests upon and is governed by rules created, not by nature itself, but by animals such as us to navigate the world safely, efficiently, and freely.

> But if historians sometimes in fact lapse into practical ways of thinking, we must not suppose that history at its best is anything but cognitive. For the modern scientific historian there is all

---

geared perfectly for flesh and blood animals on its own. So, it is important that we do not lump together the philosophy of nature with the natural sciences and investigations on one side and metaphysics on the other side. *See*, Hegel (2004); Schelling (1988).

[15] See, Kant (2007) (thing-in-itself philosophy).

> the difference in the world between the practical past as it lives in the thoughts of the patriot, for example, and the historical past, which is investigated purely for its own sake.[16]

The bottom line being that an agent is needed to set off history, morality, and any legal obligations that may follow from the agent's actions.

How we "interpret" nature is a function of our sense of survival. We are a species of animal, like other animals, which makes decisions as to its survival. Sometimes those decisions are not really decisions but automatic or "instantaneous" responses to preserve the life of that animal. In other words, an instant or instantaneous event could be a life-or-death event. It could be of an "infinite duration" within the world of microseconds. It is lived without the luxury of "interpretation" or "reading" of nature and within the domain of nature.[17] It has no historical import within nature itself. It could have historical import within historical time[18] created by culture and civilization. Nature does not create time. Time is species-conditional—that is, if an environment is harmful, an "instant" is all that animal has between life or death. So time to ponder, think, contemplate, consider, interpret a set of facts or conditions is of no use to an instantaneous event that happens "now"[19]—the "nowness" of the moment and to think or interpret will endanger that animal's survival,[20] the instantaneous has no historical import, whether an animal can plan or make arrangements for its safety and survival is a luxury afforded to animals endowed with sufficient consciousness and forethought to deliberate on its survival—that is, consciousness

[16] Walsh (1967), p. 193.

[17] The domain of nature verses the domain of civilization.

[18] Historicity of time verses the nowness of the instant.

[19] Bradley (1964), pp. 132–138. Philosophers that do not believe in the reality of time and space may view the "now" as unreal because of the status of time and space in their philosophical systems. One example here is the philosophy of F. H. Bradely. I consider the "now' from a non-metaphysical perspective and make no claim as to the whole debate as to the status of Time and Space. My use of "now" simply denotes the instantaneous status of an entity in the here and now—that complex animals undergoing change at every instant cannot be the same entity from one instant to the next in the making of duration. But a snapshot at a given instantaneous point is all that is referred to here, nothing referencing the metaphysical aspects of Time and Space, but the instantaneous now, captured in mid-stream, so to speak.

[20] Henri Bergson vitalism gave emphasis to intuition and instinct as the primal movers rather than intellect. The process of living was more important to Bergson than the process of knowing. That is, life is the ground floor of existence, knowing and intellect reside on the upper floors and could mislead the animal as to its needs, desires, expectations, simply put, its living needs—its "*elan vital*" to use his language. The picture of reality presented by the intellect is far more inferior to the picture presented by life in the raw—the blood, the guts, the intestines, the fluids, etc. all working to survive in the life of-and-with nature. Time as represented by the Intellect and Understanding could not be the same thing as Time represented by blood flow coursing throughout the body's highway of arteries and veins, fluid body dynamics, heart rate, all the other *vital signs* of life of the human animal. To scientifically dissect the human animal is nothing but understanding the composition of its cells and inorganic matter. Science will not find life by such examinations, just dead matter. Intuitions place the human animal in the jungle plane of existence. Intellect is but an afterthought, an epiphenomenon, giving the illusion of command rather than being the true servant of the instincts and bodily reactions for survival.

in-and-of-itself is "nowness"—in the moment—outside the moment lies history. So, history is secondary to the moment.

The *principle* may be stated this way:

> The historicity of Time and the facticity of Time are not one and the same thing. The Historicity of Time is the "duration" of time in the space-time plane. The Facticity of Time is the instantaneous nowness. They are worlds apart.

The interpretation of the agents actions is based within civilizational time. Moral actions sanctioned within one civilizational horizon and may no longer be accepted by another civilization. As contingent animals, our actions can only have contingency import. The permanency or durability of events set off by contingent animals has import in our historical time. It may be washed away by another civilizational time. Political, Social, and Legal institutions erected in our time simply reflect the contingency of our actions within our historical moment. Some demand stable and permanent institutions that provide solid foundations and context for our action. This may be an important goal for some, but a temporal species cannot build permanency out of thin air.

7.2 History & Causation

American pragmatist philosophy during this period (late nineteenth century) attempted to make a virtue out of ignorance. Who would dare come out against pragmatism? What could be fairer than if we could all adhere to pragmatic principles? American pragmatism[21] attempted to respond to a rival German philosophy popular at the time—Kantianism and Hegelianism,[22] two idealistic[23] philosophies that did not suit American enterprise at all. "The earliest attacks on this system of causation can be traced back to the 1870s and efforts of young American philosophers to counter a growing movement in America toward philosophical idealism."[24]

> Along with his fellow members of the informal Metaphysical Club, Oliver Wendell Holmes, Jr., "had come very early to share their deep distrust and antagonism to the *a priori* categories of Kant and the conceptual dialectic of Hegel. A philosophy of law, an analysis of legal history, which was built on Kantian or Hegelian foundations must be repudiated and cast aside." Together with future Harvard philosophers William James, Charles Peirce, and

---

[21] Rochberg-Halton (1986), pp. 3–40.

[22] From the British or Anglo-Saxon perspective, *see*, Ayer (1952) differentiation between "logical" propositions and metaphysical statements; difference between Anglo-American philosophy versus Continental philosophy; difference between "verifiable" propositions versus sheer speculation, Hegelians versus the philosophic positivism/empiricism of the twentieth century; the scientific enterprise verse the poetic-prose enterprise; etc.

[23] Immanuel Kant's idealism is a Transcendental form of idealism which is very different from the Hegelian idealism. So, it is important to keep this distinction in mind, not all idealism is equal and not all philosophers ascribe to the same idealism across the board.

[24] Horwitz (1992), p. 52; Walsh (1967), pp. 188–206.

> Chauncey Wright, Holmes shared membership in the Metaphysical Club with a young instructor at Harvard Law School named Nicholas St. John Green.[25]

The *principle* may be stated this way:

> Pragmatic philosophy is a short cut. It clears ideological or metaphysical debris of yesteryear. The gun, the plow or tractor, the builder, the capital, etc. is what is needed to clear the road. Let us do it! Do not look at metaphysics to clear the road.

This foreign invasion of critical philosophy or speculative metaphysics did not fit the American model and mindset. Experience, pragmatism, and a can-do attitude triumphed over metaphysical and speculative foreign philosophies transplanted here—attempting to find a home in the United States, be it from Germany or Continental Europe, would find it hard to find fertile soil here, given that the Anglo-Saxons already plowed it with their brand of philosophy. That is, metaphysical philosophy was a bad fit for a young nation with no interest in shaking up—pragmatism, empiricism, and utilitarianism—by disturbing the American gods of progress, prosperity, and can-do-ism. Further philosophical inquiry into 'causation' might also shake up traditional legal jurisprudence by pointing out the culprits in a chain of causal factors and agents.

The *principle* may be stated this way:

> Causation is a complex topic for the legal profession as well as the natural scientist. Moral blame cannot be assigned until the responsible free agent is identified. If the agent is not free, it screws up the responsibility scales of justice. As far as causation and science go, well, whether gravity is the causative agent that pulls things to the earth or gravity warps spacetime is neutral as far as assigning moral blame. Nature will do and respond whether it is uncovered by a human agent or not. Freedom is not a problem for nature.

What is clear is that Kant tried to respond to David Hume's theory of causation.[26] And many philosophers cut their teeth between the Hume-Kant philosophical dialectic. The attempt by nineteenth century efforts to systematize, categorize, and organize jurisprudence,[27] with the hope of objectifying law, as a neat category based on the categorizations of the natural sciences. Horwitz captures well the Nineteenth century push to 'neutralize,' or better put, make law into a "neutral" enterprise

---

[25] Horwitz (1992), p. 52.

[26] Cohen (1959), p. 224: "The Humian analysis of causation and its replacing of the ideas of production, of power and force (as synonyms of compulsion) by the idea of regular sequence, was the *coup de grace* which modern thought administered to the scholastic physics of occult qualities and powers. If we do sometimes find authoritative physicists still speaking of the operation of forces in an anthropomorphic way or lapsing into the popular manner of speaking of heat or gravity as causes, we must remember the great difficulty of freeing ourselves completely from prevailing popular use of words, and the even greater difficulty of expressing ourselves vividly without the use of metaphors, of which anthropomorphism supplies the bulk. Technical and mathematical language, however, is surely, if not slowly, replacing expressions of causal relations with mathematical functions or equations, which are neutral to all anthropomorphic theses." See further, Kant (2007), Hume (1978); *see in particular*, Cartwright (1991).

[27] Horwitz (1992), pp. 11–16; Codification Movement—attempts to generalize and purify law from its Common Law heritage.

without political or ethical bias—that would be best in dealing with corporations and other businesses—looking to limit liability by having to trace causation chains in damage suits and the need to limit damages to "proximate" cause.[28]

The *principle* may be stated this way:

> Legal systems cannot be treated like scientific systems because legal systems depend on principles of freedom and moral agency. Scientific systems are indifferent to the outcomes of investigations of praise or blame.

The philosophy of organicism, in treating the whole, as greater than the sum of the parts, goes back to Hegelian philosophy of nature, and social entities should not be fragmented into smaller and smaller pieces to discover what makes them tick. The reductionist philosophy of the natural sciences may not be applicable to the examination of life-as-a-whole, as an organism that is more than the sum of its parts. Similarly, a deductive logic is insufficient in connecting the parts to the whole. Prompting Holmes and others of his time to claim experience rather than logic as the path of the law. Logic of whatever type, deductive or inductive, like mathematics, belongs to the realm of the mind,[29] not to the world of experience and empiricism.[30]

The underlying 'chains of causation' being one thing, its power of judicial review another. If causation can be limited or cut off to the "proximate" cause, great, just as long as it does not damage the interests of property owners and corporations. Afterall, America is all about prosperity and any damage to those instruments that deliver, mobilize, or use property is bound to be *ipso facto* a bad thing. The causation of natural science, at least in the Newtonian model, of one billiard ball colliding with another billiard ball, is sufficient to show the connection of the two. David Hume set out to critique this model of causation[31] as a rather complex move the senses play on the mind—by observing sense events in nature and jumping to the conclusion that there must be a causal connection between them—but rather what the human animal sees is "constant conjunction" and assumes that A causes B. Two billiard balls collide, did A cause B to move in a particular direction? Or the two balls collide by way of the laws of moving bodies impacting one another? But showing there is no "necessary connection" between the two events, just "constant conjunction" that the

[28] Horwitz (1992), pp. 51–54; Walsh (1967), pp. 191–192; see further, Atkinson (1978), pp. 69–139.

[29] Dallmayr (1984), p. 54. "While empiricists stabilize meaning through recourse to a formal-logical idiom whose terms were expected somehow to match sense data, rationalists pursued a similar aim by focusing on language itself and—assuming a connection between language and thought—on the inherent structure and capacities of "mind." Instead of using external "reference" as a stabilizing loadstone or anchor, the moorings of language in the second case were found in pure syntax, grammar, and other "internal" factors."

[30] David Hume makes the distinction between "relations of ideas" and "matters of fact." Mathematics and logic fall in the former group. All matters that fall in the latter group can be classed as having a "cause and effect" aspect. See, Beck (1966), pp. 91–131; Walsh (1967), pp. 30–47; Miller (1987).

[31] "David Hume: Causation," in Internet Encyclopedia of Philosophy: *https://iep.utm.edu/hume-cau/.*

human animal conflates to get "causation." Experience is insufficient to show the "causation" of what happens when two billiard balls collide.

However, when dealing in the legal domain with such matters as "proximate" causation, we cannot disregard the foundational problem of causation, but must somehow limit the chain of events to a level that can be dealt with and processed by human agency.[32] When two events happen, they can be narrowed down to "proximate" cause. The relationship between two events without human agency is a facticity of the natural world, only upon the interjection of human agency can we "approximate" the causal event and attribute it to "intention," "consciousness," or "legal causation." By such attribution are we allowed to accuse a party of liability for one variation or another.

What set this "proximate" cause in motion to hit a peak in early Twentieth century America was a landmark case, *Lochner v. New York* (1905). It set off the Progressives and others in a critique of the American legal system. That is, can a legislative body legislate on behalf of workers (bakers in this case) for their "health and safety" in a free country like America? Don't these workers know how to take care of their own health and safety, must a paternalistic State do it for them? The Supreme Court, with its power of judicial review, overturned this legislation as not being the "real" reason that the legislation was passed, but that it was a redistributive plan to hurt businesses. That is, under an objective theory of contract, the employee and employer shake hands on a contract perceived beneficial by both parties. Who is the State to interfere and jump in to stop them? America is a free country and free citizens should be free to conduct their own business, deals, or bargains as they see fit, not as to what the state thinks is good for them. And furthermore, how was the State to determine the "proximate" cause of injury to their health simply by working too many hours in a bakery? Is a baker's job that dangerous that the workers' need in *loco parentis* to ensure their safety? Be that as it may, "proximate" cause, as far as legal system and legal determination is concerned, need a cutoff point if blame or injury is to receive weight on the scales of human justice. And if historical inquiry is to make any sense, the "proximate" cause is all that is given in most events. As for the ultimate cause, we leave to the gods.

[32]Walsh (1967), pp. 191–192. Walsh best summarizes just how troublesome a concept such as "cause" can be for historian—that there are historians that want to use it and those that shun it: "Philosophers of various schools have cast doubt on the propriety of the very notion of an historical cause or have urged that the term 'cause' can be properly used in historical contexts only when understood in a restricted way. According to Collingwood, for instance, historians, 'unless they are aping the methods and vocabulary of natural science', use 'cause' in a sense in which 'that which is caused is the free and deliberate act of a conscious and responsible agent, and "causing" him to do it means affording him a motive for doing it.' [B]ut Collingwood on this subject is moderation itself when compared with Professor Oakeshott, who argues in effect for the expulsion of the term 'cause' from the whole field of historical thought and, as if answering Collingwood in advance, describes Thucydides as 'not only peculiar, but also a defective historian' because, for him, 'personal character and motive is a first cause behind which, as a general rule, he does not press.'"

"David Hume: Causation." In: Internet Encyclopedia of Philosophy: *https://iep.utm.edu/hume-cau/*.

References

Atkinson RF (1978) Knowledge and explanation in history: an introduction to the philosophy of history. Springer, New York
Ayer AJ (1952) Language, truth & logic. Dover Publications, Garden City
Beck LW (ed) (1966) Eighteenth-century philosophy. The Free Press, Los Angeles
Bergson H (1913) Time and free will: An Essay on the Immediate Data of Consciousness (Dover). Mineola, NY
Bradley FH (1964) The unreality of space and time. In: Smart JJC (ed) Problems of space and time. The Macmillan Comp., London
Cartwright N (1980) The truth doesn't explain much. Am Philos Q 17
Cartwright N (1991) The reality of causes in a world of instrumental laws. In: Boyd R, Gasper P et al (eds) The philosophy of science. MIT Press, Cambridge
Cohen MR (1959) Reason and nature. Dover Publications, Garden City
Collingwood RG (1945) The idea of nature. Oxford University/A Galaxy Book, Los Angeles
Dallmayr F (1984) Language and politics. University of Notre Dame, Notre Dame
Godfrey-Smith P (2003) An introduction to the philosophy of science: theory and reality. University of Chicago, Chicago
Hegel GWF (1956) The philosophy of history (trans: Silbee J). Dover, Garden City
Hegel GWF (1988) Introduction to the philosophy of history. Hackett Publishing, Indianapolis
Hegel GWF (2004) Hegel's philosophy of nature (trans: Miller AV). Clarendon Press, Oxford
Hegel GWF (2005) Philosophy of right. Cambridge University, Cambridge
Hempel CG (1942) The function of general laws in history. J Philos 39(2):35–48
Horwitz MJ (1992) The transformation of American law: the crisis of legal orthodoxy 1870-1960. Oxford University, Oxford
Hume D (1978) Treatise on human nature. Oxford University, Oxford
Kant I (2007) Critique of pure reason (trans: Weigelt M). Penguin Classics, New York
Kuhn T (2012) The structure of scientific revolutions. University of Chicago, Chicago
Lauer Q (1987) A reading of Hegel's phenomenology od spirit. Fordham University, New York
Maritain J (1951) Philosophy of nature. Philosophical Library, New York
Miller RW (1987) Fact and method: explanation, confirmation and reality in the natural science. Princeton University, Princeton
Minkowski H (2012) Space and time. Minkowski Institute Press, Quebec
Rochberg-Halton E (1986) Meaning and modernity: social theory in the pragmatic attitude. University of Chicago, Chicago
Schelling FWJ (1988) Ideas for the philosophy of nature, 2nd edn. Cambridge University, Cambridge
Taylor C (1975) Hegel. Cambridge University, Cambridge
Vico GB (2001) New science. Penguin Classics, New York
Walsh WH (1967) Philosophy of history. Harper Torchbooks, New York
Whitehead AN (1985) Process and reality. Free Press, Los Angeles

Chapter 8
CONCLUSION: The Horizon and Limits of Human Nature, Democratic Roads and Constitutionalism

As I initially promised the reader to "unbalance" the empirical and the rational by crisscrossing the linear and non-linear routes to reach this end point. Hopefully, we are able to see landscapes that otherwise might be bypassed in the name of efficiency. It is hoped that the reader was able, at the very least, able to see alternative roads and scenes not provided by traditional sources as to the disposition of the human animal, the institutions capable of arising in any given civilizational time, and in particular the problems that can be generated in building "democratic" institutions in a non-democratic civilization.

All institutions are grounded within the civilizational time they are built into. Just as the human animal cannot change its species-nature overnight, so too civilizations capture the human animal in the condition it is found between its sunrise and sunset. No one choses when to be born and which type of civilization is suitable for them. Only looking backwards is it possible to see the domains of passing civilizations. Our own civilization provides the scope and horizon of the possible institutions available to us. So, civilizational time is grasped *post hoc*. Our traditions, ways of being, and our institutions pass historical eras as the river to the ocean. The temporality of these institutions is a given to the extent, regardless of how well built, that they too will eventually be rolled over by civilizational time.

Legal and Social Institutions are the product of civilizational time horizons. Our civilizational time provides the parameters of the possible as the state of our species is found. The institutions that are available to us are the products of our own making. Civilizations of the past are closed to us because we cannot re-enter them from the future. Civilizations that are in front of us or in the future are beyond the scope of our experience and comprehension. That is a way of saying that we are stuck in our own civilizational time or prisoners of our time. Whether democratic institutions can be built is a function of the civilizational time one tries to birth them into. However, just because a particular institution—here a democratic one—is attempting to be born in our civilization time, it does not mean that such an institution can be given birth to. It could be the case it is stillborn because the civilization is not prepared for its birth.

G. Skouras, *Constitutionalism and Democracy*,
https://doi.org/10.1007/978-3-031-66906-4_8

This is the case with trying to give birth to democratic institutions within our civilizational time. They are an impossibility. So, the question arises: is it worth the effort to continue trying to give birth to one or is all that can be expected are stillborn ones? At the opening of this book a similar question was put in for answer: whether democracy is possible or a utopian/metaphysical enterprise. The answer was a compromised one. Democracy is indeed a utopian idea, but some form or variation despite how imperfect was worth trying to work out. It was labeled a "pragmatic" democracy. The reason for this continued effort at establishing a fallen but "workable" or pragmatic version of democracy is that if the individual person has dignity, then it is worth the effort to give that person voice by way of a vote.

We have found our modern efforts to breed democracy an utter failure. Not due to any lack of trying but for such a system to be birthed in our civilizational time maybe a mountain too high to climb. Maybe a future civilization will be able to create such an institution. As for us, we are left with stillborn entities. Nevertheless, we said, it is worth the effort to give voice/vote to the ordinary/common citizen because, if they are to put themselves, their bodies, under the direction of a given polity, they should have a voice as to what happens to them in that polity. We hoped that perhaps a "workable" or "pragmatic" model of democracy can be developed, so that each citizen has a voice as to what happens to them as members of a wider political community. However, how workable such a model can be is unclear to me. But the goal being to give equal voice in the polity to all members is worthy of continuous attempts to make it happen. The exact parameters of that goal remain unclear to me. But given some of the philosophers we encountered here, along with the condition of the modern commoner, the solution to giving the vote to all is still worth the effort regardless of how uniformed the average citizen might be. The fact that he/she is thrown in our civilization time is no fault of their own. And as long as they remain here, as contingent animals, it is worthwhile that they have a say on maintaining their life and the choices available to them to reach their potential. No true State can afford to treat its citizens as cattle. An attack on one person's dignity diminishes us all.

Hopefully, it has been amply pointed out that the history of democratic systems is very recent. As to the internal plumbing of democracy, it is left to experts of one sort or another. The façade of democracy looks prettier than the internal plumbing of the system. We have pointed out several features of the system that feed the anti-democratic foundationalism that the Founders laid into the construction of the edifice. Due to the 'experimental' nature of democracy during its American construction, the Founders placed many traps into the foundation of the structure in case *We the People* either wanted to dismantle their handy work or reconstruct it. If we take the Founders building effort as a first pass, we might take their "phrases and clauses" as a first pass at democracy building. That we should try to use the initial concepts, by their use, as a builder selects "tools"[1] from a box and applies them for a particular function. And, understanding that ideal concepts should not be barriers to

[1] Wittgenstein (2009); see further, *https://plato.stanford.edu/entries/wittgenstein/*

praxis or pragmatic success[2] and utility.[3] As long as we do not misunderstand efficiency and productivity for fairness and justice—that would be using the wrong toolset for the job.

The *principle* may be stated this way:

> Perfection is in the eye of the beholder. Concepts such as Democracy, Justice, Fairness, Equality, etc. are words of management. They connect the aspiration to reality during any stage of Civilizational development. They are not static or immortal.

As we saw in previous chapters, the challenge to produce law without politics or see law as a "neutral" entity, might sound good on paper, but, with the roll of historical time has eroded or vaporized as a "realistic" possibility. That is, there is no law without politics. Neutral law is a myth.[4]

This means that there do not exist perfect tools that will distribute or allocate services and goods justly and fairly to all in the polity. "Justice" does not come from above the human animal (from the clouds or heavens) but is embedded in the human animal (instinctual and biological needs of the animal for survival). Justice is what the human animal determines it to be based on instincts, experience, and knowledge. It does not stem from without or implanted from outer space but from within. That is, justice cannot be an "objective" fact but a subjective resolution of the facts. That justice is not an "abstraction" but a stimulus-response to pragmatic conditions and situations that the human animal finds itself in. The instinctual life can be as determinative of justice as the contemplative life.

This being the case, new developments in the democratic process become imperative to minimize any unfairness or damage done to those left out of the polity if the Legislative branch becomes the final arbiter of law. I already discussed why the Supreme Court must be stripped of the power of judicial review and will not belabor the point here. But clearly branches of government, or officials unaccountable to *We the People*, can become a serious threat to all the people if they are elevated or "crowned" through the spoils of electoral politics or through any other means of assuming power.

The *principle* may be stated this way:

> Justice comes from within the human animal, not from without. Standing apart neutrally and fairly weighing the scales of justice is a metaphysical idea, like God in the heavens dispensing justice to the good and punishment to the evil. Plato might find justice in the heavens or perfect sphere. We flesh and blood and bone animals find justice in the sinews of our flesh, veins, arteries and marrow in our bones and teeth.

---

[2]For a critical school thinker perspective, see: Habermas (1984, 1989).

[3]For a utilitarian school perspective, see: Bentham (2010); Mill (2001), on utilitarian philosophy.

[4]Horwitz (1992), pp. 194–195 "The appearance of pragmatism in American philosophy around the turn of the century represents a challenge to the prevailing process-oriented conception of justice that had dominated late-nineteenth-century American thought. This turn to consequentialism in social thought is an important expression of the gradual disintegration of the belief in neutral processe[s]."

As we saw in Chap. 2, religious wars can spill over to civil wars, as is the case over property protection. The Framers of the American Constitution, being good students of history and knowing of wars fought over religion for centuries, for millennia, may we dare to speculate that they may have been fought the minute the human animal came off the trees, perhaps one tribe's magic was stronger and better than another tribe's magic. The Founders may even have concluded that religion may have been the "cause" or spark over many battles and wars spanning all human history. If religion might be trouble, why not allow each to pray their way without the imposition of uniformity and church mandates from the government. That it might be necessary to protect one religion from attack by another religion, the same way they protected property from attack—that is, wall off these "hot and troublesome" topics, in the Constitution, from human meddling and consign them divine protection. Natural rights and natural law would do nicely—a metaphysics of law protections from the human animal. That is, attempt to tame the human animal by the application of natural law or divine law. Give each human animal the freedom to practice whichever religion suits their taste. And by placing such protections within the Constitution, as walled off from positive law—from those in power wanting to use the power of the state to impose religious conformity and regulate orthodox uniformity or interfere or confiscate private property—by providing a way of special protection around say "property" and "religious freedom"—why not provide or attach a *Bill of Rights* to the U.S. Constitution to insure that these troublesome topics are walled off under divine protection and at the same time protect *We the People* from war, revolution, battles, and all other manner of ways used in history by one group of people to bloody another group of people? That is, give religious freedom to all, and prohibit state or non-state actors from telling people how to pray, to whom to pray, and what doctrines or rituals to exercise with their prayers and beliefs. And let people keep their property from theft by the government or the public.

The *principle* may be stated this way:

> Religion and property have been historical troublemakers. Is there a way to wall off these troublesome characters by way of divine protection and intervention? That is, what if we state these troublemakers should enjoy natural rights protections, and place them under the protection of the more powerful and universal law—natural law, under the cover of a Bill of Rights, or, better yet, under the protection of divine law?

But, nevertheless, the American-British, if you will, tossed off the British system in part—so what was leftover? They kept British philosophy and common law—political and of legal philosophy, of such philosophers as Hobbes and Locke and Coke and many others, which achieved philosophical sophistication left deep marks on the American Founders and the American system of government. As I said before, to the Founders' Locke was to America what Aristotle was to the medieval world. Their guide, their philosopher.[5]

---

[5]It has been argued and debated, by scholars especially after the Second World War, that the British influence or Lockean or the Whig tradition had a competitor, and that was the continental

As we further saw in earlier chapters, the British were not the sole determinant of American constitutional action. That the French, and in particular Montesquieu, was instrumental in carving up the American Constitution separate branches of government. Early Americans were God believers even though America was not set up as a theocracy. The Constitution embeds God—albeit a (a nondenominational) natural god—in order to give natural rights protections to all citizens without interfering with human law—embedding doctrines of property protection and religious liberty, immune from majoritarian or electoral politics, by way of *Bill of Rights* protections. So which branch of government was best equipped to monitor and interpret the Constitution for compliance with these God-given natural rights? Obviously, Hamilton, a hidden monarchist, at the Constitutional Convention ventured to set up the judiciary as the guardian of these eternal rights—and thought that the judiciary was the "least dangerous branch" and should hold the power of judicial review. Of course, we saw other members, either at the Constitutional Convention or subsequently, argue against giving this ultimate power to one of the branches of government. That debate started before the drafting of the Constitution and continues unabated to this day—through wars, upheavals, economic collapses, presidential power grabs, etc., the debate goes on today.

Whether it be Jefferson or Madison early in the Nineteenth century or Tocqueville or Lincoln later in the century or Franklin Roosevelt fighting a major Depression and World War in the Twentieth century—and threatening to pack the Supreme Court if they did not back down and stop acting like a super-legislature—what is clear is the debate has not been settled or put to rest. That is, a resolution of this judicial power grab will remain elusive until a new restructuring of the Constitution is undertaken—that is, the internal plumbing undergoes renewal and updating—and a new principle is embedded in the new Constitution "explicitly" forbidding the Supreme Court from engaging in the practice of judicial review. Constitutions were meant to be sturdy things, but not last forever. All must die. The Constitution is no exception. We can only hope that upon its rebirth *We the People* are the true sovereign and not the Nine Justices of the Supreme Court.

Justice must arrive in equal measure at the level of the people, in the civilizational mode they happen to exist in. Now, someone by this stage of the book might put two and two together and ask a rather embarrassing question: if, as you assert, the Supreme Court should be stripped of the power of judicial review, and you further admit that the Founders wanted property protection, then what exactly is your complaint? Admittedly, yes, they have. Unfortunately, they have done more than their job. They have done two jobs: the legislatures' job and the judiciary's job. A foundational document, like the Constitution, must make it clear as to who speaks for the People.

---

republican-communitarian tradition that was overlooked or forgotten during the course of the nineteenth century. That is, the republicanism of Machiavelli also played a strong role in the formation of the American State and Constitution. *See generally*, Pocock (2016).

As I presented the conditions of early America, the justice meted out to the Native Americas was brutal. Tocqueville, for example, encountered a civilization of Natives out-of-our-time—that is, the native peoples of North America belonged to itself in a time for-itself and could not go out of its time to join or become a civilization for-our-time. Consequently, the two civilizational time zones/horizons—Western and Native—could not be bridged or made to co-exist with one another. Either the native tribes destroyed Western civilization in North America or Western civilization destroyed the Native Americans. This is because there could be no translation of cultures across civilizational timelines/timeframes. History marks civilizational time. Those that fall outside that time zone are in trouble. Why? Because the human animal, as it evolved and evolves, is an extremely dangerous animal.[6] It has survived this long, under both natural time and civilizational time, because of fighting, re-fighting *ad infinitum*, within its own species and with other species for land, resources, safety or any other natural or artificial goods needed for its survival or aggrandizement, a running battle for survival under earthly conditions as found in the past and as currently existing. Simply because one civilization turns over, and another rolls over it, that means that the laws of animal survival become suspended.

These battles for survival are not only true at the species-individual level but also at the civilizational level. Not only at the level of the passing of biological traits and information from individual to individual but also at the cultural level by the passing of historical, technological, and cultural knowledge from one passing generation to the next and ultimately from one civilization to the next civilization. And as different civilizations encounter one another they will inevitably clash, especially if one civilization is stronger than the other. That is, one civilization—out-of-time that could not be synchronized with another civilization of a different time-horizon. For example, there is no particular reason the Western civilization destroyed the native civilization. The two civilizations collided under different capabilities and different conditions—it was not a matter of the Western was stronger in hand-to-hand combat than the native. It might be the case that Native Americans possessed equal, if not greater strength, to the Westerners in hand-to-hand combat. But the collision of civilizations simply was out of sync—in time or out of time, generally put—in history or outside of history. One civilization transmitted to its descendants' knowledge, techniques, and technology that was superior to those left behind to the descendants of the native/tribal peoples of North and South America.

[6] Thomas Hobbes was right as to the dangers posed by human animals. He recognized that such animals would be at each other's throats without a strong sovereignty that can secure their safety. However, Hobbes prescription of a powerful monarch, government, or sovereignty may resolve one problem but opens up a pandoras box of other problems for mammal animals such as us that like to also think they possess traits beyond self-preservation traits, that can also be observed in other mammals to one degree or another traits such as nurturing, caring, nourishment, compassion, growth, etc. that could also be killed off by attempting to protect the self at all costs. That is, the medicine prescribed by Hobbes may be worse than the disease. Nevertheless, Hobbes remains correct that without the preservation of the animal's life all else becomes epiphenomenon.

So, any question of justice at the civilizational mode level is inapplicable. One does not choose the civilization into which one is born. The Justice one gets is the justice each civilization is prepared to dispense. But once born into a community, then it behooves that community that all are treated fairly. That justice is measured out in equal doses or in equal measure. Having an unelected body dispense justice is a mismeasure of the law of community. The Framers of the Constitution made the mistake, in believing that the "better sort of people," to the extent that an aristocratic class of people existed, that they were in a better position to best judge what was best for "all" the people or the "commoners" than anybody else.

What is clear is that property relations are critical to any civilization. There is not a single civilization since humans came down from the trees that are free of strife. Civilization after civilization, era after era had to deal not only with the mythological, religious, and metaphysical universe/world of the mind but also the concrete reality of property acquisition, utilization, and protection, regardless of being-in-time or being-out-of-time. The Framers of the American Constitution inherited beliefs and doctrines of Western civilization regarding property matters. As we saw in a previous chapter, the passage from the Agricultural Age to the Age of Modern Industry created a class struggle between workers and capitalists. Many times, in history, many other issues, such as religion and the like, cloud the property matter. That is, the economic acquisition, distribution, and control of property (of whatever form) is darkly seen in its existential clashing—but during periods of transition, it can become clear and highlighted to the average worker or capitalist as an era passes (Agricultural) and another era (Industrial) arrives on the scene of history. Usually, it is clothed with other matters than the simple combat of opponents struggling to survive.[7] The pitting of human animals in an "artificial" environment (or urban jungle) or a rural environment (or a farmer's jungle) will under all conditions struggle for scarce resources and nourishment similar to placing them into a real jungle.

The *principle* may be stated this way:

> What is key and central is the American Framers of the Constitution embedding property so deeply into the sinews of the Constitution that for all intents and purposes mention of America has become synonymous with property protection. The Supreme Court and the Nine Justices that serve as the high priests of constitutional interpretation continue give us

[7] Justice Holmes, took the position, that it was not his job as a Justice of the Supreme Court to kill legislation that the government thought it was needed—like the *Lochner* decision—the protection of individual rights of workers from capitalists and the State stepping in to limit the working hours of bakers to 10 hours per day/60 per week. ("Of course, the laissez-faire conservatives cared little about the "right" of employees to work fourteen-hour days at rock-bottom wages; they were really protecting the ability of employers to get cheap labor. [W]hat irked him [Holmes] about those decisions was the focus on individual rights in general, implying that there are limits on what a democratic majority can do. Holmes would have none of it. "Every society rests on the death of men," he liked to say. If a nation needs soldiers, it seizes young men and marches them off to war at the point of a bayonet. If an epidemic breaks out, it forces the public to get vaccinated.""), Healy (2013), p. 6.

their exclusive opinion as to what the Constitution means. Presumably, they have the authoritative manual to deconstruct for us the Constitution's clauses and sayings.

Now comes the Supreme Court and places its thumb on the scale of justice on the side of the capitalists over and above *We the People*. I would think that the People have a right to demand an explanation as to who gave the Supreme Court the authority and the legitimacy to tip the scale of justice on behalf of the capitalists rather than *We the People*? We saw the Fuller Supreme Court, during the Gilded Age and Progressive Era, protect the property of the few over and against the needs of the many. What justified or legitimated that action? First, property protection is the centripetal force that governs the American Constitution and society, and second, those in power know how to appoint Justices that will not rock the boat—with the use of the appointment process to bypass the public in the appointment of Justices.

America always puts out the propaganda that there are no classes in America—*We are all Middle class*—some may move into the upper class, some may fall to the lower class but eventually things balance out if you wait long enough. We as a people hopefully can recognize propaganda for what it is. But regardless, once the Congress is boxed in from below and freed from the top—elimination of the Senate—the Congress can protect the People by positive law that is tied to the ground floor of democracy, not from the ceiling of aristocracy, the Senate, and the Presidency. And the need for the Lower House of the Congress, once the Senate has been dispensed with, and the power of judicial review added to its portfolio, becomes grounded from below, by a network of worker unions and other civic organizations, that will provide the anchorage necessary that it does not abuse it additional powers—to ensure that *We the People* and *We the Workers* remain free to fulfill our human potential and guard against Legislative tyranny.

The role of judicial review in a democracy is a contradiction. Why? Because it aims to place the judiciary in between the legislature and *We the People* in filtering and serving as the ultimate arbitrator of the law. There is no reason that the judiciary cannot settle disputes, but beyond that it must confine itself to dispute settlements, not policy making. It appears also at the structural level the judiciary serves to dampen radicalism, at any given time, by having a bunch of lawyers interpret the Constitution. For one thing lawyers are not known for being radicals as a group or profession. So, the views of *We the People* might be very different from the lawyering class.

On another matter regarding the foundational principle of the existence of Natural Rights, during the establishment of the United States and drafting the Constitution, was no small matter, but the placing of a Natural law Deity into the Constitution was in essence to place a natural religion into the document or framework of the American system. This concept of Natural Rights is a metaphysical concept, and the historical record seems to indicate that although the Founding Fathers did not explicitly, or directly, endorse any religion, they could not escape the period of civilization development that they existed in—the need for embedding a natural religion into the Constitution—even one the operates on Newtonian principles. Nevertheless, today we are skeptical of basing the Constitution on such metaphysical rights. However, the Founders were British byproducts of a Lockean persuasion that drafted the *Declaration of Independence*, incorporation of Deism into the Constitution, and the addition of a *Bill of Rights* to ensure their progeny of the Western tradition and civilization that they were the inheritors of this tradition. But clearly even if the Framers were Deists of one sort or another, the masses and general public were mostly of the Protestant religion of one sect or another—and that they could never forget or neglect the inclusion of natural law as a hint that the Almighty dwelt therein—in between the words, paragraphs and ideas—and the *Bill of Rights* is the product of those efforts of the inclusion of a powerful metaphysic of rights that were granted by God to the human animal that has been ever present in America and the world as they knew it—being men of a pre-Darwinian generation. The whole social and political structure rested on a foundation of Deism and God given rights—that is, rights given to all people by the First Mover of human existence. So, the Constitution, just like the *Declaration of Independence*, could be no other than an infusion of God given/natural rights.

Further, the general proposition, as understood by an American Aristocratic gentry class of men, seemed to select the lawyering class as the intermediary between *We the People* and the governing bodies—that the lawyering class would make good protectors of property interests. That is, it was best left to judges and the lawyer class to serve as gatekeepers and final arbiters of law for the public. So, the Framers of the Constitution believed that placing the legal class as intermediaries between *We the People* and property owners was to add safety for the protection of property. The main purpose of the Constitution as a whole was the protection of property, everything else was secondary. People that were not property owners had no business serving as interpreters or arbiters over the interests of the propertied class. Consequently, utility, efficiency, and property became the cornerstones of the American legal tradition. Property was the be all and end all of everything. Without its protection nothing else mattered or matters because it is the resting foundation and security needed for a good life or happiness. And a happy society is a propertied society. This philosophy became the basis of all else that followed. Everything was measurable in property terms, everything revolved around property—how to grow it, make it, expand it and so on. America may have been the world's first country explicitly founded on the property matrix.

The Industrial Revolution also spurred Congress to act in containing monopoly, accommodate taxation, and perhaps ease the burden of workers under the boot of capitalism. But, with Supreme Court blockage, these efforts eventually fizzled. That is, attacks to eradicate monopoly fizzled and ended with mixed results with the occasional victory for the anti-monopolists. So, basically, within the last 50 years of American history, and the rise of the Republican Party post-1970s, has resulted if not the abandonment but the curtailment of any need to control monopoly in the United States. As to easing the burden of workers-labor, it took major fights, over course of the Twentieth century, to attempt to bring a safe work environment. As to the taxation end, to say there is a hatred of taxes is an understatement. Besides the Supreme Court blocking taxation statutes in the early Twentieth century, it took a

Constitutional Amendment[8] to even consider federal income taxation power. It is fair to say there can be no civil society without taxation. In some utopia, taxation may be dispensed with, but in our civilization a state without taxation is a state of barbarism.

Now, one might say: where was the Democrats and the Democratic Party in all this? After the 1970s, and with the collapse of unions and union support, the Democratic Party has been defaced and moved to the center. So that, to be sure, the Democrats will yell and scream a bit louder than the Republicans, in hopes to control monopoly power, but the truth is that each of these parties are the other side of the same coin. That is, they are both corporate based parties. So, the battle and efforts of early Americans (late nineteenth century and early twentieth century Americans) to control this evil practice of monopoly has been lost to history, as the two major parties fight each other over the crumbs that the corporations might throw at them.

The *principle* may be stated this way:

> Monopoly power has won in the United States. True enough, from time to time, the threat of busting up monopoly power grows louder, and maybe one or two corporations are sacrificed to appease the anti-monopolists, but in the end concentration of power and monopoly power wins over We the People.

We also saw in the last 50 years the rise of "originalism" jurisprudence. We were not able to give a complete exposition of this doctrine here. However, we laid out some hints that this type of jurisprudence is faulty because it seeks to recover a document in its exact form and interpretation as if it was the Eighteenth century. All we can say to these "originalist" thinkers is that they are confused about their time horizon and principles of linguistic slippage.

Now that we have said something on the legal plane, it must not be forgotten that the law rests upon historical time, philosophical time, sociological time, and nature's time. Each of these levels of time, with the exception of nature's time, are based on civilizational time. As to reaching bottom, at nature's Quantum level, Time is meaningless, or on reaching a philosophy of Simples, time is irrelevant; they cannot undergo further decomposition or decay. The philosopher's Simples and the scientist's quarks or subatomic world have no need for time. Similarly, our perception and our belief in empty Space, or Newtonian space filled with "ether", may appear to our senses and based on our sense knowledge to have an independent existence of us. There must exist some sort of empty space in which physical bodies are contained, but when looking under the hood, there may be less than meets the eye. Our consciousness, intentionality, and finality are all intertwined within the existential plane. Creatures such as us live and build our nests on an existential and civilizational plane that has birthed us. As to the dimensions of the subatomic world or the cosmological world, they are beyond the plane of our experience and

[8] *16th Amendment* (1909) to the Constitution of the United States to allow the Federal government to collect income taxes without apportionment regarding the States. This was a response to the Supreme Court negating taxation in the 1885 case of *Pollock v. Farmers' Loan & Trust Comp.*

lives. The history of philosophy and the philosophy of nature meet on the civilizational plane.

Can there really emerge a "democracy", as theoretically understood, in our civilizational time? That is a good question. History, so far, has unfolded by showing that such a question must be answered in the negative. In the red tooth and claw world that human animals find themselves, such a question as the possibility of democracy may have to be postponed until the horizon of another civilization comes into view. We, here today, can only make use of the tools at our disposal that the human animal can have dignity, regardless of whether such dignity is respected under nature's grip. It is a dream, perhaps, to bring forth democracy in our time, but hopefully, amply shown here, such a system is froth with problems. We at least can try or aim for a "skinny" version of it. Why? Because the principle is right that if one is worthy of dignity, one is also worthy of a voice in the political arena.

As to the constitutionalism side of the equation, history and experience show that without the "rule of law" there exists the jungle or, better put, "the law of the jungle." Constitutionalism or the jurisprudence of constitutionalism is how to create fair rules that respect human animals with dignity. That the human animal is simply not disposable by the powers that be or by a "justice" unworthy of giving dignity to each individual. Of course, as I indicated in the text, grand concepts such as "Justice" may have a place in Plato's metaphysical universe but little application in civilizational time. Nevertheless, even if the odds of obtaining "justice" are against each and every individual in their time, there is at least the satisfaction of aiming high to attempt to reach it.

A key subset in this is the Supreme Court with the power of judicial review. The Court, being a leader in support of the "rule of law," as I argued, cannot be both legislator and judge. I hope, at least, I made some progress showing why the Court must be stripped of judicial review power. Having now operated for more than 200 years with such a power, it may strike many as to why strip the Court of this power now? The answer is clear: the concentration of power entrusted to only one entity can be very dangerous to *We the People*.

References

Bentham J (2010) A fragment of government. Cambridge University, Cambridge

Habermas J (1984) The theory of communicative action: reason and the rationality of society, vol 1. Beacon Press, Boston

Habermas J (1989) The theory of communicative action: lifeworld and system: a critique of functionalist reason (trans: McCarthy T), vol 2. Beacon Press, Boston

Healy T (2013) The great dissent: how Holmes changed his mind---and changed the history of free speech in America. Picador, New York

Horwitz M (1992) The transformation of American law 1870-1960: the crisis of legal orthodoxy. Oxford University, Oxford

Mill JS (2001) Utilitarianism, 2nd edn. Hackett Publishing, Indianapolis
Pocock JGA (2016) The Machiavellian moment: Florentine political thought and the Atlantic republican tradition. Princeton University Classics, Princeton
Wittgenstein L (2009) Philosophical investigations (eds & trans: Hacker PMS, Schulte J), 4th edn. Oxford-Wiley Blackwell, Oxford

The manufacturer's authorised representative in the EU is Springer Nature Customer Service Centre GmbH, Europaplatz 3, 69115 Heidelberg, Germany. If you have any concerns regarding our products, please contact ProductSafety@springernature.com

Printed and bound by CPI Group (UK) Ltd, Croydon, CR0 4YY
30/09/2026
02225608-0020